International Statebuil[

This concise and accessible new text offers original and insightful analysis of the policy paradigm informing international statebuilding interventions. The book covers the theoretical frameworks and practices of international statebuilding, the debates they have triggered, and the way that international statebuilding has developed in the post-Cold War era.

Spanning a broad remit of policy practices from post-conflict peace-building to sustainable development and EU enlargement, Chandler draws out how these policies have been cohered around the problematization of autonomy or self-government. Rather than promoting democracy on the basis of the universal capacity of people for self-rule, international state-building assumes that people lack capacity to make their own judgements safely and therefore that democracy requires external intervention and the building of civil society and state institutional capacity. Chandler argues that this policy framework inverses traditional liberal–democratic understandings of autonomy and freedom – privileging governance over government – and that the dominance of this policy perspective is a cause of concern for those who live in states involved in statebuilding as much as for those who are subject to these new regulatory frameworks.

Encouraging readers to reflect upon the changing understanding of both state–society relations and of the international sphere itself, this work will be of great interest to all scholars of international relations, international security and development.

David Chandler is Professor of International Relations, Department of Politics and International Relations, University of Westminster and is the founding editor of the *Journal of Intervention and Statebuilding*.

Critical Issues in Global Politics

This series engages with the most significant issues in contemporary global politics. Each text is written by a leading scholar and provides a short, accessible and stimulating overview of the issue for advanced undergraduates and graduate students of international relations and global politics. As well as providing a survey of the field, the books also contain original and groundbreaking thinking which will drive forward debates on these key issues.

1. **Global Ethics**
   Anarchy, freedom and international relations
   Mervyn Frost

2. **International Statebuilding**
   The rise of post-liberal governance
   David Chandler

International Statebuilding

The rise of post-liberal governance

David Chandler

LONDON AND NEW YORK

First published 2010
by Routledge
2 Park Square, Milton Park, Abingdon, Oxon OX14 4RN

Simultaneously published in the USA and Canada
by Routledge
270 Madison Avenue, New York, NY 10016

Routledge is an imprint of the Taylor & Francis Group, an Informa business

Transferred to Digital Printing 2010

Typeset in Times New Roman by
Pindar NZ, Auckland, New Zealand

British Library Cataloguing in Publication Data
A catalogue record for this book is available from the British Library

Library of Congress Cataloging in Publication Data
Chandler, David, 1962-
International statebuilding : the rise of post-liberal governance / David
Chandler.
    p. cm. — (Critical issues in global politics ; 2)
    Includes bibliographical references.
    1. Nation-building. 2. Intervention (International law) I. Title.
    JZ6300.C535 2010
    327.1—dc22   2010002460

ISBN: 978-0-415-42117-1 (hbk)
ISBN: 978-0-415-42118-8 (pbk)
ISBN: 978-0-203-84732-9 (ebk)

For my boys Harvey Tate and Oliver Finley . . . But not for selling at Your Local Shop!

Contents

Acknowledgements

This book is, in many respects, a culmination of an academic journey which started during my PhD; when I found out, in 1997, that the Organization for Security and Co-operation in Europe (OSCE) had just established a Democratization Branch, as part of their ongoing mission in Bosnia-Herzegovina. It had done so in the wake of the extension of the powers of the international administration after the main nationalist parties attained a landslide victory in the first state-level elections in 1996. At the time, I could not understand how the international administrative powers could conceive of extending their mandates of regulation and control as mechanisms of bringing 'democracy' to the people of Bosnia. I considered this to be a contradiction in terms – as I thought of democracy as synonymous with political autonomy and self-rule, rather than with the extension of international protectorate powers. However, it appeared that – with the birth of international statebuilding, as a set of interventionist capacity-building practices – what once made no sense was now widely considered to make perfect sense and these policies were widely supported.

For many years I have struggled with trying to theorize or to understand the bundle of practices and meanings which we now call international statebuilding; with trying to understand how a set of policies that could not make sense in the past could apparently make sense to us today. This journey has been a hugely fulfilling one for me, lasting long beyond my PhD studies, through numerous publications in this area, the establishment of the *Journal of Intervention and Statebuilding,* and through engagements in a number of theoretical contestations with other academics in this field and in international relations more broadly. Over this time, my debts, both in terms of academic support and collegial encouragement, have become so extensive that it is probably best merely to say that I am confident that those concerned know who they are and also that I am, and shall remain, extremely grateful to them.

In the immediate context of the completion of this book, I wish to thank those friends and colleagues who engaged with the problematic of 'The Future of International Statebuilding' at the conference organized by the Department of Politics and International Relations, University of Westminster, 9–11 October 2009, particularly: Christopher Bickerton, Berit Bliesemann de Guevara, Adam Branch, Susanna Campbell, Simon Chesterman, Philip Cunliffe, John Heathershaw, Aidan Hehir, Lee Jones, Roland Paris, Michael Pugh, Vanessa Pupavac, Meera Sabaratnam, Oliver Richmond, Oisín Tansey and Giulio Venneri. I also wish to thank Paulina Tambakaki for her encouragement, support and suggestions. In so far as this book draws on the powerful framing of the shift in liberal discourses of government, presented by Michel Foucault in his *Birth of Biopolitics*, I especially wish to thank Julian Reid for his critical insights, challenging disagreements and friendly advice.

The specific themes of this book were developed in the preparation and teaching of an intensive course on international statebuilding at universities in Kobe and Tokyo in the summer of 2009. I would like to thank Professor Hiroyuki Tosa at Kobe University for generously facilitating my time in Kobe, as Visiting Professor at the Graduate School of International Cooperation Studies (GSICS), Kobe University, my teaching assistant Kenji Wada and the MA and PhD students who attended my classes there. I would also like to extend special thanks to those students and practitioners who attended my course at the National Graduate Institute for Policy Studies (GRIPS), Tokyo, especially: PhD students Zubair Poplazi and Girum Abebe; programme advisors at the Cabinet Office, Satoko Okamoto and Megumi Yoshii; Takeshi Yuasa, Senior Research Fellow at the National Institute for Defense Studies; and Major Norisa Uragami an instructor in the CIMIC division of the Ground Self-Defense Force.

The key themes were also developed in a number of invited seminar papers in late June and early July 2009: 'Foucault and the Critique of Liberalism in IR', Kwansei Gakuin University, Osaka, 27 June; 'Why Japan Can't Think the Global', Institute of Comparative Culture, Sophia University, Tokyo, 30 June; 'The Resilient Subject and Statebuilding', College of International Relations, Ritsumeikan University, Kyoto, 3 July. I would like to thank the Japanese International Studies Association for their sponsorship and those involved in organizing and participating in these seminars, including Hiroyuki Tosa, Sorpong Peou, Giorgio Shani, Julian Reid, Gideon Baker, Kosuke Shimizu and Mustapha Pasha.

Last, but by no means least, I would like to thank Craig Fowlie, the commissioning editor at Routledge, who I first met in a previous life when I worked as the press officer for a Race Equality Council in the North East of

England, and who has been tireless in his encouragement and faultless in his patience with me in regard to this book project.

Parts of this book draw on recently published or forthcoming material: Chapter 2 is an amended version of 'The Uncritical Critique of Liberal Peace', forthcoming in the *Review of International Studies*; Chapter 3 draws upon material published in 'Great Power Responsibility and "Failed States": Strengthening Sovereignty?' in Julia Raue and Patrick Sutter (eds) *Facets and Practices of Statebuilding* (Martinus Nijhoff Publishers, 2009); Chapter 5 is an amended version of 'The EU and Southeastern Europe: The Rise of Post-Liberal Governance', in *Third World Quarterly*, Vol. 31, No.1 (2010), pp. 69–85; Chapter 6 draws on 'Unravelling the Paradox of the "Responsibility to Protect"', *Irish Studies in International Affairs*, Vol. 20, (2009), pp. 27–40; Chapter 7 uses material from an unpublished paper presented at the sixth SGIR Pan-European Conference on International Relations, Turin, Italy, 12–15 September 2007 and from an Internet piece, 'Forcing Africans to "Adapt" to Poverty', published on *Spiked*, 1 February 2007, available at: http://www.spiked-online.com/index. php?/site/article/2799/ (accessed 29 March 2010); Chapter 8 is an amended version of 'Race, Culture and Civil Society: Peacebuilding Discourse and the Understanding of Difference', a paper written for the workshop on 'Liberal Peace and the Ethics of Peacebuilding', organized at the International Peace Research Institute (PRIO), Oslo, 9 November 2009.

1 Introduction
The statebuilding paradigm

Introduction

This book deals with the question of how we can conceptualize the policies and practices of international statebuilding. There is little doubt that international statebuilding – with the goal of developing and exporting frameworks of good governance – has become a key policy field for leading states and international institutions. These policy practices have increasingly become internationally accepted as central mechanisms through which the problems of weak or failing states can be addressed. International statebuilding is no longer something that just happens after the event – western military interventions for humanitarian or security reasons (Kosovo, Afghanistan and Iraq) or post-conflict peacebuilding (Bosnia and East Timor) – but is increasingly seen as a vital package of policy measures designed to prevent states from sliding into economic and political collapse. As a set of international policy prescriptions, the frameworks of good governance are seen as a 'silver bullet' capable of assisting states in coping with the problems of our complex globalized world: facilitating sustainable development, social peace and the development of democracy and the rule of law.

At the same time as international statebuilding is seen to be the preventive solution to a wide range of economic, social and political problems facing much of the world, there is much less agreement on how these policies can be adequately developed and implemented. It is widely recognized that policy practices are running ahead of clear understandings of how international engagement can be most effectively maintained and coordinated. Statebuilding appears to be something that western governments and international institutions are compelled to do despite the fact that much of the policy-making and implementation appears to be ad hoc and there is little conception of what 'works'. The perceived need to act and to develop policy in this area – in the face of, what are generally agreed to be disappointing, even counterproductive, results – has driven policy and academic discussion. Most of the books written in this policy area therefore consider past engagements and practices with the intention of learning from mistakes and ensuring that these 'lessons learned' can inform future and ongoing interventions.

While there is little evidence that, on the ground, frameworks of intervention are more successful, it is nevertheless the case that the boom in academic and policy study in this area can be seen to be a constructive and highly informative one. In fact, I would argue that this policy sphere is one of the most important areas of study for students of international relations and of politics in general. This is because, as a subject area that has only emerged in the post-Cold War era, it tells us a lot about how international policies are worked through and reflected upon today. In the working through of problems of international intervention, academics and policy advisers reflect the changing nature of how we understand the world around us and how we construct problems and solutions at both a policy level and at a more reflective or theoretical level.

This book is concerned with these broader policy and theoretical reflections, which enable us to see the export and development of good governance practices as a way of addressing problems of development, democracy and international security. In this way, it seeks to construct or draw out the meaning and implications of today's paradigmatic framing of international statebuilding and the centrality of ideas of good governance to this. The central argument, drawn out in this book, is that international statebuilding is understood to be possible – in fact, understood as being a necessity – on the basis that, in today's (globalized) world, policy-making autonomy – government – is much more problematic than in the past. Statebuilding, as a policy package of preventive international intervention, is understood as a mechanism of ongoing relationship management which is capable of ameliorating the problems of autonomy, or of government, through the extension of internationalized mechanisms of governance.

Inherent to the logic of statebuilding is an understanding of the world in which modern, rights-based assumptions of government – of the operation of politics and law – are inverted and transformed. At the heart of this transformation of modern, liberal, frameworks of state–society relations is the problematization of autonomy. For classical liberal framings, the autonomy of the subject is the basis upon which the institutions of government are constructed and upon which the market is legitimized. Equality at the ballot box or before the law depends on the assumption that political and legal subjects are moral, rational and self-determining actors. Autonomy is the necessary starting point upon which modern liberal democratic forms of government are constituted. However, the paradigm of international statebuilding appears to be one in which the relationship between autonomy and institutions is inversed: autonomy appears to be the problem which requires management rather than the unproblematic starting assumption. The consequences of this transformation in our understanding of autonomy and its discursive role in the construction of how political power operates are as profound as they are misunderstood, in a subject area in which attention has been largely placed on technical and administrative problems of policy-making rather than upon conceptual analysis. However, it is only once this transformation is grasped that statebuilding becomes a meaningful set of practices; a meaningful way of constructing problems and solutions. For example, in Chapter 3 we will consider the problematic of sovereignty (a core concept in international relations). In the past, sovereignty was the basis upon which international law was constructed and upon which the discipline of international relations, in so far as it was a sub-branch of political theory, was based. Sovereignty implied the capacity of states to act as rational and moral actors, therefore as equals; with the right of sovereignty being the basis of the core principle of non-intervention. The statebuilding discourse or policy paradigm understands sovereignty not as a ban on intervention but rather as necessitating intervention. The fact that states, which are held to lack capacity – or to potentially lack adequate capacity – are making sovereign decisions is held to be a major threat both to their own citizens and to the security of the international society of states itself. It is the fact that non-western states have sovereignty, the rights of independent decision-making, which is understood as making international intervention necessary as both an act of altruism (on behalf of the citizens of that state) and an act of self-interest (in order to promote the security of intervening governments and international society more broadly).

To take another example, in Chapter 5 on the European Union's export of good governance and in Chapter 8 on the reinvention of civil society, this apparent inversion of the relationship between the subject of rights and political power is drawn out in relationship to the formal political process. It is only in the context of international statebuilding that democratization or civil society-building become possible. In a classical liberal framework, the starting assumption is that individuals are rational and moral actors. In this framing, the promotion of democracy meant the freeing of popular autonomy from the barriers imposed, for example, by Stalinist or right-wing military regimes: therefore, to promote democracy was to promote freedom. The statebuilding framework is very different; here it is autonomy or freedom which is the problem. Democratization implies building the capacity of individuals to be able to use their already existing autonomy safely and unproblematically. In this context, civil society intervention is central to statebuilding, on the basis that people lack an adequate understanding to cope with freedom and autonomy without this leading to conflict or oppression. While democracy promotion was premised on people's capacity for freedom, international statebuilding's project of democratization is premised on the assumption that people lack this capacity. For international statebuilding, expressions of popular autonomy or freedom, such as elections, are particularly problematic and are arguments to justify international intervention rather than reasons for opposing external interference.

In order to emphasize the importance of the problematization of autonomy in the framework of international statebuilding, and in the policy packages of good governance which are central to it, this book on the key issue of international statebuilding is subtitled 'The rise of post-liberal governance'. The use of the expression 'post-liberal' is intended to highlight how classical liberal, rights-based, framings of law and politics are inverted and transformed through the paradigm of international statebuilding. The desire to draw out the distinctive use of familiar political concepts, in ways which transform their meaning and interrelationship, is the central purpose of this book. The following section of this introductory chapter expands a little more on the importance of understanding international statebuilding as a paradigm or particular set of interlinked discourses, and after this the contents of the book will be briefly sketched out.

The paradigm of international statebuilding

Over the last decade, international statebuilding has become one of the most important areas of policy discussion in the international arena. It seems that, regardless of the issue of concern, whether it is that of war and conflict, of development and poverty reduction, of human rights and democracy, of the threat of terrorism, or how we might respond to global economic problems, questions of environmental degradation or of health and reproductive rights, the conceptual framework of international statebuilding has been central to how these problems are posed and how the solutions to these problems are constructed.

For example, in the current discourses of international security, statebuilding is seen as central to address the threats allegedly posed by weak states, which are understood to harbour terrorists, drug traffickers and international criminal networks and therefore export instability, refugees, crime and terror. The 2002 US National Security Strategy sums up these prevalent fears in its assertion that: 'America is now threatened less by conquering states than we are by failing ones' (NSS 2002: Section 1). According to Francis Fukuyama, 'state-building is one of the most important issues for the world community because weak or failed states are the source of many of the world's most serious problems, from poverty to AIDS to drugs to terrorism' (Fukuyama 2004:

ix). Robert I. Rotberg does not exaggerate in arguing that statebuilding has 'become one of the critical all-consuming strategic and moral imperatives of our terrorized time' (Rotberg 2004: 42).

For leading policy analysts, Ashraf Ghani and Clare Lockhart, the key problem 'the failed state – is at the heart of a worldwide systemic crisis that constitutes the most serious challenge to global stability in the new millennium' (2008: 4). The problems of global insecurity, poverty and underdevelopment, war and conflict are alleged to be found in the widespread existence of dysfunctional states that have formal sovereignty but lack the capacities to safeguard the welfare of their own citizens and thereby put the stability of other states at risk:

> A number of contemporary global crises have their roots in forty to sixty fragile countries. As these states have experienced prolonged conflict or misrule, networks of criminality, violence, and terror have solidified, providing an ever expanding platform that threatens the entire globe.
>
> (Ghani and Lockhart 2008: 23)

These states – alleged to form an 'arc of crisis' extending from Africa through the Middle East and Central and East Asia – are held to lack the necessary capacities for good governance. While, in the west, it is understood that the state provides the institutional framework enabling its citizens to pursue their personal and economic interests within a framework of order and security, the failing state is seen to lack this institutional framework; making autonomy problematic at the level of both the individual and society as a whole. Here, it is clear that external intervention in traditional terms is no longer adequate. The watchword of international statebuilding is increasingly that of prevention (as will be considered at greater length in Chapter 6); accordingly, international statebuilding approaches are posited as a preventive alternative to costly military interventions: 'No international police or army can substitute for a combination of well-ordered markets and states' (Ghani and Lockhart 2008: 23; see also, Collier 2007).

It is important to establish the similar discursive framing of policy problems and potential solutions in policy spheres such as democracy, development and security, which were considered to be separate areas of concern until the 1990s and are now considered to constitute an interlocking nexus. There is little doubt that: 'solutions to our current problems of insecurity, poverty, and lack of progress all converge on the need for a state-building project' (Ghani and Lockhart 2008: 4). At the same time as a common framework for viewing problems has arisen, so has the policy response of international statebuilding:

Aiding collapsed and incapable states could previously be seen as an altruistic, idealistic . . . 'optional' matter of concern . . . But in a post-9/11 world, this has become a global issue. Like it or not, we are moving toward a common security-development paradigm. It is increasingly clear that one key phenomenon – the failed state, or the sovereignty gap – connects the entire complex of these problems.

(Ghani and Lockhart 2008: 26)

The basis of this 'common paradigm' is the understanding of a wide range of social, economic and political problems as the products of the autonomy of the non-western state: the fact that autonomy or sovereignty is the precondition for institutional frameworks upon which poor decisions are made by both states and societies. The solution to these problems is therefore that of enabling states and societies to make better choices and decisions and at the same time ensuring that decision-making is more constrained by international frameworks of regulation. As World Bank policy guru Paul Collier explains, while excellent government policies may help failing states there is not that much that can be expected in the short-term with regard to economic development, at the same time, very poor policies have an asymmetric effect of a rapid destructive impact. Therefore: 'Because of this asymmetry, the implementation of restraints is likely to be even more important than the promotion of government effectiveness' (Collier 2007: 64).

The institutional framework, or the 'rules of the game' – the context in which autonomous actors make their decisions – are seen to produce counterproductive results: the pursuit of individual interests does not lead to the collective good, but, on the contrary, to economic and social collapse and disintegration. Autonomy on the basis of a poor institutional framework is held to block the citizens of these states from having access to the benefits of economic growth and globalization:

The rules of the game in failing states – the parameters that people impose upon themselves to shape their interactions – are poor governance and rampant corruption. The very means that could bring prosperity to billions – global capital – cannot find a home in such countries.

(Ghani and Lockhart 2008: 24)

International statebuilding is therefore conceived in terms of overcoming institutional blockages, or changing the 'rules of the game', through turning bad governance into good governance. It is held that the export or development of good governance can remove the institutional blockages which prevent state–society relations from creating a stable social order and which prevent the state from benefiting from the stable social and economic order of international society. In fact, it has been through discussions of economic development that the framework of international statebuilding policy practices has become cohered, rather than in the higher profile ad hoc experiences of international administration. This institutionalist approach of what could be described as post-liberal governance (the subject of this book) flows from the economic framing of the problems of development as lying with the institutions of the failing state rather than operations of the world economy itself. It is due to the institutional forms taken by failing states that global capital is understood as being prevented from operating efficiently.

For international statebuilding discourse, the problem is not that of the market per se or of a lack of resources; the explanation for the lack of economic development is held to be that of bad governance and poor institutional choices at the level of elites and societies. It is important to note, as in the previous quote from Ghani and Lockhart, that these institutional frameworks are often understood to be freely chosen: they are 'the parameters that people impose upon themselves'. The autonomy of the state and society is held to pose a deep and underlying problem, in that self-determined decisions create historical path-dependencies whereby institutional problems at both formal and informal levels are reproduced and have deep social and historical roots. The export of good governance solutions is therefore no easy matter as the copious 'lessons learned' studies all point out: it is held that there are no 'quick fixes', whether in terms of military interventions, international aid or the export or imposition of policy frameworks. The good governance project is increasingly seen to be a long-term one, operating at both the formal level of state institutions and the informal level of civil society (see also, Chapter 5 on the European Union).

The discourse of international statebuilding presupposes that whatever problems there might be with the workings of the global economy, states and societies can be made more sustainable or resilient if they operate in order to respond to the needs of the market and other external pressures, such as those of environmental sustainability. Ghani and Lockhart provide a typical perspective, arguing that the problem is not the market itself but the institutions of weak or failing states which fail to facilitate the market and, therefore, do not enable it to function efficiently. Bad governance is alleged to block 'good globalization', development and prosperity, resulting in 'bad globalization': 'the unattractive side of the global economy – rent seeking and depredation' (2008: 153–54). Here, rather than critique global capitalism or the assumed harmony of globalization, it is understood that there is no such thing as 'global capitalism' or 'globalization' per se but rather good or bad capitalism or globalization depending on the institutional framework of states.

This institutionalist paradigm of post-liberal governance has risen from the margins of social and economic theory to the mainstream of government and international institutional policy practice in the past two decades. In the discourses of poverty reduction and international development, state-capacity has become central to international concerns and 'enhancing the capacity of African states has risen to the top of the continent's development agenda' (Léautier and Madavo 2004: v). These concerns, and policy interventions in response to them, were highlighted in the World Bank's *World Development Report 1997: The State in a Changing World* and in the 2000 follow-up study, *Reforming Public Institutions and Strengthening Governance: A World Bank Strategy* (WB 1997; WB 2000). The UK government's 2005 Commission for Africa report argued that failures in state-capacity had been the central barrier to development in the continent (CfA 2005: 14). The UN Millennium Project expert panel, directed by Jeffrey Sachs, suggested that the central problem faced by poor and heavily indebted states was weak governance, caused not so much by 'corrupt' governments but those that 'lack the resources and capacity to manage an efficient public administration' (UNMP 2005: 113). The World Bank's perspective has become an international consensus, or policy paradigm, upheld by all the leading western governments, including the United States, and the United Nations, European Union and other inter-governmental actors and international organizations.

Conceptualizing international statebuilding

International statebuilding is often approached in different ways: for some policy-makers and academics, the focus has largely been on international administrations; for some, the concern has been a broader one of post-conflict peacebuilding; for others, the focus has been that of increasing state capacity to address the risks of state failure or the problems of under-development. These approaches serve to help us delimit a subject area; they help to divide the social world in ways which enable us to identify certain policy practices according to the problem which is being addressed or the policy responses to these problems. Breaking down policy practices or areas of policy-making in different ways enables policy-actors and academics to make comparative judgements between different policy approaches addressing similar problems or to undertake analysis seeking to develop these policies differently in response to the outcomes of certain policies in certain contexts. These approaches often involve 'lessons learned' analyses and are held to be useful to policy-makers and to facilitate the making of better or more effective policy.

   This book is less concerned with breaking down international statebuilding into separate areas of policy-making. Rather it is concerned with how international statebuilding approaches are framed or given meaning: how the world and its problems are constructed and how policy interventions into this world are understood. International statebuilding is more than a set of policy solutions to a set of policy problems; for the purposes of this book, international statebuilding will be understood as a paradigm through which the world is understood and engaged. Certain problems are posed or constructed in certain ways and the way of posing these problems facilitates or makes possible certain answers to these problems.

The question of how we might conceptualize international statebuilding is the question of how we might understand international statebuilding theoretically. When we theorize, we attempt to establish a framework that helps to clarify the subject of our investigation. Clarifying the subject is more than a matter of categorizing and describing the policy responses to certain problems, it concerns revealing the mechanisms through which it is possible to construct problems and policy responses in certain ways. This process of clarification is one of abstraction: we abstract from the concrete mass of facts and information the key aspects or essential assumptions which can then enable us to make sense of the material.

The conceptualization of international statebuilding will be undertaken here through the clarification or construction of what could be called a paradigm of international statebuilding and through an analysis of the implications of this paradigm, as outlined briefly earlier. A paradigm is a framework or model which facilitates a way of understanding and engaging with the world: it is a shared way of undertaking academic or policy work, in which there is a consensus on the approach taken. This consensus could include how the world is described, i.e. what is to be observed and scrutinized (in academic discourse this is termed the ontological focus), it could also include a broad agreement on the kind of questions that are supposed to be asked, the kind of answers probed for, and how the findings should be interpreted (this is sometimes termed the epistemological focus, i.e. how knowledge is understood to be generated).

In his 1962 book, which established the importance of the social construction of knowledge, *The Structure of Scientific Revolutions*, Thomas Kuhn set out the thesis that the way we understand and relate to the world develops unevenly, in what he termed 'paradigm shifts' (Kuhn 1996). The important claim which he made was that paradigms were not commensurable, which meant that two paradigms could not be reconciled with each other because they could not be subjected to the same measure or common standard of comparison. That is, no meaningful comparison between them was possible, not because they dealt with a fundamentally different subject matter but because their frameworks of meaning were fundamentally different: the concepts being used were not mutually compatible or mutually intelligible. The fact that a new paradigm replaced an old paradigm did not necessarily mean that it was better in some objective sense of understanding the external world or in terms of policy-making. This was because the criteria of judgement also depended upon the paradigm itself and on the conceptual framework which defined it and gave it its explanatory value.

Conceptualizing international statebuilding as a paradigm is particularly useful for students and policy analysts as it enables us to see that international statebuilding appears to be premised on a very different criteria of meaning or a very different way of understanding the problems of the world and of making policy in relation to these problems, than was the case prior to the rise of international statebuilding. It also enables us to understand how the concepts being used in the paradigm have a different meaning and a different inter-relationship than do similar concepts which hold a different set of meanings and relations in other paradigmatic framings of problems and policy-solutions. It will be the purpose of this book to draw out and clarify the different meanings that these concepts have today – the key concepts are ones that the reader will most likely already be familiar with: ones such as state sovereignty, democracy, the rule of law, empowerment, resilience, sustainability, good governance and civil society. Understanding international statebuilding as a paradigm – or theorizing international statebuilding – does not involve any complicated language; in fact, it involves clarifying what these basic concepts might mean in a specific paradigmatic or discursive context.

Understanding international statebuilding as a paradigm also helps us to take some academic distance from the subject matter. The purpose of this book is to clarify what international statebuilding is. The sorts of questions we will be concerned with are:

• How do international statebuilders understand the world?
• How are different problems constructed or understood within an international statebuilding paradigm?
• How are policy solutions formulated within an international statebuilding paradigm?
• How does the international statebuilding paradigm relate to previous paradigms of understanding and theorizing the world?

It should be noted that explaining the specificity of the statebuilding approach to the world and to policy practices could also be done through applying similar methodological frameworks to those of Kuhn's use of paradigms and paradigm shifts. For readers interested in the methodological importance of conceptualizing international statebuilding as an internally unified set of understandings, Louis Althusser's conception of a problematic (outlined most lucidly in his 1961 work 'On the Young Marx') is well worth consideration (2005: 55–71). Althusser explains the ways in which conceptual frameworks have to be understood not merely in terms of their answers or policy conclusions but, more crucially, as including the questions which they pose (their hidden and often unconscious assumptions) (Althusser 2005: 66–69). The problematic, thus established, derives its inner coherence from the way its elements are combined together, the way in which they form a systematic structure. Starting out from an analysis of isolated concepts or policy aims therefore fails to grasp the bigger picture of how these are understood and acted upon (2005: 66–69). The point which I want to make is that of the need to reflect on the meaning of concepts and to consider their use within specific policy contexts, rather than to take their meaning for granted and assume that it is constant regardless of the context in which the concept is deployed.

Michel Foucault, who we will be focusing on through much of this book, was also concerned with the need to consider how the meaning of concepts developed and was deployed in specific contexts. He used a number of conceptual terms, such as discourses, epistemes, apparatuses and dispositifs, to indicate the importance of analysing the concrete interrelation between sets of ideas and policy-practices. For Foucault, these conceptual treatments of the ways in which ideas and practices developed and interrelated were heuristic devices enabling us to understand how governments and institutions formulated policy in specific ways on the basis of certain guiding assumptions which gave these policy practices their meaning and coherence.

In the opening lecture in his book *The Birth of Biopolitics*, Foucault expands on the importance of his methodological approach, which was sensitive to how different discursive frameworks enabled concepts to take on very different meanings:

> ... I would like to point out straightaway that choosing to start from governmental practice is obviously and explicitly a way of not taking as a primary, original, and already given object, notions such as the sovereign, sovereignty, the people, subjects, the state, civil society, that is to say, all those universals employed by sociological analysis, historical analysis, and political philosophy in order to account for governmental practice. For my part, I would like to do exactly the opposite and starting from this practice as it is given, but at the same time as it reflects on itself and is rationalized, show how certain things – state and society, sovereign and subjects, etcetera – were actually able to be formed, and the status of which should obviously be questioned.
>
> (Foucault 2008: 2–3)

Rather than starting from universal concepts, which were often treated as if they had a life or a logic of their own, which could be traced and understood in their development over time, Foucault started from the methodological basis that presupposed that universals did not exist, enabling him to more sharply consider the historically specific contextual meaning of fundamental concepts – such as the state or civil society – rather than taking them for granted. In this way, he was able to locate the existence and development of different problematics, discourses or paradigms, through which the policy-practices of government were understood very differently and, in fact, were based upon distinct operative principles and attempted to achieve different objectives. Through this framework of analysis Foucault studied how different and distinct 'governmental rationalities' overlapped or became contested (2008: 313).

Despite the differences between Foucault, Althusser and Kuhn, these theorists are useful in highlighting how different policy paradigms, problematics or discourses can be incommensurable with each other. This incommensurability is a product of the fact that our understandings of ourselves and the world in which we live are contingent, socially constructed, products which do not immediately or necessarily stem from the external world which we are observing or engaging with. These ideas are socially mediated and do not change merely in response to 'objective' changes in the external world but also in response to political or 'subjective' factors. In some cases, as in the paradigm shift analysed in this book, the change in perspective can be so sharp that it can be like seeing the world through different glasses, in which the problems are different as well as the policy solutions and the rationality behind acting.

Foucault explains how certain practices and discourses come together to construct a paradigm (or a pair of glasses) through which the world can be understood and certain policy frameworks – such as, in our case, international statebuilding – can become possible:

> [This methodological approach is] a matter of showing by what conjunctions a whole set of practices – from the moment they become coordinated with a regime of truth – was able to make what does not exist [e.g., international statebuilding] nonetheless become something, something however that continues not to exist. That is to say . . . not how an error . . . or how an illusion could be born, but how a particular regime of truth . . . makes something that does not exist able to become something. It is not an illusion since it is precisely a set of practices, real practices, which established it and thus imperiously marks it out in reality.
>
> (2008: 19)

Where other books on international statebuilding are concerned with the discrete practices and policies of international statebuilding as a subject matter in themselves, this book is concerned with the paradigm of international statebuilding: with what makes this bundle of practices and ideas a coherent whole. With how, what we call, international statebuilding came to exist and how it can be conceptualized or academically understood. It is important to emphasize that our concern in this chapter and those which follow is not primarily to provide a history of international statebuilding or to learn policy lessons from the experiences of international statebuilding, but to critically investigate and reflect upon the bundle of ideas and practices which, as a whole, constitute and make possible international statebuilding.

It should also be borne in mind that this is an exercise of critical theorizing – of understanding international statebuilding theoretically or academically – the purpose is not primarily that of normative critique. The purpose of this book is not to expose or condemn international statebuilding as an exercise in colonial thinking or of hegemonic western power but to understand it from the viewpoint of its practitioners and advocates: to understand it within its own terms. Readers of this book are perfectly capable of drawing their own normative or political judgements about international statebuilding. This book is essentially concerned with understanding the paradigm through which international statebuilding can be understood, by its practitioners and supporters in academia, as not just a rationale for policy-making but as the only framework for understanding and engaging with the world; one, that, on its own terms, appears to be commonsense or self-evident. The point is not so much to prove whether this paradigm is 'right' or 'wrong', but rather to understand the logic and the political context which makes international statebuilding appear to be rational and legitimate. In fact, to understand why international statebuilding appears to its practitioners and advocates as an externally-imposed necessity: one which must be pursued even if policy-practices seem to be running ahead of the available policy information relating practices to outcomes.

A post-liberal paradigm

As will be discussed in more detail (in Chapter 4 on post-liberal governance) the paradigm of international statebuilding – what makes international statebuilding possible – is conceived here in what are described as post-liberal terms. It is analysed as a policy discourse and set of practices which make sense on their own terms, judged by their own criteria, but which make little sense in terms of traditional or classical liberal frameworks of political and legal theory. For this reason, this book does not set out to critique international statebuilding from the position of modern liberal democratic theory, i.e. from the position of the normative defence of autonomy – of the rights to self-government, to democracy and to sovereignty; the focus is instead upon explaining the consequences of operating from within a post-liberal paradigm.

Much of the current literature on international statebuilding is concerned with the contradictions or dilemmas of international intervention with the intention of reconstructing states and societies (see for example, Paris and Sisk 2009a; Pugh *et al.* 2008; Newman *et al.* 2009). It is often asserted that these dilemmas, problems and contradictions, which are increasingly seen to explain the lack of success of international statebuilding in practice, are the product of international statebuilding's construction as a liberal project. It is asserted that the goal of external policy intervention is the construction of a sovereign state and that international policy frameworks pose the importance of the market and of democracy to the success of the statebuilding process. It is also held that the key concerns expressed in the policy frameworks of good governance – such as the rule of law, human rights, economic development and the development of civil society – are the products of a universalized liberal view of the autonomous individual. As we shall consider, in the chapters which follow, though these concepts and terms may sound familiar as part of the 'liberal' political cannon, it is important to consider their reinterpretation within the international statebuilding paradigm. In Chapter 2 it will be suggested that the critique of allegedly 'liberal' frameworks of intervention has facilitated the development and coherence of the international statebuilding paradigm on the basis of its acceptance of difference and the limits of international actors' capacity to develop, secure or democratize failing states and societies.

It has been through reflections on the experience of international intervention in the 1990s and the discussions of the 'lessons learned' that the limits of international policy interventions have been highlighted in ways which have cohered and articulated the post-liberal paradigm of the problematic of autonomy in more overt ways than have been possible in domestic discussions within western polities – although similar shifts in approaches to the meaning and purposes of government have been in the process of development (most clearly noticeable in the discussion of the European Union as an institution of governance rather than government, see EU 2001b). In the discourses of the problems and practices of international statebuilding, the rationality of government – i.e. our understanding of the role of the state, its relationship to society and to the international system – has been posed in ways which have challenged the traditional rights-based assumptions of classic liberalism, which grounded the legitimacy of government on the state's capacity to express collective agency and on its representative accountability.

The view that states and societies, subject to the gaze of international statebuilders, cannot be left to develop their own solutions to social, economic and political questions has increasingly gone along with the idea that international intervention cannot solve these problems or questions on their behalf. The people and the elites of states and societies intervened upon are assumed to be incapable of bearing policy responsibility but at the same time the frameworks of statebuilding intervention deny capacity or policy responsibility to the international interveners themselves. It appears that the policy paradigm of international statebuilding lacks a clear conception of the political and legal subject as the domestic and international arenas increasingly appear to merge and lines of political accountability become blurred. International statebuilding operates in a world without either the liberal conception of the sovereign or the liberal conception of the citizen, as political autonomy has become increasingly problematized at the level of individuals, societies and states. In this context, rights-based accounts of policy legitimacy, based on ideas of the social contract and the primacy of the political subject, have been displaced by what could be described as post-liberal framings, which seek to secure stability through balancing internal and external interests and concerns as matters of technical and administrative competence in the formulations of good governance.

Structure of the book

Criticism of international statebuilding, as it has been implemented as a set of concrete policy practices, has come from a wide range of academic and policy perspectives and the limited nature of policy successes has been highlighted as much by the advocates of statebuilding intervention as by its more radical critics. However, these critics of international statebuilding have only rarely or indirectly highlighted the core conceptual aspect of the statebuilding paradigm: its critique of modern liberal-democratic assumptions about the operation of states and societies. In fact, quite the opposite: rather than statebuilding being understood as premised on a critique of liberal assumptions of the autonomous political subject, the dominant critical analytical framing, amongst both advocates and policy-critics, is that of the 'liberal peace'. In Chapter 2, we will analyse this approach, which criticizes international statebuilding for being *too* liberal and understands the limited success of external intervention as a result of the liberal, universalist, frameworks held to inform international policy-making. We consider the problematic nature of the consensus that international statebuilding should be analysed as a liberal or neoliberal set of practices, which then are held to be in need of adaptation, in order to fit the context of the problems of weak and fragile states in our uncertain and globalized times. This dominant framing often asserts that international statebuilding policy practices have either been too non-interventionist, on the basis of the liberal assumptions that the market or democracy will work 'naturally' without a strong regulatory external presence, or, alternately, that past policy practices have been too interventionist, on the liberal assumption that external interveners can manage the process of state construction without needing to take on board the knowledge and interests of those who live in these societies. In this chapter, it will be argued that these critiques, of the two 'liberal' extremes of international intervention, have driven the international statebuilding discourse in what can be described as 'Third Way' or post-liberal terms.

In Chapter 3, on rethinking the state, the transformation of the understanding of sovereignty is analysed, as a way of highlighting how the post-liberal paradigm of international statebuilding reflects the attenuation or implosion of the liberal framework of political understanding. This can be clearly observed in the redefinition of sovereignty and its inversion from a liberal concept, marking out autonomy as the precondition for the international legal and political order, to the post-liberal framework of governance, in which the problematization of autonomy means sovereignty appears only as a dangerous illusion or idealized goal of external intervention. In the post-liberal paradigm, international policy-practices are legitimized precisely on the basis of the need to preventively intervene to facilitate the safe operation of autonomy.

The chapter goes on to consider the changing approach to sovereignty within the discipline of international relations and the understanding of the problematization of autonomy as the product of globalization which is held to make sovereignty a 'fiction'. It then analyses how sovereignty has been deconstructed in the policy discourse of international statebuilding, through which the traditional conceptualization of sovereignty as synonymous with autonomy and self-government has been inversed to separate sovereignty from statehood. While the international recognition of autonomous statehood remains, this recognition is now seen to necessitate international intervention to ensure that autonomy is made safe through governance mechanisms which assert the need to build sovereign capacities through the internationalization of the production of sovereignty.

The inversion of liberal conceptions of state–society relations is drawn out in more detail in Chapter 4, on post-liberal governance. The key point which this chapter seeks to highlight is that the paradigm of international statebuilding is dependent upon a framing of international regulation in terms of governance rather than government. This shift from government to governance is understood as having less to do with the technical or administrative nature of international regulation or the international order, than with the way in which policy interventions are rationalized and understood. Today, we have an international order which is still based on the nation state as the key actor and policy-making focus – and the construction or reconstruction of the state as the key policy goal – but, nevertheless are witnessing a fundamental shift in our understanding of the operation and management of this order: a shift from government to governance. Post-liberal governance will be analysed as not so much about replacing the nation state with other actors – whether they are trans-national companies or non-governmental organizations – but about how the nation state is understood to develop and implement policy. We thereby highlight that the concept of governance concerns the way that governments govern: the rationality of government, its goals and objectives and its methods of relating to domestic society and to the international sphere.

The chapter expands upon the concept of 'post-liberal', explaining the distinction between this conception and the use of the terms liberal or neoliberal and then goes on to draw out how this distinction impacts upon our understanding of the differences between the concept of government and that of governance. We then turn to the paradigmatic shift in understanding, which international statebuilding highlights, and to briefly analyse the critique of the liberal subject from within the disciplines of economics and sociology and how both these critiques have impacted on the discipline of international relations. Finally, we consider two fundamentally important turning points in the development of post-liberal governance as a coherent bundle of ideas and policy practices: first, in response to the crisis of legitimacy of the post-war West German state, which was to serve as a template for the development of the European Union (analysed by Foucault in the *Birth of Biopolitics*); and, second, as a response to the failure of post-colonial development, which was to become paradigmatic to an institutionalist understanding of the problems of international development today (through the influential policy work of Douglass C. North).

In Chapter 5, the European Union and its export of 'rule of law' and 'good governance' policy frameworks to Southeastern European states is analysed, drawing out how international statebuilding operates on an institutionalist understanding of blockages to democracy and development at two levels, those of the formal state-level institutions and the informal level of civil society. The EU's discourse of governance asserts that it is supportive of sovereignty but here sovereignty is understood as a capacity to manage autonomy, rather than being a product of autonomy and co-determinate with it. This framework enables the EU's interventionist practices and conditionalities to be posed as capacity-building the Southeastern European candidate states rather than as impositions denying or undermining their sovereignty. We consider how the policy practices bound up with the discourse of governance are explicitly those of statebuilding: whereas traditional liberal discourses presupposed sovereignty and political autonomy as the condition of statehood, the governance discourse sees statehood as separate from sovereignty (seen as the capacity for good governance). It highlights how the institutionalist approach of governance understands economic, social and political problems as products of poor institutional frameworks, which have been unable to constrain actors' autonomous pursuit of self-interest in irrational or destabilizing ways.

This chapter also explores how the export of good governance under the EU depends upon an understanding of the rule of law developed within the post-liberal paradigm. It is this framing that enables the EU to export its regulatory regime in its dealings with other actors and potential members, such as the states of Southeastern Europe. In the paradigm of post-liberal governance, the rule of law is understood in terms which are not compatible with the conceptual frameworks of classical liberalism. Whereas, in liberal modernity, the rule of law was understood to derive from the legal subject, in post-liberal frameworks, the rule of law is held to constitute the legal subject or citizen. This inversion of the classical liberal framing of law enables law to be understood and to be legitimized as something external to the state and society being intervened in and as something which can be exported as part of the statebuilding process. The legitimization of the export of the rule of law, on the basis of the problematic nature of the autonomous subject, has meant that external regulation by the EU lacks a framework of legitimation from with the liberal paradigm and, in fact, is constituted in opposition to it.

Chapter 6 considers how the post-liberal paradigm of international state-building has become increasingly central to international security discourses, in the shift from the interventionist frameworks of the 1990s, which clearly posed external intervention as a response to exceptional problems, to the statebuilding approach, which repackages intervention in the terminology of prevention. The shift to a post-liberal paradigm is analysed in the shifting understanding of security at the international level, particularly how the classical subject-based approach of international relations and political theory – the understanding of security in relation to the autonomy and freedom of the political subject – has been rearticulated from the assumptions of the rationalist approach of realism, via the 1990s debates on the 'right of intervention', through to the post-liberal framings of the Responsibility to Protect and international statebuilding.

In the heuristic terms of paradigm shifts, this chapter will draw out three stages: first, the subject-based framing of security as a product of self-help in the anarchical sphere of international relations, which dominated the traditional discipline of international relations; second, the shift towards a liberal discursive framework of intervention posed in terms of the weighing of competing concerns of security and freedom, reflected in debate on the alleged clash of the human rights of individuals and the sovereign rights of states, which was dominant in the 1990s; and third, what we describe in this book as the post-liberal paradigm, cohered in the 2000s, which moved beyond the liberal security/freedom problematic, reformulating the political subject in relation to security in terms of resilience (the capacity to manage internal and external security threats) rather than autonomy (the capacity to strategically project interests). In this framework, international security is no longer concerned with the problematic of securing autonomy but with the problematic of preventively securing the international community against the dangers of state autonomy. This post-liberal paradigm shift will be analysed through an in-depth consideration of the discursive framing of the Responsibility to Protect (R2P). The doctrine of R2P was initially developed in response to the destabilizing consequences of the 'liberal turn' of the 1990s, which appeared to remove the limits to the use of unilateral force and the restrictions of international law. As it has developed, R2P has reflected the shift away from the liberal framing of international intervention as enhancing autonomy, towards the post-liberal framing of resilience through limiting autonomy; in the phraseology of R2P this can be understood as the shift from intervention to prevention.

Chapter 7 analyses the institutionalist approach to development and traces the ways in which current discussions of 'development as freedom' reproduce previous understandings of difference in the international sphere. In the post-liberal discourse of 'human development', freedom and autonomy are foregrounded but development lacks a transformative or modernizing material content. The individualized understanding of development takes a rational choice perspective of the individual or 'the agent-orientated view', in which development policy is orientated towards enabling individuals to make effective choices by increasing their capabilities. The outcome of development can therefore not be measured by any universal framework; different individuals have different development priorities and aspirations and live in differing social and economic contexts. It is highlighted that, while this approach can be understood as a critique of top-down or state-led approaches to development, the post-liberal framing should not be confused with neoliberal advocacy of the free market. Markets are not understood as being capable of finding solutions or leading to development themselves and are seen to depend on the formal institutional framework and the informal institutional framework of social culture, ideas and 'behavioural ethics'.

We will consider how the post-liberal paradigm of international statebuilding builds on earlier discursive framings of development, in stressing the need for ownership, but is distinct from these approaches in that it inverts and transforms the traditional liberal paradigm which understood economic development and political autonomy as mutually supportive aspects of liberal modernity. Earlier development discourses sought to adapt liberal approaches to the colonial or post-colonial world through the emphasis on the problems of material development. The statebuilding paradigm inverses the problematic – the framing of the relationship between development and autonomy: posing the autonomy of the post-colonial or post-conflict subject as a problem for development rather than the lack of development as a problem for political autonomy. In this chapter, the discourse of development as freedom, increasingly central to understanding development within the international statebuilding paradigm, will be traced out in relation to two earlier framings of the problematic of development and autonomy, under the colonial Dual Mandate and in the early post-colonial period. This chapter draws out the changing nature of western discourses of development and the understanding of policy practices as promoting the empowerment of the post-colonial other.

In Chapter 8, the centrality of civil society to international statebuilding will be analysed, considering the ways in which difference has been historically rearticulated, from approaches which have sought to highlight racial or cultural explanations to today's understanding of the centrality of civil society. This chapter seeks to draw out an understanding of the role of narratives and discourses of race, culture and civil society, within international statebuilding, through the location of the discourse of culture as a transitional stage between interventionist and regulatory discourses of race and civil society. It particularly seeks to highlight that earlier discourses of cultural difference have been a key precondition for the post-liberal paradigm of international statebuilding intervention and policy regulation as it has become cohered in the last decade. This is important, as the discourse of culture has, in many respects, been displaced by the discourse of civil society. In drawing out the links between the framings of race, culture and civil society, this chapter seeks to explain how the discourse of civil society intervention has been reinvented on the basis of the pre-existing moral divide reflected through the discourse of culture and highlights that the discourse of civil society contains a strong apologetic content, capable of legitimizing and explaining the persistence of social and economic problems or political fragmentation while simultaneously offering statebuilding policy programmes on the basis of highly ambitious goals of social transformation.

We will consider how, in the policy framings of international statebuilding, the concept of civil society is used very differently to how the concept was deployed in traditional political discourses of liberal modernity. This chapter will clarify some of these differences and highlight that, whereas for traditional conceptions of civil society, autonomy was seen as a positive factor, in the international statebuilding discourse, autonomy is seen as a problematic factor and one which necessitates regulatory intervention. Civil society discourse highlights the problematic nature of autonomy, understood as irreducible differences which risk conflict if not regulated via the correct institutional mechanisms. In the distinctive privileging of difference, in this context of external engagement, the concept of civil society is used in ways which reflect and draw upon pre-modern concepts of difference, especially the pre-existing colonial and post-colonial discourses of race and culture.

Conclusion

It is hoped that, through grasping international statebuilding as a paradigm of discourses and policy practices, this book will enable the reader to reflect upon the changing understanding of both state–society relations and of the international sphere itself, expressed through these policy discourses. It is this change of understandings – this paradigm shift in the way that the political sphere is perceived and policy interventions rationalized – which is the subject of this book. The debates and discussions of international statebuilding are therefore of more importance than merely those of 'learning lessons' for improving policy practices in the international sphere. This book suggests that the stakes involved are potentially much higher.

How we discuss and understand international statebuilding is also important for what it reveals about us; about how we reflect on our own understandings of the political sphere, both domestically and internationally. These discussions highlight that we increasingly understand the liberal framework – and its assumptions about the autonomy of the political subject – as one which today is unworkable or as only feasible if it is subordinated to a series of transitions and inversions. It therefore seems that the question of whether liberalism can or should be replaced or transformed and the consequences of any such replacement or transformation are as pressing for those of us who live in states which have assumed the tasks of international statebuilding as for those who are the subject of these new and intrusive regulatory frameworks.

2 The 'liberal peace' critique of international intervention

Introduction

For many commentators, the lack of success in international intervention since the early 1990s has been explained through the critical discourse of 'liberal peace', where it is assumed that 'liberal' western interests and assumptions have influenced policy-making, leading to counterproductive results. At the core of the critique is the assumption that the liberal peace approach has sought to reproduce and impose western models: the reconstruction of 'Westphalian' frameworks of state sovereignty; the liberal framework of individual rights and winner-takes-all elections; and neoliberal free market economic programmes. This chapter challenges this view of western policy-making and suggests that post-Cold War post-conflict intervention and statebuilding can be better understood as a critique of classical liberal assumptions about the autonomous subject – framed in terms of sovereignty, law, democracy and the market. The conflating of discursive forms with their former liberal content creates the danger that critiques of liberal peace can rewrite post-Cold War intervention in ways that exaggerate the liberal nature of the policy frameworks and act as apologia, excusing policy failure on the basis of the self-flattering view of western policy-elites: that non-western subjects were not ready for 'western' freedoms.

Since the late 1990s, commentators have developed critical frameworks of the 'liberal peace' to understand the new, more interventionist, approaches to the problems of post-conflict rebuilding and the threat of state failure (see, for example, Duffield 2001; Paris 2002; Pugh 2005; Richmond 2005; Richmond and Mac Ginty 2007). In essence, the 'liberal peace' is held to go beyond traditional approaches of conflict prevention, or 'negative peace'; towards the external engineering of post-conflict societies through the export of liberal frameworks of good governance, democratic elections, human rights, the rule of law and market relations (see Richmond 2008a for an overview). As Alex Bellamy and Paul Williams summarize: 'The principle aim of peace operations thus becomes not so much about creating spaces for negotiated conflict resolution between states but about actively contributing to the construction of liberal polities, economies and societies' (2008: 4–5).

The critical discourse of the liberal peace flags up the problem that – under the guise of universalizing western liberal frameworks of democracy and the market – the needs and interests of those subject to intervention are often ignored, resulting in the maintenance of inequalities and conflicts and undermining the asserted goals of external interveners. The critique of international intervention and statebuilding, framed by the construction of the liberal peace, has been highly effective in challenging assumptions of easy fixes to post-conflict situations (see, for example, Chesterman *et al.* 2005; Dobbins *et al.* 2007; Paris and Sisk 2009a).

This chapter forwards an alternative framework, one which questions the use of the 'liberal peace' rubric to describe and analyse post-conflict and international statebuilding interventions in the post-Cold War period. It will be argued that the critique of liberal peace bears much less relation to policy practice than might be assumed by the critical (radical and policy) discourses and, in fact, appears to inverse the relationship between the critique of the liberal peace and the dominant policy assumptions. The critical construction of the liberal peace leads to a set of assumptions and one-sided representations that portray western policy-interventions as too *liberal*: too fixated on western models and too keen to allow democratic freedoms and market autonomy. It will be explained here that this view of 'liberal' interventions transforming post-conflict societies through 'immediate' liberalization and 'rapid democratization and marketization' is a self-serving and fictional policy narrative (Paris 2004: 235). This narrative fiction is then used, in the frameworks of policy-orientated critiques, as the basis upon which to reflect upon western policy and to limit policy expectations (while often extending regulatory controls) on the assumption that the aspirations of external interveners were too ambitious, too interventionist, and too 'liberal' for the states and societies which were the subject of intervention.

It is unfortunate that this policy narrative is given support by more radical critiques of post-Cold War intervention, similarly framed through the critique of liberal peace. For example, Oliver Richmond is not exceptional in re-reading the catastrophe of the invasion and occupation of Iraq in terms of an 'attempt to mimic the liberal state', which has 'done much to discredit the universal claims of the transferability of the liberal peace in political terms' (2008b: 458). Michael Barnett argues that 'liberal values' clearly guide peacebuilding activities and that their 'explicit goal' is 'to create a state defined by the rule of law, markets and democracy' (2006: 88). Beate Jahn has argued that 'the tragedy of liberal diplomacy' lies in the ideological drive of liberalism, in which intervention is intensified despite the counterproductive results (2007a; 2007b). Foucauldian-inspired theorists, Michael Dillon and Julian Reid, similarly reinforce the claim, that the key problematic of intervention is its liberal nature, in their assertion that we are witnessing a liberal drive to control and to regulate the post-colonial world on the behalf of neoliberal or biopolitical power, seeking 'to globalize the domesticating power of civil society mechanisms in a war against all other modes of cultural forms' (Dillon and Reid 2009: 20).

This view of a transformative drive to regulate and control the post-colonial world on the basis of the liberal framings of power and knowledge stands in stark contrast to the policy world, in which, by the end of the Cold War, leading policy institutions were already highly pessimistic of the capacities of what were seen as 'non-liberal' subjects to cope with liberal political, economic and social forms. This pessimism extended to a widespread suspicion that even East and Central European states would be unable to cope with democracy and the market, let alone the states of sub-Saharan Africa. Bringing the critique back in relation with the policy practices seems to suggest that the policy critics of the liberal peace offer succour and consolation to the policy-makers rather than critique. This leads to the concern of this chapter that radical critiques of international intervention on the basis of its 'liberal' nature may be contributing to the development of the policy project of post-liberal governance, which is cohering frameworks of intervention on the basis of a critique of traditional liberal framings of the political subject.

There are many different approaches taken to the critique of liberal peace approaches and often authors do not clearly stake out their methodological frameworks or develop a 'scattergun approach' using a range of different critiques (see Richmond 2005). Nevertheless, for heuristic purposes, it will be useful to frame these diverse critiques within two broad, distinctive, but often interconnected, approaches; which are here categorized as the radical, 'power-based', and the more policy-orientated, 'ideas-based', critiques. The former approach tends to see the discourse of liberal peace as an ideological and instrumental one, arguing that the rhetoric of freedom, markets and democracy is merely a representation of western self-interest, which has little genuine concern for the security and freedoms of those societies intervened in. The latter approach suggests that rather than the concepts being misused, in the discursive frameworks of the projection of western power, the problem lies less with power relations than with the universal conceptualization of the liberal peace itself.

The 'power-based' critique

In this framework, the liberal peace approach is critiqued on the basis that it reflects the hegemonic values and the political, economic and geo-strategic needs of western states. This critique focuses on the role played by the interests of western powers in shaping policy and the impact of the economic and structural inequalities of the world economy. It also pays attention to the naturalizing of policy assumptions based upon this perspective. There are three main versions of this power-based perspective.

First, there is a critical approach which tends to engage with a left or neo-Marxist structural critique of liberal peace approaches. This framing suggests that western intervention is inevitably reproducing hierarchies of power due to the structural constraints of neoliberal market relations – opening up societies and economies through the demands for democratization and the free market (see, for example, Pugh 2005; Pugh *et al.* 2008). This approach focuses on the problems of neoliberal economic policies for the reconstruction of post-conflict societies and suggests that, in serving the interests of dominant western powers and the international financial institutions, the policies of the liberal peace inevitably reproduce the conditions and possibilities for conflict (see also, Abrahamsen 2000; Barbara 2008; Cramer 2006; Jacoby 2007).

This approach often draws upon Robert Cox's critical theory to suggest that the narrow problem-solving approach taken by western policy-makers is problematic as it takes for granted the interests of these actors and treats market-based economic solutions as merely technical 'problem-solving' approaches to address problems of post-conflict development (Cox 1981). These critical approaches to the liberal peace suggest that it is necessary to reflect on these assumptions to reveal the power interests that lie behind them and to question the presentation of these policies in policy-neutral technical terms (see Bellamy and Williams 2008). Michael Pugh, for example, has consistently highlighted how neoliberal economic practices are naturalized as technical solutions to development and reconstruction, marginalizing or preventing political discussions of economic alternatives better suited to post-conflict societies.

Second, there is a more Foucauldian structuralist approach, which critiques the 'liberal peace' not so much on the liberal basis of its interventionary policies per se as on the interests behind these policies: understood as perpetuating the needs and interests of liberal, neoliberal or biopolitical capitalism in the west. Mark Duffield has pioneered this approach in his book *Global Governance and the New Wars* (2001). Here, the focus is less on the opening up of non-western economies to the world market and more on the reshaping and transformation of these societies in order to prevent instability. In his 2001 work, Duffield argued that the project of 'liberal peace reflects a radical development agenda of social transformation' with the aim 'to transform the dysfunctional and war-affected societies that it encounters on its borders into cooperative, representative and, especially, stable entities' (2001: 11).

This transformative liberal intervention is held to have necessitated the radicalization of both development and security discourses, giving the external institutions of global governance new mandates to: 'shift the balance of power between groups and even to change attitudes and beliefs' (Duffield 2001: 15). In his later work, Duffield expanded on this framework of the projection of liberal interests in stabilizing 'zones of conflict' through the use of the Foucauldian conception of biopolitics, where intervention was understood as saving, developing, or securing the other, at the same time legitimizing and extending external regulatory control (Duffield 2007; see also, Dillon and Reid 2009). Duffield argues that in the interests of stabilizing the neoliberal economic order, the divisions between the 'developed' and the 'undeveloped' world are reproduced through policies of containment such as 'sustainable' or 'community-based' development. This approach is echoed by Vivienne Jabri, in her exposition of a Foucauldian framing of the divisive politics of neoliberal intervention. She states, for example:

> The discourse, from Bosnia to Kosovo to Iraq is one that aims to reconstruct societies and their government in accordance with a distinctly western liberal model the formative elements of which centre on open markets, human rights and the rule of law, and of democratic elections as the basis of legitimacy. The aim is no less than to reconstitute polities through the transformation of political cultures into modern, self-disciplining, and ultimately self-governing entities that, through such transformation, could transcend ethnic or religious fragmentation and violence. The trajectory is punishment, pacification, discipline, and ultimately 'liberal democratic self-mastery'.
>
> (Jabri 2007: 124)

The third approach engages from the perspective of critical theory and human security. Like the first approach, it highlights that 'liberal peace' policies should be seen as political and power-based, rather than as purely technical solutions (for example, Bellamy and Williams 2008). However, the focus is less on the assumptions about market relations or securing the needs of global neoliberal or biopolitical power and more on the assumptions made about the political and institutional framework and positivist and rationalist forms of western knowledge. For writers, such as Alex Bellamy and Paul Williams, a central concern is the problematic focus on the rebuilding of Westphalian state forms (2008); for Oliver Richmond, the focus is on the liberal assumptions of political community assumed in the approach of 'liberal peace', which tends to ignore vital local concerns of identity and culture (Richmond 2008a).

The power-based approaches in this third category clearly take on board the concerns over universalizing western liberal assumptions which will be dealt with in the following section, sketching the 'ideas-based' critiques. However, they are classed within the first category as the conception of western 'power' still plays a vital role. Unlike the first two approaches, these more subjective or constructivist frameworks of critique suggest that frameworks of liberal peace, projected through western power, can be successfully challenged by other more reflective, emancipatory, or 'bottom-up' approaches to liberal peace; suggesting that there is not necessarily a clash of interests between those intervening and those intervened upon. As Richmond states:

> Interdisciplinary and cross-cutting coalitions of scholars, policy makers, individuals – indigenous, local, transnational – and civil society actors can develop discursive understandings of peace and its construction . . . [facilitating] a negotiation of a discursive practice of peace in which hegemony, domination, and oppression can be identified and resolved.
> (2008b: 462)

Some commentators from within this perspective would argue that elected western politicians could pursue alternative polices by constructing their interests in a more enlightened way, for example, through pursuing more human security orientated policies, which could be conceived as in western self-interest, in a globalized and interconnected world, or that non-state actors may be able to intervene in ways which engage more equally and empathetically with those on the ground (for example, Tadjbakhsh and Chenoy 2007; Maclean *et al.* 2006).

The 'ideas-based' critique

The 'ideas-based' critique of liberal peace presents itself as a critique of the grounding universalizing assumptions of the liberal policy discourse itself, rather than merely as a critique of the forms of its implementation. These critics of liberal peace advocate less liberal frameworks of intervention, with less attention to the reconstruction of sovereign states, democracy and the free market. While upholding the values of democracy and the free market as ideals, these critics argue against the liberal peace approach on the basis that it is unsuitable in the context of post-conflict states and situations of state failure.

This approach tends to focus on the problem of western interventionist 'ideas' or 'values' rather than on interests or power relations. While their critique of the liberal peace thesis therefore may appear to be more radical, their intentions can also be understood as more conservative or policy-orientated.

Nevertheless, authors such as Roland Paris have defended their position on the basis that policy interventions cannot simply be understood as reflecting power interests, asserting that:

> Peacebuilding missions have taken place in some of the poorest and most economically stagnant parts of the world . . . countries that, to put it bluntly, have little to offer international capitalists . . . The balance sheet of peacebuilding simply does not sustain the economic exploitation thesis.
>
> (Paris 2002: 653)

Rather than problematizing relations of power or the interests behind policy-making, there is a tendency here to view the liberal peace approach as a projection of western ideals in a context where they can be counterproductive. This critique has been developed by Jack Snyder (2000), Fareed Zakaria (2003), Stephen Krasner (2004; 2005), Robert Keohane (2002), and Roland Paris (2004), amongst others, who argue that liberal peace assumptions have undermined the effectiveness of international statebuilding.

One of the core liberal assumptions problematized in this approach is that of sovereign statehood. These critics argue that focusing on (re)constructing sovereign states is unlikely to solve the problems of post-conflict societies, merely to reproduce them. Krasner argues that sovereignty is problematic for many states because they lack the capacity for good governance and require an external regulatory framework in order to guarantee human rights and the rule of law (2004: 89; see also, Fearon and Laitin 2004). Robert Keohane forwards a similar perspective with differing levels of statehood applicable to different levels of governance capacity: 'We somehow have to reconceptualise the state as a political unit that can maintain internal order while being able to engage in international co-operation, without claiming exclusive rights . . . traditionally associated with sovereignty' (2003: 277; see also, Keohane 2002).

Pursuing a similar approach, Paris argues that the assumptions of liberal peace – that democracy and the free market will ensure social progress and stability – neglect to consider the problematic nature of transition. Questioning the assumption that 'liberalization fosters peace', Paris advocates less emphasis on interventionist policies which promote democracy and the market, both of which can encourage competition and conflict without adequate institutional frameworks (2004: 40–51). Instead, Paris advocates a policy of 'Institutionalization before Liberalization' in order to establish the regulatory frameworks necessary to ensure that post-conflict societies can gradually (and safely) move towards liberal models of market democracy (2004: 179–211). This critique of the export of liberal models to non-liberal societies echoes that made in the 1960s by Samuel Huntington (1968; see also, Chapter 7; Chandler 2006c).

These critics of liberal peace do not argue that they are anti-liberal; merely that liberalism, as projected in liberal peace frameworks, has to take into account the non-liberal context in which intervention takes place. Fareed Zakaria, for example, argues that, while in the west, we have historically associated liberalism and democracy, in much of the non-western world we have to make a choice between liberalism and democracy as, without the institutional framework of limited government, 'elections provide a cover for authoritarianism' and are 'merely legitimized power grabs'; in this context, therefore, 'what Africa needs more urgently than democracy is good governance' (2003: 98–99; see also, Snyder 2000).

This critique of the liberal peace is that, rather than being based on the needs and interests of western hegemonic powers and international financial institutions, the problem is one of projecting an idealized understanding of the west's own historical development; one which tends to naturalize the smooth working of the market and understand liberal political frameworks as an organic product of democratic processes such as free elections. For these critics, the founding assumptions of the liberal peace are the problem: attempts to universalize western models in non-liberal contexts, will merely reproduce, and maybe even exacerbate, the problems of conflict and instability.

A 'critical' consensus?

This chapter highlights that the critical intent of academics seeking to construct a radical critique of interventionist western policies has been blunted by their articulation within the problematic of a 'liberal peace'. As the dominant reflections on policy reform similarly seek to pose policy in response to the alleged failings of liberal approaches, this critique easily becomes assimilated into the policy discourse of how policy might be reformed and legitimated, in less allegedly liberal ways, after the policy debacles of Iraq and Afghanistan. The two fairly distinct critical framings of the 'liberal peace' stem from very different methodological perspectives and political and policy intents. While the 'ideas-based' critics tend to seek to defend and legitimate regulatory external intervention, the 'power-based' critics tend to challenge and oppose these frameworks as the projection of western power and interests. Nevertheless, in critiquing western policy interventions, developed since the end of the Cold War, within the problematic of 'liberal peace' it seems that there is often much less distance between the radical approaches and the policy approaches than might be assumed on the basis of political intent and occasionally there is a surprisingly large area of confluence.

It seems that both sides of the divide, regarding the dynamics driving frameworks of liberal peace, start from the basis that the liberal peace (in its various framings) is actually an adequate description of the policy framework being devised and implemented in international intervention and external statebuilding approaches since the end of the Cold War. This would, of course, appear to make intuitive sense if we understood the post-Cold War period as one in which there was a new confidence in the power of liberal frameworks, with assumptions that the collapse of non-market alternatives meant the 'End of History' and the end of any political or ideological challenge to the ascendency of liberal perspectives and discursive judgements on the economic, political and social frameworks of states and societies. However, it will be suggested here that, in order to understand the paradigm of international statebuilding, we need to highlight that the rise of critiques of liberal peace is, in fact, indicative of widespread lack of confidence in classical liberal assumptions about human behaviour and the political and socio-economic institutions needed for human flourishing.

In the critiques of the liberal peace, this growing consensus on the problematic nature of liberalism appears to cross the political and policy spectrum. The fundamental and shared claim of the critics is that the lack of success of external interventions, designed not only to halt conflict but to help reconstruct the peace, is down to the liberalism of the interveners. If only they were not, in various ways, so *liberal*, then it is alleged external intervention or assistance may potentially be much less problematic. It can appear that the main academic and political matter of dispute is whether the liberal peace discourse is amenable to policy change. Here the divide seems to roughly approximate to the division highlighted earlier, in terms of the heuristic categories of 'power-' and 'ideas-based' liberal peace critics. The more radical, 'power-based', critics, with a more economic-determinist approach to the structural dynamics or the needs of 'neoliberalism' are less likely to be optimistic of reform. On the 'ideas-based' side, those critics of liberal peace frameworks who tend to be more engaged in policy-related work are more optimistic with regard to a shift away from the policy emphasis of liberal peace.

In a recent article, Endre Begby and Peter Burgess (2009) argued that the majority of the critics of the liberal peace seemed to share two key assumptions about external intervention: first, that external western intervention (of some kind) was necessary, and second, that the goal of this intervention should be the liberal one of human freedom and flourishing. They stated that, in this case, the problem was not so much with the aspirations or goals of 'liberal peace' but with the practices of intervention itself. They have a valid point regarding the limited nature of much of this 'critical' discourse, but do not reflect adequately on the diminished content of the 'liberalism' of the policy interventions themselves nor the 'liberal' aspirations of those who advocate for the reform of practices of external intervention. It seems that the common ground, in the broad and disparate critiques of the liberal peace, is not the critique of the external practices of intervention as much as of the classical assumptions of liberalism itself.

The critique of liberalism as a set of assumptions and practices seems to be driving the approach to the study of post-Cold War interventions in ways which have tended to produce a fairly one-sided framework of analysis, in which the concept of liberalism is ill-equipped to bear the analytical weight placed upon it and appears increasingly emptied of theoretical or empirical content. Liberalism appears to be used promiscuously to explain a broad range of often contradictory policy perspectives and practices, across very differing circumstances and with very differing outcomes. In this sense, it appears that liberalism operates as a 'field of adversity' (see Foucault's use of this term, 2008: 106) through which a coherent narrative of post-Cold War intervention has been articulated both by critical and policy-orientated theorists. The promiscuous use of liberalism to explain very different policy approaches is, of course, facilitated by the ambiguous nature of the concept itself.

It is this ambiguity which enables liberalism to be critiqued from opposing directions, sometimes by the same author. Good examples of this are Roland Paris and Timothy Sisk who criticize 'liberal' peacebuilding for being both too laissez-faire and too interventionist in its approach to the regulation and management of conflict. In the peacebuilding literature today, the experience of the early and mid-1990s and the 'quick exit' policies of the 'first generation' peacebuilding operations in Nambia, Nicaragua, Angola, Cambodia, El Salvador, Mozambique, Liberia, Rwanda, Bosnia, Croatia and Guatemala has been repackaged as evidence that western interveners had too much faith in the liberal subject (for example, Paris and Sisk 2009b). Similarly, the ad hoc responses to the problems of the early 1990s in the development of 'second generation' peacebuilding, with protectorate powers in Bosnia, Kosovo and East Timor, have been criticized as liberal hubris, on the assumption that international overlords could bring democracy, development and security to others. It seems that, rather than adding clarity, the critique of the 'liberalism' of intervention tells us very little.

The mechanism through which these liberal framings have been facilitated and critiqued is that of the discursive centring of the non-liberal other; on whose behalf the policy critics assert the need for different policy practices. In this way, the policy critics of past policy approaches evade a direct critique of liberal assumptions about equality, autonomy, and transformative capacity, instead, arguing that the non-liberal other (in various ways) invalidates, challenges or resists (passively as well as actively) policy practices which may otherwise have been less problematic.

Rather than a critique of liberalism for its inability to overcome social, economic and cultural inequalities, both the policy, 'ideas-based', critique of the liberal peace and the more radical, 'power-based', critiques argue that social, economic and cultural inequalities and differences have to be central to policy practices and invalidate universalizing liberal attempts to reconstruct and rebuild post-conflict societies. In this context – in which the dichotomy between a liberal policy-making sphere and a non-liberal sphere of policy intervention comes to the fore – there is an inevitable tendency towards a consensual framing of the problematic of statebuilding intervention as a problem of the relationship between the liberal west and the non-liberal other.

The non-liberal other increasingly becomes portrayed as the barrier to western liberal aspirations of social peace and progress; either as it lacks the institutional, social, economic and cultural capacities that are alleged to be necessary to overcome the problems of liberal peace or as a subaltern or resisting subject, for whom liberal statebuilding frameworks threaten their economic or social existence or fundamental values or identities. The 'critique' becomes apology in that this discursive focus upon the non-western or non-liberal other is often held to explain the lack of policy success and, through this, suggest that democracy or development are somehow not 'appropriate' aspirations or that expectations need to be substantially lowered or changed to account for difference (see also, Chapter 7).

International statebuilding and the critique of liberalism

It would appear that the assumptions held to be driving liberal peace approaches are very much in the eye of their critical beholders. The most obvious empirical difficulty is that international policy regarding intervention and statebuilding seems to have little transformative aspiration: far from assumptions of liberal universalism, it would appear that, with the failure of post-colonial development, especially from the 1970s onwards, international policy-makers have developed historically low expectations about what can be achieved through external intervention and assistance. The lack of transformative belief is highlighted by one of the key concerns of the policy critics of the liberal peace – the focus on capacity-building state institutions and intervening to construct 'civil' societies. The focus on institutional solutions (at both the formal and informal levels) to the problems of conflict and transition is indicative of the narrowing down of aspirations from transforming society to merely regulating or managing it – often understood critically as the 'securitizing' of policy-making. This is a long way from the promise of liberal transformation and the discourse of 'liberating' societies economically and politically.

In fact, it is the consensus of opinion on the dangers of democracy, which has informed the focus on civil society-building and good governance. For the policy and radical critics of liberal peace, liberal rights frameworks are often considered problematic in terms of the dangers of exclusion and extremism. As already noted (in Chapter 1), today's 'post-liberal' peace approaches do not argue for the export of democracy – the freeing up of the political sphere on the basis of support for popular autonomy. The language of post-liberal institutionalist approaches is that of democratization: the problematization of the liberal subject, held to be incapable of moral, rational choices at the ballot box, unless tutored by international experts concerned to promote civil society and pluralist values (see also, Chapter 5). In these frameworks, the holding of elections serves as an examination of the population and the behaviour of electoral candidates, rather than as a process for the judgement or construction of policy (which it is assumed needs external or international frameworks for its production).

The focus on institutionalism does not stem from a 'lessons learned' critique of liberal peace programmes; institutionalist approaches developed from the 1970s onwards and were rapidly mainstreamed with the end of the Cold War. These policy frameworks originated, in part, as a response to criticism of US-led development policies and sought to explain why the introduction of market-orientated policies did not lead to the equalization of development possibilities but instead appeared to perpetuate inequalities (see the theoretical framing developed in North and Thomas 1973; see also, North 1981; 1990). For institutionalist approaches, the problem is not the market but the formal and informal institutions of the societies concerned, which are held to prevent or block the market from working optimally (see also, Chapter 4). From 1989 onwards, western governments and donors have stressed that policy interventions cannot just rely on promoting the freedoms of the market and democracy, but need to put institutional reform and 'good governance' at the core. This shift was highlighted in the seminal World Bank papers highlighting the growing policy consensus around institutionalist approaches (WB 1989; 1992; 1997; 1998). Even in relation to Central and Eastern Europe it was regularly stressed that the people and elected representatives were not ready for freedom and that it would take a number of generations before it could be said that democracy was 'consolidated' (for example, Dahrendorf 1990). The transitology literature was based on the critique of liberal assumptions – this was why a transitional period was necessary. Transition implied that markets and democracy could not work without external institutional intervention to prevent instability. While markets needed to be carefully managed through government policy-making it was held that civil society was necessary to ensure that the population learnt civic values to make democracy viable (see, for example,

Fukuyama 1995; Schmitter and Karl 1991; O'Donnell 1996; Gunther *et al.* 1996).

It was through the engagement with 'transition' and the problematic negotiation of European Union enlargement that the discursive framework of liberal institutionalism – where human rights, the rule of law, civil society, and anti-corruption are privileged over democracy – was programmatically cohered (see also, Chapter 5). It was also through the discussion of 'transition' that the concept of sovereign autonomy was increasingly problematized, initially in relation to the protections for minority rights and then increasingly expanded to cover other areas of domestic policy-making (see, for example, Cordell 1998). It would appear that the key concepts and values of the 'liberal peace', held to have been promoted with vigour with the 'victory of liberalism' at the end of the Cold War, were never as dominant a framing as their radical and policy critics have claimed. In fact, recent studies show that where there has been the rhetorical use of liberal claims of promoting democracy and the market, this has often been a post-hoc response to policy failure, used for public relations rather than as a driver of policy-making (Hehir 2008).

Rather than attempting to transform non-western societies into the liberal self-image of the west, it would appear that external interveners have had much more status-quo aspirations, concerned with regulatory stability and regional and domestic security, rather than transformation. Rather than imposing or 'exporting' alleged liberal western models, international policy-making has revolved around the promotion of regulatory and administrative measures which suggest the problems are not the lack of markets or democracy but rather the culture of society or the mechanisms of governance. Rather than promoting democracy and liberal freedoms, the discussion has been how to keep the lid on or to manage the 'complexity' of non-western societies, usually perceived in terms of fixed ethnic and regional divisions. The solution to the complexity of the non-liberal state and society has been the internationalization of the mechanisms of governance, removing substantive autonomy rather than promoting it.

While it is true that the reconstruction or rebuilding of states is at the centre of external projects of intervention, it would seem to be mistaken to understand the project of international statebuilding as one which aimed at the construction of a liberal international order (see also, Chapter 4 on post-liberal governance; Devji 2008: 173). This is not just because external statebuilding would be understood as a contradiction in liberal terms but, more importantly, because the states being constructed in these projects of post-conflict and failed state intervention are not liberal states in the sense of having self-determination and political autonomy. The state at the centre of statebuilding is not the 'Westphalian state' of classical international relations theorizing. Under the internationalized regulatory mechanisms of intervention and statebuilding the state is increasingly reduced to an administrative level, in which sovereignty no longer marks a clear boundary line between the 'inside' and the 'outside' (see Walker 1992). Whether we consider EU statebuilding, explicitly based on a sharing of sovereignty, or consider other statebuilding interventions, such as those by the international financial institutions in sub-Saharan Africa, it is clear that the state is central as a mechanism for external coordination and regulation rather than as a self-standing actor in so-called 'Westphalian' terms (see Ghani and Lockhart 2008; Chandler 2006a; Harrison 2004).

Too liberal?

There is little evidence here of the assertions of the critics of the liberal peace, that external interveners imagine that they have the power to reshape state institutions and societies in accordance with western norms. The limited results would appear to demonstrate that the process of internationalizing the governance of non-western states, through the process of state institution-building has increasingly resulted in states that have little connection with their societies, and where the formal political process is increasingly marginalized. Empirically, the radical critics of liberal peace may be correct to argue that external policies of intervention – which operate at the formal level of exporting administrative frameworks, such as the rule of law and mechanisms of 'good governance' – marginalize the people of these societies. This, however, is not the same as arguing that this is because the frameworks of intervention are too *liberal*.

It is quite possible to argue that external mechanisms of international engagement ignore the economic and social context of these societies and are satisfied with non-western states paying lip-service to external donor and institutional requirements without asserting that these external actors are attempting to transform these states into Westphalian liberal democracies. At the empirical level, it is unproblematic to argue that the result of these external programmes of intervention might be seen as 'façade democracy' or as 'reproducing state failure' (Bickerton 2007; Chopra 2003) or to highlight that western policy aspirations have little purchase on very different realities and often therefore result in 'hybrid polities' where the state formally accords to western norms but informally still operates on the basis of traditional hierarchies and exclusions (see, for example, Roberts 2008; 2009).

Where this critical discourse becomes problematic is in the confidence with which its proponents assert that the reasons for these policy failings can be located in the liberalism of the interveners or the illiberalism of the subjects of intervention. Roland Paris, for example, argues that 'there is no logical requirement for international agencies to resurrect failed states *as states*, rather than [as] some other type of polity', and argues that this is the 'latest chapter in the globalisation of the Westphalian state', where this state form is being propped up despite its failings (2002: 654). Paris argues that just as the non-liberal other cannot deal with the liberal state form, they are similarly ill-suited to handle electoral democracy, warning particularly against the holding of elections in post-conflict situations. It is asserted that holding elections when societies are still divided or segmented will be counterproductive, often giving enhanced legitimacy to warring parties and bolstering the legitimacy of the forces successful in conflict. Often the solutions advocated by the policy critics are along similar lines with regard to both sovereignty and democracy: the need for greater international engagement in the state institutions, under the guise of guaranteeing that no voices are 'excluded' and the need to constrict the autonomy of elected authorities. Under the rubric of the critique of the liberal peace, these critics of the liberal peace universally advocate the reform of policy interventions away from the focus on liberal rights frameworks and electoral democracy.

Dominik Zaum, for example, through a series of case studies, argues that the aspirations of the technocratic approach of international statebuilding fails to appreciate that the liberal discourse of self-government undermines the authority of external interveners and enables local elites to assert pressure and influence (2007). These liberal normative commitments are held to mean that international interventions are limited both in time and scope and therefore find it difficult to resist compromising their initial goals through giving greater authority to local actors (see also, Ignatieff 2003). Other authors have a similar perspective, explaining the failures of international intervention as a product of external actors assuming that liberal models can merely be exported, rather than understanding the contradictions involved in bringing liberalism to non-liberal societies. Michael Barnett and Christopher Zürcher, for example, have sought to analyse why liberal interventions tend to be no more than surface phenomena, on the basis that elites at both national and subnational levels can 'capture' and 'compromise' statebuilding, leading to the reproduction of existing state-society relations and patrimonial politics (2009). Miles Kahler argues that this thesis of 'policy capture' by local elites is the key to solving the 'recurring puzzle' of 'the absence of a clear relationship between an apparent asymmetry in bargaining power between the international coalition and local political agents on the one hand, and statebuilding outcomes on the other' (2009: 296).

Some of the policy critics argue not merely that these western models are perverted by the power of the non-liberal other but that the attempt to export western models to non-liberal societies is inevitably going to fail to bridge the gulf between liberal and non-liberal state-society forms. Noah Feldman, for example, suggests that these non-western states and societies are so alien to western liberal interveners that 'the high failure rate strongly supports the basic intuition that we do not know what we are doing' (2004: 69). Feldman suggests that we need to continue to provide external assistance but should reject the idea that 'our comparative advantages of wealth and power [give] us any special ability to identify the institutional structures that will succeed in promoting democracy' (2004: 71). Michael Ignatieff similarly argues that 'we do not actually know how to make states work in non-liberal societies that are poor, divided on religious or ethnic lines or lacked a substantial state tradition in the first place' (2005: 73). The work of Roland Paris and Timothy Sisk, supports this view, suggesting that, in dealing with the non-liberal other, the issues are so complex and dilemma-laden that pragmatic 'muddling through' is the only solution (2009c).

Discursively, the alleged 'voice' of the non-liberal other has also been central to the shifting discourse of development. While some commentators suggest that little substantive has changed in the shift from the modernizing frameworks of the liberal 'Washington Consensus' to the post-liberal, post-conditionality, 'New York Consensus' focus on pro-poor policy making, sustainable development and poverty reduction strategy papers (for example, Pugh 2005; Cammack 2004, 2006; Harrison 2001), there is little doubt that the aspirations for social and economic transformation have been scaled back (see Crawford 2006; Easterly 2006). It is quite clear that the broad frameworks of development intervention have much lower horizons than during the Cold War period (Leys 1996; Pender 2001); for example, the replacement of Cold War desires for modernization with the Millennium Development Goals (MDGs). The MDGs focus not on social and economic transformation but on the situation of the poorest in society with the aspiration that, by 2015, people will be able to live on $1 a day (Sachs 2005). The view that there is a universalizing transformative liberal agenda is a peculiar way to understand the focus on sustainable development, small and medium enterprises and the shift away from large development projects. Mark Duffield's work on the divisive effects of post-Cold War development policies draws out well what could more critically be understood as the 'post-liberal' nature of the shifting discourses on development and security (2007; see also, Chapter 7).

With regard to the critique of universal liberal aspirations for progress, it is often difficult to tell the policy perspectives apart from the viewpoints of some of the more radical critics of the liberal peace. There is a noticeable slippage from liberalism being criticized for its inability to universalize economic growth and overcome the problems of combined and uneven development to the problem of liberalism appearing to be the universalist aspiration for development itself. For example, Michael Pugh asserts that rather than the 'economic rationalism of (capitalistic) entrepreneurship', other, 'non-liberal', values need to be taken into account. Following the work of those critical of liberal development models, such as Amartya Sen (see also, Chapter 7; Sen 1999), he argues that in non-liberal societies:

> Inequalities and non-physiological needs are considered more significant than either absolute poverty or, beyond a survival point, physiological needs. This means that provided people are not destitute . . . they may choose to live humbly in order to be fulfilled. Such an approach recognises that the paths to modernisation may not be convergent at all, and the marginalised peoples of the world are entitled to choose the extent to which, and how, they integrate in the global economy.
>
> (Pugh 2005: 34)

It would seem that at the core of the policy and radical critiques of the liberal peace is a critique of liberal aspirations rather than a critique of international interventionist policies and practices. The critique reflects the ease with which liberalism has become a 'field of adversity', through which both policy reform and critical claims for theoretical advance can both be made. The construction of a liberal 'field of adversity' seems to have little relation to policy realities. This is reflected in the fact that, while there is a consensus on the view that western policies are problematic in that they are too liberal, there is much less attention to how the problems of the post-colonial world might be alternatively addressed. Here, as discussed later, the discursive critique of the liberal peace unfortunately has very little to offer in ways that go beyond present policy perspectives.

Beyond the critique of the liberal peace?

It would appear that the ostensibly more radical critics, those who draw out the problematic nature of power relations – the aforementioned 'power-based' critiques – in fact, have very little to offer as a critical alternative to the current policies of intervention and statebuilding, other than a scaling back of the possibilities of social change. The leading critics of the liberal peace, like Mark Duffield, Michael Pugh and Oliver Richmond – working through critical theoretical frameworks which problematize power relations and highlight the importance of difference – suggest that the difference between the liberal west and the non-liberal other cannot be bridged through western policy-making. For Pugh, as we have seen earlier, taking critical theory to its logical conclusion, capitalist rationality is itself to be condemned for its universalizing and destabilizing impulses. Similarly, for Duffield, it seems that the problem of hegemonic relations of power and knowledge cannot be overcome, making any projection of the ideals of development or democracy potentially oppressive (2007: 215–34). Oliver Richmond, has systematized this perspective, highlighting the problems of the disciplinary forms of knowledge of 'liberal peace' approaches and suggesting that while it may be possible to go beyond them through the use of post-positivist and ethnographic approaches – enabling external interveners to have a greater access to the knowledge of 'everyday life' in non-liberal societies being intervened in – any attempt to know, rather than merely to express 'empathy', is open to hegemonic abuse (2008a: 149–65).

It would appear that, without a political agent of emancipatory social change, the radical 'power-based' critics of liberal peace who draw upon the perspectives of critical theory, cannot go beyond the bind which they have set themselves, of overcoming hegemonic frameworks of knowledge and power. In fact, it could be argued that these critical approaches, lacking the basis of a political subject to give content to critical theorizing, ultimately take an uncritical approach to power. Power is assumed rather than theorized; making the limits to power appear merely as external to it. It is assumed that there is an attempt to transform the world in liberal terms and that the failure to do so can therefore be used to argue that liberal forms of knowledge are inadequate ones. The critique is not essentially of power or of intervention but of the limited knowledge of liberal interveners. The alternative is not that of emancipatory social transformation but of the speculative and passive search for different, non-liberal, forms of knowledge or of knowing. This comes across clearly in the conclusions reached by Duffield, Richmond and others, and highlights the lack of a critical alternative embedded in these approaches.

The more ostensibly conservative critics of the liberal peace, drawn largely to the policy-making sphere, have much clearer political aims in their critique of the liberal peace. This is manifest in their focus on institutional reform, understood as a way of reconciling non-liberal states and societies both to the market and to democratic forms. This, like the transitology discourse before it, is a radical critique of classical liberal assumptions. In their advocacy of these frameworks, discursively framed as a critique of the 'liberal peace', they have a clear point of reference. Although, as highlighted earlier, this point of reference is a fictional one: a constructed narrative of post-Cold War intervention, which enables them to ground the scaling-back of policy expectations against a framework of allegedly unrealistic liberal aspirations.

This critique of liberalism is not a critique of interventionist policy-making but rather a defence of current practices on the basis that they have not been properly applied or understood. Institutionalist approaches, which have informed the interventionist frameworks of international institutions and donors since the early 1990s, are explicit in their denunciation of the basic assumptions of classical liberalism. This critique of liberalism is, however, an indirect one, inevitably so, as the institutionalist critique developed at the height of the Cold War (see Leys 1996). This is why, while the classical concepts of the liberal rights framework remain – 'sovereignty', 'democracy', 'rule of law', 'civil society' – they have been given a new content, transforming the universal discourse of the autonomous liberal rights-holder from that of the subject of rights to the object of regulation. This new content has unfortunately been of little interest to the more radical 'power-based' critics of the 'liberal peace'. But, in understanding the content of institutionalist approaches, it is possible to tie together the superficial nature of external engagement with the fact that it has a post-liberal content rather than one which is too liberal.

As we shall analyse in the chapters that follow, the institutionalist discourse of intervention and regulation is not one of liberal universalism and transformation but one of restricted possibilities, where democracy and development are hollowed out and, rather than embodying the possibilities of the autonomous human subject, become mechanisms of control and ordering. Institutionalization reduces law to an administrative code, politics to technocratic decision-making, democratic and civil rights to those of the supplicant rather than the citizen, replaces the citizenry with civil society, and the promise of capitalist modernity with pro-poor poverty reduction. To conceptualize this inversion of basic liberal assumptions and ontologies as 'liberalism' would be to make the word meaningless at the same time as claiming to stake everything on the assumed meaning and stakes involved in the critique of the 'liberal' peace.

Conclusion

The critique of the liberal peace is based upon the assumption that western intervention is too 'liberal'. The fact that it is too liberal is alleged to be revealed in its lack of success on the ground; in its failure to achieve liberal outcomes. For the policy critics, the sources of this failure are held to be located in the non-liberal nature of the societies intervened upon. In the dominant policy framing of interventionist agendas, this failing is because of the lack of capacity of domestic societies and political elites; for more radical readings, the problematic impact of external policy-making is often re-read as the resistance of indigenous ways of life and knowledges, which should instead be understood and empathized with.

If the critique of intervention is for its liberalism, then it suggests that the self-image of the west is being projected where it cannot work. The critique can easily flatter the self-understanding of international interveners that if they are incapable of transforming the post-conflict societies and failing states that they are engaged with it is merely because they cannot easily be anything other than liberal and that the societies being intervened in are not ready for liberal frameworks of governance. This critique, can, in fact, result in the reproduction of the ideological binary of the civilizational divide between the interveners and the intervened in, which is seen to be confirmed the more interventionist approaches appear to have little impact and to have to be scaled back.

There are a number of problems with the critical construction of 'liberal peace'. These stem not merely from the fact that the interventionist policies being critiqued seem to be far from 'liberal'. Of greater concern is the way that the term 'liberal' appears to have become an easy and unproblematic assertion of critical intent. The critique of the 'liberal peace' – and its ability to encompass both policy advocates and radical critics of intervention – appears to reveal much more about the problematic state of radical and liberal thought than it does about the policies and practices of intervention and statebuilding. The ostensible framework of the 'liberal peace' – of the transformative dynamic ontology of the universal rational subject – had already long since been critiqued and displaced by the framework of governance and regulatory power. It is peculiar, in these circumstances, that the dominant policy discussion and the radical discursive framing of post-Cold War intervention should both therefore take this form.

While apologetic intent can perhaps be reasonably applied to some critics working within policy-making circles and attempting to justify the continuation and revamping of current policy framings, this charge cannot so easily be placed at the feet of those articulating more 'power-based' critiques of the liberal peace. That the radical critique of the 'liberal peace' should reproduce similar framings to that of the policy-oriented institutionalist critique of liberal peace, highlights the use of the liberal paradigm as a 'field of adversity' to give coherence to radical frameworks of critique. However, in focusing on the target of liberalism rather than starting from the policy practices and discourses themselves, there is a danger that radical criticism not only misses the fundamental transformations in the way that international policy-making is being constructed but that it can also be enlisted in support of the institutionalist project, which seeks to rewrite the failures of post-Cold War intervention as a product of the universalizing tendencies of a liberal approach and suggests that we should give up on the liberal aspirations of the past on the basis of an appreciation of the irreconcilable 'difference' of the non-liberal subject.

The following chapters consider the post-liberal nature of international statebuilding policy discourse in more depth, drawing out the implications of this new policy consensus which problematizes the universal categories of liberal frameworks of democracy and market development on the basis that societal differences need to be better understood and adapted to. It is upon the basis of the recognition of differences in institutional capacities that universal liberal framings of the autonomous subject have been critiqued and traditional rights-based approaches to sovereign equality and non-intervention have been reinterpreted as barriers to international stability rather than as the bulwark of the international order. As we shall see in the following chapter, state sovereignty has become an argument for the necessity of international statebuilding intervention rather than a reason to resist this intervention. This inversion of liberal framings of autonomy, as a precondition for the interventionist order of post-liberal governance, is discussed at greater length in Chapter 4 and, as a set of developing policy practices, in Chapter 5.

3 Rethinking the state

Introduction

In what is described here as the post-liberal paradigm of international statebuilding, the most important conceptual shift from that of a classic liberal framework is in the meaning of the term sovereignty. The meaning of sovereignty within the international statebuilding paradigm is incommensurable with the meaning of sovereignty in the classic liberal account of politics and of international relations. Sovereignty, as a concept marking out the autonomy of the state – indicating its monopoly of rule over a territory and its autonomy to act in the international sphere – was a central concept in the classical political theory of liberalism and in the division between the disciplines of political theory and international relations.

The post-liberal paradigm of international statebuilding reflects the attenuation or implosion of this liberal framework of political understanding. This is highlighted in the redefinition of sovereignty and its inversion from a concept marking out the centrality of autonomy, for liberal approaches to government, to the centrality of the problem of autonomy, in what is described here as the post-liberal framework of governance. Where autonomy was central to the understanding and legitimization of the liberal political order, both domestically and internationally, in the post-liberal paradigm, autonomy is problematized and international policy-practices are legitimized precisely on the basis of the need for external intervention as the precondition for the safe operation of autonomy.

The following section considers the changing approach to sovereignty within the discipline of international relations and the understanding of the problematization of autonomy as the product of globalization, which is held to make sovereignty a 'fiction'. It then analyses how sovereignty has been deconstructed in the policy discourse of international statebuilding, through which the traditional conceptualization of sovereignty as synonymous with autonomy and self-government has been inversed to separate sovereignty from statehood. While the international recognition of autonomous statehood remains, this recognition is now seen to necessitate international intervention to ensure that autonomy is made safe through governance mechanisms which assert the need to build sovereign capacities through the internationalization of the production of sovereignty.

The 'fiction' of sovereignty in international relations

International relations developed, in the post-Second World War period, as a sub-branch of the academic discipline of political theory; conceived of as a political discipline but one that was distinct from political theory due to the specific nature of its subject matter. Whereas political theory dealt with the internal politics of sovereign states, with the relationship between sovereign and society or state and citizens, international relations attempted to understand the international polity: one which operated in the absence of a sovereign; in the absence of an international hierarchy or order. Whilst hierarchical order was held to exist within sovereign states, the international sphere was conceived of as anarchical, akin to a Hobbesian state of nature.

This understanding of the problematic of the discipline of international relations – how autonomous (state) subjects maintained order in the absence of a sovereign – was framed in the terms of classic liberal political theory, but as a negative image. Liberal theory qualitatively distinguished between domestic societies framed by a formal institutional sphere of law and politics – institutionalizing the division between political and legal equality and economic and social inequality – and a sphere where liberal order was not possible: the international sphere. This liberal framing of the distinction between the domestic sphere and the international sphere constituted the basis upon which international relations could appear as a distinct sub-discipline of politics, marked out by the absence of a sovereign.

In the absence of a sovereign, it was understood that international relations was limited in its ability to theorize politics. The politics of the international sphere was understood to be little more than *realpolitik*: the politics of power relations. In this context, there was a much weaker constitution of international society, and international law was understood to be a product of power rather than consent, with little room for ethical discussions of justice rather than order, or progress rather than cycles of war and peace. In fact, the dominant concern was highlighted in Martin Wight's article, which asked the question: 'Why is there no international theory?' (Wight 1966).

The paradigm of international statebuilding is based on a third approach, quite distinct from the liberal framings which sharply distinguished between the existence of a sovereign order, making progress, justice and ethics possible, and the inter-sovereign order of the international in which security involved self-help mechanisms of the balance of power (see also, Chapter 6). Its conception of the international order is one of shared or overlapping regimes of governance in which autonomy is problematized at the level of sovereignty. The solution to the lack of sovereign order in the international sphere is not that of constituting a global sovereign – the nation state writ large – but of restricting sovereign autonomy at the level of the state. While, discursively, it may be concerned with strengthening states, it conceives of this as a process of limiting or regulating their autonomy.

Once autonomy is problematized, the concepts of sovereignty or of self-government or self-determination mean something very different within the post-liberal paradigm. Sovereignty or self-government apply to a range of capacities for self-help and being able to manage the administrative and technical requirements of autonomy, rather than to self-direction or the establishment of autonomous political goals or aspirations. In fact, autonomy is seen to impose external duties and responsibilities on states rather than expressing their freedom of agency. Sovereignty is redefined from an attribute of autonomy, denoting control over a territory, to the recognition of the limits and dangers of autonomy or control. It is only once, allegedly, failing states recognize that they should not aspire to control that they are said to have sovereignty: i.e. to be able to manage the policy equilibrium necessary for good governance in reflective modernity.

The fact that states are sovereign, i.e. self-governing actors, is seen as necessitating international regulatory control. Autonomy is therefore not the goal of statebuilding but rather its precondition; on the starting assumption of the need for external assistance or the internationalization of the process of ensuring this autonomy is governed safely. Sovereignty, in this sense, is the problem rather than the solution. In this framing, the problem of failed and failing states is precisely that they are autonomous, that they control themselves. In which case, they lack the international framework of regulatory norms and intermeshing institutional frameworks held to be necessary for effective and functional states. It is their autonomy that is understood to be cutting them off from developmental opportunities, preventing sustainable solutions to conflict, facilitating environmental degradation, and so forth.

The problematization of autonomy is given the status of commonsense in the paradigm of international statebuilding as there is an assumption that autonomy is no longer a positive attribute even for advanced western states. The desire for autonomy is increasingly seen as a hubris or prejudice in itself: that any assertion of the importance of autonomy is already a problematic denial of the realities of the international sphere and potentially destabilizing and conflictual. To attempt to assert or defend autonomy against the discursive dynamic of the international statebuilding paradigm is therefore, in itself, considered to be a problematic sign. It is the discussion of autonomy, in the context of globalization, which perhaps most clearly highlights the shift in dominant understandings of autonomy and the incommensurability between the liberal paradigm and what is described here as the post-liberal one. According to leading social theorists, such as Anthony Giddens, David Held and Ulrich Beck, globalization undermines the previous rationale of sovereign autonomy: the idea that states could both collectively represent society and that they could instrumentally act on its behalf. Sovereignty was legitimized as a collective expression of popular will in the classic assumptions of liberalism. However, if it is the case that citizens are much more reflexive in their identities and interests, seeing themselves more as global citizens than as bound to a particular territorial community, then the state is not capable of fulfilling the task of representation and therefore of legitimizing itself in relation to its society (Giddens 1994: 10).

More importantly, globalization is held to invalidate sovereign claims of control and direction over society – the ability to act instrumentally or as a social agent. In this way, globalization has been held to make sovereignty meaningless (in ways which will parallel our discussion of the shift from government to governance in Chapters 4 and 5). This lack of instrumental capacity is conceived of as invalidating claims to sovereign status both domestically and in the international arena. In fact, globalization is held to undermine the notion of a division between these two spheres of activity. For Ulrich Beck, national sovereignty is undermined by the fact that globalization disrupts the links between territory and authority, making the distinction between territories, and the framework of legitimacy for government power, increasingly problematic (Beck 1997; 2005). Taken to its extreme, Giddens refers to the work of business guru Keniche Ohmae that: 'we live now in a borderless world, in which the nation state has become a "fiction" and where politicians have lost all effective power' (Giddens 1998: 29; Ohmae 1990; 1995).

Globalization, here acts as a shorthand explanation for why it appears that state autonomy can no longer be the central way of conceiving the legitimacy of governmental power or of rationalizing policy practices, either domestically or internationally. The importance of the globalization thesis lays less in its explanatory claims for this shift than in its widespread acceptance as a marker for the transformed nature of our understanding of autonomy. In a complex, global, interconnected and increasingly insecure and uncertain world it appears that policy-making autonomy is a problem rather than a framework for resolving problems of politics or of policy-making. Globalization poses the question that if autonomy is potentially dangerous and destabilizing, how should governments govern, the answer to this question can be seen in the rationalities for governance developed in the discourses of international statebuilding, in which sovereignty is reinterpreted as the institutional mechanism through which the dangers of autonomy can be ameliorated.

Sovereignty without autonomy

Sovereignty in classical framings of international relations signified political and legal autonomy: constitutional independence. It was a legal concept which was understood to be unconditional and indivisible. As Robert Jackson summarized:

> [It is] legal in that a sovereign state is not subordinate to another sovereign but is necessarily equal to it by international law . . . Absolute [unconditional] in that sovereignty is either present or absent. When a country is sovereign it is independent categorically: there is no intermediate condition. Unitary [indivisible] in that a sovereign state is a supreme authority within its jurisdiction.
>
> (1990: 32)

Prior to decolonization in the last century, the sovereign state form was only one of several kinds of international status. Under European colonialism territorial entities took the form of 'colonies', 'protectorates', 'mandates', 'trust territories', or 'dominions' (Jackson 1990: 33). What these various forms had in common was formal legal subordination to a foreign power; they were a denial of sovereignty. There was nothing inevitable or natural about the sovereign state form or about its universalization in the twentieth century, in the wake of the First and Second World Wars (Wight 1979: 23; Morgenthau 1970: 258–61).

Few people engaged in the field of international statebuilding would argue that international policy interventions in non-western states should be based on the desire to create or support traditional sovereign entities. This can be seen clearly in practice in the cases of international engagement in Bosnia, Afghanistan, the handing over of 'sovereignty' in Iraq, and moves to make Kosovo an independent state in 2008, and more broadly in the UN and G8 proposals for state capacity-building in Africa. The sovereign state forms are held up but sovereignty is being redefined – or 'unbundled' in Stephen Krasner's phraseology (1999) – emphasizing the administrative and technical responsibilities of the state while abandoning its political content of self-government and autonomy.

This is done in three ways: first, by redefining sovereignty as a variable 'capacity' rather than an indivisible right, thereby legitimizing a new hierarchy of variable sovereignty and invalidating the UN Charter principle of sovereign equality; second, by redefining sovereignty as a duty or responsibility rather than a freedom, legitimizing external mechanisms of regulation, held to enhance 'sovereignty' despite undermining the traditional right of self-government or autonomy; and, third, by exaggerating the formal importance of international legal sovereignty so that this formal shell then facilitates the repackaging of external regulation as 'partnership' or 'country ownership' and the voluntary contract of formally equal partners.

Sovereignty as capacity?

The most important challenge to traditional conceptions of sovereignty has been the conflation of the formal political and legal right to self-government (an absolute quality) with the question of state capacity (a variable quantity), usually formulated in terms of 'good governance'. The conception of sovereignty as a capacity, rather than as a formal legal right to self-government and international legal equality, creates a structure of a 'continuum' of sovereignty or a hierarchy of sovereignty where some states are considered to be more sovereign than others. This approach was notably developed by Robert Jackson, with his conception of 'quasi-states' (Jackson 1990). For Jackson, the sovereignty granted to post-colonial states was artificial. Not because they were often still under the influence of their former colonial rulers, but because many of these states did not have the capacity to regulate and control their societies to the same extent as states in the west. Jackson argued that these states possessed 'de jure' sovereignty, formal international legal rights, but lacked 'de facto' sovereignty, the capacity to govern effectively.

This idea of the 'unbundling' of sovereignty into its different attributes was popularized by Stephen Krasner in his 1999 book *Sovereignty: Organized Hypocrisy*. In his more recent work, he has focused on sovereignty as a 'bundle' of three separate attributes: 'domestic sovereignty', the capacity of domestic governance structures; 'Westphalian/Vattelian sovereignty', i.e. self-government or political autonomy; and international legal sovereignty, formal juridical independence (Krasner 2004: 87–88). Krasner uses the problem of weak state capacity to argue that self-government should not be a barrier to international intervention but, in fact, makes intervention a necessity. Whereas in the 1990s intervention would have been posed as a conflict between human rights (or the right of intervention) and the right of state sovereignty (self-government and autonomy), in Krasner's terminology there is no conflict with sovereignty because human rights would be protected if governments possessed adequate governing capacity ('domestic sovereignty'):

> Honoring Westphalian/Vattelian sovereignty . . . makes it impossible to secure decent and effective domestic sovereignty . . . To secure

decent domestic governance in failed, failing, and occupied states, new institutional forms are needed that compromise Westphalian/Vatellian sovereignty for an indefinite period.

(2004: 89)

The discovery that the formal legal equality of sovereignty hid the inequality of state capacities was not a new one. The same problem, although to a lesser extent, is present in domestic politics, where equality at the ballot box or under the law in liberal democracies does not necessarily ameliorate social and economic inequalities between individuals. In the domestic context, of course, relatively few people would argue that these inequalities should mean that formal political and legal equalities should be abandoned. In the international sphere, the existence of vast inequalities of power was one of the reasons that state sovereignty, held to be unconditional and indivisible, was the founding principle of international society. It was only on the basis of formally upholding the equality and autonomy of states, and the sovereign rights of non-intervention, that post-colonial societies could be guaranteed the rights to self-government. UN General Assembly declarations during the Cold War regularly asserted that differences in state capacity could never be grounds for undermining the rights of state sovereignty.

The affirmation that differences in capacity were no justification for the inequality of treatment as sovereign equals was confirmed most notably in the UN General Assembly Declaration on the Granting of Independence to Colonial Countries and Peoples of 14 December 1960 (Resolution 1514 [XV]) which proclaimed that: 'all peoples have the right to self-determination; by virtue of that right they freely determine their political status and freely pursue their economic, social and cultural development' and that 'inadequacy of political, economic, social or educational preparedness should never serve as a pretext for delaying independence' (UN 1960). This was passed in the General Assembly by a vote of 89 to 0, with 9 abstentions. Even the colonial powers were unwilling to reject it (Jackson 1990: 77). This was followed by the Declaration on the Inadmissability of Intervention in the Domestic Affairs of States and Protection of their Independence and Sovereignty of 21 December 1965 (Resolution 2131 [XX]) and the Declaration on Principles of International Law Concerning Friendly Relations and Co-operation among States in Accordance with the Charter of the United Nations of 24 October 1970 (Resolution 2625 [XXV]). The latter declaration making it clear that: 'All States enjoy sovereign equality. They have equal rights and duties and are equal members of the international community, notwithstanding differences of an economic, social, political or other nature' (UN 1970).

By associating sovereignty with a sliding scale of 'capacities', rather than political and legal rights of equality, not only is a new international hierarchy legitimized but intervention can be framed as supporting 'sovereignty' at the same time as it is undermining the rights of self-government. This inversion of the concept of 'sovereignty' was formulated in very clear terms in a 2005 UK Overseas Development Institute working paper report 'Closing the Sovereignty Gap'. In this report, by Ashraf Ghani, Clare Lockhart and Michael Carnahan, sovereignty is understood in terms of administrative functions rather than in political or legal terms:

> The consensus now emerging from global economic, military and political institutions signals that this gap between de jure sovereignty and de facto sovereignty is the key obstacle to ensuring global security and prosperity. The challenge is to harness the international system behind the goal of enhancing the sovereignty of states – that is, enhancing the capacity of these states to perform the functions that define them as states. Long-term partnerships must be created to prepare and then implement strategies to close this sovereignty gap.
>
> (2005: 4)

Here, sovereignty is no longer conceived of as a right to self-government. Sovereignty is merely a capacity which can be 'enhanced' or, presumably 'weakened'. The conflation of external intervention for the purposes of 'capacity-building' with enhancing state sovereignty and independence has become central to the statebuilding discourse.

In a later full-length book, *Fixing Failed States* (2008), which has been highly influential in the field of international statebuilding policy-thinking, Ghani and Lockhart develop further on their thesis of the 'sovereignty gap', asserting the need for an equilibrium between core functional responsibilities:

> The performance of these . . . functions produces a clustering effect . . . [Performed] simultaneously, the synergy creates a virtuous circle . . . and thereby produces a 'sovereignty dividend'. Conversely, when one or several of the functions are not performed effectively, a vicious circle begins. This negative cycle creates the sovereignty gap.
>
> (2008: 163)

Here, the key to sovereignty in functional terms is not measured in narrow indices of growth or stability but rather the capacity of balancing the functional requirements in equilibrium, ensuring that a 'synergy' is produced rather than a 'vicious circle'. How these functional requirements are brought into balance and managed and regulated 'simultaneously' is understood to

be the key to sovereignty, in terms of the post-liberal paradigm of governance: 'a state's ability to execute its functions coherently is what renders it
truly sovereign' (2008: 164). In Africa, where state capacity is held to be a
fundamental concern for external powers engaged in supporting a multitude
of empowering projects, headlined by the UN's Millennium Development
Goals, these governance interventions have gone furthest (see, for example,
the Sachs report (UNMP 2005) and Tony Blair's Commission for Africa
report (CfA 2005: Chapter 4)).

If sovereignty is defined as the capacity of non-western states for 'good
governance' there would seem to be little wrong in external institutions
implementing strategies for long-term engagement in these societies in
order to enhance their 'sovereignty'. In fact, governments which resisted
this external assistance could, in the Orwellian language of international
statebuilders, be accused of undermining their own sovereignty. The key to
the success of this conceptual conflation is not in its legitimization of external
intervention (already accepted in the 1990s) but in its portrayal of external
regulation as somehow empowering or strengthening non-western states.
Here is the virtuous circle for intervening powers, one that was not possible
in the post-conflict interventions of the 1990s: the more intervention there
is the more the target state is held to be responsible and accountable for the
consequences of these practices.

This approach, of understanding sovereignty as functional capacity,
clearly removes sovereignty from a classic liberal paradigm in which sovereignty was understood in terms of autonomy. This functionalist approach is
one which attempts to legitimize policy in the post-liberal terms of technical
and administrative outcomes rather than representational legitimacy. Not
only does this approach legitimize interventionist practices independently
of a liberal framing of autonomy: it operates on the basis of a problematization of autonomy itself. It is clear that from a functionalist perspective of
administrative and technical efficiency, the world of sovereign nation states
is a suboptimal one: the more that government can be organized on a larger
scale the more efficient it could be. It appears that the only barrier to technical
and administrative efficiency is the vested interests of political elites, who
are more interested in power than in technical efficiency.

From the approach of functional efficiency, it would appear that autonomy
can only be a potential problem, where the competition for representational
authority and political power encourages an emphasis on divisive political
questions and political elites need to reward their constituencies or influential supporters rather than focusing on the functional needs of society as a
whole. The basis of enhancing sovereignty in terms of capacity is in fact an
approach which legitimizes the limitation of autonomy in order to safeguard
technical or administrative efficiency from the 'distortions' of the political

process. This paradigm legitimizes the authoritative role of external experts, held to be best placed to put functional requirements 'above politics'. This technical and administrative approach can best be described as post-liberal, lacking any framework of legitimization in society itself, but rather being legitimized in terms of the external capacity to neutrally manage governance requirements.

The functionalist approach inverses the classic liberal assumptions, deriving the legitimacy of the state from societal processes, instead replacing 'the government of men' with 'the administration of things'. As James Heartfield perceptively comments, in relation to the functionalist approach of David Mitrany – for whom 'all knowledge is knowledge of the relation of things' (Mitrany 1975: 650) – this technicist approach implies that the tasks of government are set externally rather than derived internally (Heartfield 2010). It is the changing external relationships between things rather than the subjective ambitions or aspirations of political subjects which determine the tasks of governance. From a greater understanding of external relationships between things – affecting how economies work or societies develop – governance can be a task of administration rather than politics; or a task of 'technical self-determination' (Mitrany 1975: 118).

In this functionalist framework, sovereignty no longer exists as an expression of a self-determining collective political subject, but merely at the level of administrative decision-making. It is the task of governance to ensure that the 'relationship between things' is managed correctly. The good management of these relationships (the 'good governance' which is the subject of the following chapter) is then a reflection of the capacity of a state to be able to govern itself, to possess 'self-determination' or have 'self-government'. Sovereignty is redefined as the capacity to govern administratively, recognizing that autonomy implies not self-direction but the ability to respond adequately to external contexts. In this context, it is little surprise that sovereignty can be redefined in terms of 'responsibility', as we consider next.

Sovereignty as responsibility?

The second shift, articulated by the advocates of post-liberal approaches to statebuilding, is the assertion that non-western states have the 'responsibilities' of sovereignty rather than the rights of sovereignty. What these 'responsibilities' consist of is not held to be a decision made solely by the citizens of the state or their representatives, but one made in 'partnership' with external bodies. Rather than being a barrier to external interference, sovereignty becomes a medium through which non-western states and societies become integrated into networks of external regulation. International regulatory mechanisms of intervention are legitimized, first through the role of international institutions in deciding the content of the 'responsibilities' of sovereignty, and, second, through holding states to external account for 'failings' in the exercise of sovereignty (now discussed in the language of responsibility/capacity).

Sovereignty as 'responsibility' enables a new consensual or 'partnership' approach to statebuilding. Non-western states are in a poor position to resist new international mechanisms of regulation which come replete with carrots of international aid, trade privileges, debt forgiveness, or integration into international organizations, in return for external support for governance reforms and institutional capacity-building. Statebuilding or 'sovereignty-building' involves non-western states being firmly embedded in international institutional frameworks, over whose decision-making processes they have little influence. For the UK Overseas Development Institute, the focus on strengthening sovereignty entails a much more interventionist role by external institutions:

> We define a sovereignty or statebuilding strategy as . . . the alignment of the internal and external stakeholders . . . In order to design and implement statebuilding strategies, the operation of the current international system must be reorientated towards a model where partnership and co-production of sovereignty becomes the aim of both national leaders and international partners.
>
> (Ghani *et al.* 2005: 13; see also, Ghani and Lockhart 2008: 166)

This 'co-production of sovereignty' follows the strategies adopted by the European Union towards Southeastern European states from 2000 onwards; where international partnerships enmeshing applicant states in a network of international institutional processes which were coordinated through the Stability Pact, the Stabilisation and Association Process, the Community Assistance for Reconstruction, Development and Stabilisation programme, and the 'European Partnership' process. The prospect of future EU membership was explicitly offered to Albania, Bosnia, Croatia, Macedonia and Federal Republic of Yugoslavia at the Feira European Council in June 2000. At this point the EU shifted away from external conditionality and towards statebuilding in the region, initiating a project of 'reforming and reinventing the state in Southeastern Europe' (ESI 2007: 18) (see also, Chapter 5).

This shift from external relations of aid and trade conditionality to 'partnership' in domestic governance is symbolized by the dropping of the term 'Balkans' by international institutions, as too 'negative' and 'hegemonic' and its replacement by 'Southeastern Europe' symbolizing that this is a joint project of partnership, addressing 'European problems' with 'European solutions' (see, for example, *Balkanologie* 1999; Hatzopoulos 2005). The EU argued that it was well placed to assist these states in developing governance capacity which was identified as not just their main barrier to progress but also an area where the EU held a vital 'comparative advantage' and could 'provide real added value' (EU 2001c: 9). This engagement in domestic policy-making was held to have 'both pedagogical and political' benefits for the candidate states (EU 2001d: IIIc). Although talking-up the partnership between international institutions, the EU and prospective member states; the statebuilding process has been directed by close cooperation between the EU and international financial institutions which together have provided 'an effective means of focusing authorities' minds on essential reforms and of engaging with them in a sustained way to secure implementation' (EU 2001d: IIIc).

Since 2000, the concept of statebuilding through international partnerships to enhance governance capacities has increasingly replaced external pressures. Where the incentive of European membership is not available a wide range of other governance partnerships have been established around acceptance that the core problem of non-western states is that of state capacity and that the solution lies with the shared 'responsibilities' of both the non-western state and international institutions. The general rule of thumb appears to be that the greater the inequalities at play in the relationship between non-western states and international institutions the more grandiose the language of partnership. As would be expected, it is in relation to Africa that the rhetoric and reality are most out of step. Here the language is of 'African leadership' and an entirely 'new kind of partnership' not based on inequality and hierarchy but 'mutual respect and solidarity' (CfA 2005: 17). The UN Millennium Development Goals (MDG) project, following and extending the 'country ownership' approach of the interventionist World Bank Poverty Reduction Strategies, requires that states engage in far reaching governance reform and open up every area of domestic policy-making to international scrutiny and involvement. The 'responsibilities' or 'leadership' or 'ownership' lie with the domestic state but their partners (or joint 'stakeholders') decide the policies:

> The host country should lead and own the effort to design the MDG strategy, drawing in civil society organizations; bilateral donors; the UN specialized agencies, programs, and funds; and the international financial institutions, including the IMF, the World Bank, and the appropriate regional development bank. The contributions of the UN specialized agencies, programs and funds should be coordinated through the UN Country Team, and the UN Country Team should work closely with the international financial institutions.
>
> (UNMP 2005: 53)

The 'host country' books the meeting rooms but the 'guests' come along with the policy frameworks. These external policy prescriptions closely tie international aid to new institutional frameworks of regulation and monitoring. In effect this transforms external assistance from being a subject of international relations, between states, to one of domestic politics, of management and administration. This radical transformation in the relationship between non-western states and international institutions is highlighted forcefully by the Commission for Africa report which stresses that it is: 'not simply recommending throwing money at the problems' but a 'fundamental change in the way in which aid works' (CfA 2005: 94).

Once international financial institutions have a more direct role in the *internal* governance mechanisms of non-western states, aid is much less likely to be based on overt external regulation in the form of *external* conditionality. Graham Harrison usefully highlights the 'post-conditionality' regimes of international financial institutions in states like Tanzania and Uganda, where the influence of external donors is better conceived not as a 'strong external force' but as 'part of the state itself', through direct involvement in policy-making committees (2001: 669; see also, Harrison 2004). The undermining of sovereign autonomy and the enmeshing of subject states in international institutional frameworks fundamentally blurs the lines of accountability and control and the relationships of power behind these mechanisms. The relationship between western institutions and non-western states is a highly coercive one which forces these states to cede their sovereign powers to external institutions; the fiction of 'partnership' then relies heavily on an exaggeration of the importance of international legal sovereignty.

International legal sovereignty?

Today, despite the new interventionist consensus and the international attention given to 'failing' states and the lack of governance capacities in 'zones of instability', there is surprisingly little support for the return of international protectorates and direct external administrations. Only a small number of commentators argue that states should, in fact, be 'allowed to fail' and more capable neighbours allowed to directly govern these territories (for example, Herbst 2004) or that the UN Security Council should establish new international trusteeships (Helman and Ratner 1993).

Intervening powers and international institutions seem to have a particularly strong desire to preserve the formal trappings of sovereignty. The contradictory desire to intervene but also to avoid political responsibility is most sharply posed in questions of military intervention, such as post-9/11 'regime change' in Afghanistan and Iraq. Few acts are as fundamentally undermining of sovereignty as the external removal of a state's government.

Yet, no sooner have intervening actors destroyed sovereignty than they are talking-up its fundamental importance and pledging to restore authority to local actors at the soonest possible moment. Statebuilding is the process of negotiating these contradictory drives towards intervention and away from responsibility for outcomes.

Leading US policy advisors and international think tanks are increasingly singing from the same hymn sheet, suggesting that international regulation should no longer be seen in the old ways. In fact, the maintenance of formal sovereignty is at the heart of new approaches to 'neo-trusteeship' (Fearon and Laitin 2004), 'pooled sovereignty' (Keohane 2002), or 'shared sovereignty' (Krasner 2004). In the words of Krasner:

> Shared sovereignty would involve the engagement of external actors in some of the domestic authority structures of the target state for an indefinite period of time. Such arrangements would be legitimated by agreements signed by recognized national authorities. National actors would use their international legal sovereignty to enter into agreements that would compromise their Westphalian/Vatellian sovereignty [self-government/autonomy] with the goal of improving domestic sovereignty [governing capacity]. One core element of sovereignty – voluntary agreements – would be preserved, while another core element – the principle of autonomy – would be violated.
>
> (2004: 108)

The key difference between new forms of external regulation – 'neo-trusteeship' or, the even more user-friendly, 'shared sovereignty' – and traditional notions of a trust or protectorate is that, today, the subordinated territory will formally be a contracting legal equal. International legal sovereignty is maintained while political autonomy – self-government – is given up. The Bosnian peace agreement at Dayton in 1995 is the classic example of the voluntary surrender of sovereignty; the 'neo-trusteeship' was legitimized not through war and coercive power but through international legal agreement; through the signature of the Bosnian parties (Chandler 2005).

Law and reality no longer coincide when considering the location of sovereign power and authority (see Yannis 2002: 1049). Kosovo, for example, was until recently formally part of the Serbian state, the lack of fit between the formal location of sovereignty and external mechanisms of regulation made discussions of final status hard to resolve as decision-making authority lay neither with the elected Kosovo government in Pristina nor the Serbian government in Belgrade. Afghanistan and Iraq have the juridical status of independent states despite their dependence on the political and security role of the US. The artificial nature of these regimes is highlighted by the fact that their governments' writs seldom extend outside the protected security zones of the capitals. The restrictions on the Iraqi interim government's authority meant that the formal transfer of Iraqi sovereignty from the US-led Coalition Provisional Authority to an Iraqi government in June 2004 did not reflect any change in the real relations of authority (see, for example, Klein 2005). Here we have sovereign states without sovereign autonomy. States exist on paper, in terms of juridical status – for example, as members of the United Nations – with national flags, and maybe their own currencies, but not as independent political subjects capable of self-government. The states which are the products of international statebuilding are more like administrative bodies than political subjects with independent agency. As Robert Keohane argues:

> We somehow have to reconceptualize the state as a political unit that can maintain internal order while being able to engage in international co-operation, without claiming the exclusive rights . . . traditionally associated with sovereignty . . . The same institutional arrangements may help both to reconstruct troubled countries that are in danger of becoming 'failed states', and to constrain the autonomy of those states.
>
> (2003: 277)

He suggests that statebuilding can establish the 'institutional arrange-ments' which are capable of taking responsibility for maintaining order ('domestic sovereignty') but without giving rise to rights of self-government ('Westphalian sovereignty'). He recommended the exit strategy chosen for Kosovo, where there was a shift from existing trusteeship status, which could be called 'nominal sovereignty', to the independence of 'limited sovereignty' with external powers able to override domestic authorities, with a future final stage of 'integrated sovereignty' where the state is locked into the interna-tional institutions of the EU, able to override domestic authorities (2003: 296–97). This was held to resolve the problem of Kosovo's independence as it would never achieve independence beyond the purely formal trappings of statehood: 'Westphalian sovereignty . . . is simply bypassed in the movement from limited to integrated sovereignty' (2003: 297).

His proposals were strikingly similar to those later advocated by the International Commission on the Balkans. The commission's April 2005 report, *The Balkans in Europe's Future*, talked about Kosovo's 'independ-ence without full sovereignty', to be followed by 'guided sovereignty' with 'reserve powers' for the EU and a final stage of 'full and shared sovereignty' (ICB 2005: 18–23). Here statebuilding was held to be able to build a new type of state; one which has 'sovereignty' but is still in essentially the same position that it was when it was formally a protectorate. The difference being that formal accountability has been shifted back to the non-western state. James Fearon and David Laitin suggest a similar approach, arguing that a return to traditional forms of sovereignty is not the solution, but instead that the transfer of power in cases of post-conflict intervention and regime change should be 'not to full sovereignty but rather as a state embedded in and monitored by international institutions' (2004: 42). Krasner argues the point even more openly in his support for the concept of 'shared' sovereignty, which similarly uses 'sovereignty' as a means for enabling external regulation. Here, international legal sovereignty allows non-western states to enter into 'partnerships' which informally violate their sovereign rights:

> For policy purposes, it would be best to refer to shared sovereignty as 'partnerships'. This would more easily let policymakers engage in organized hypocrisy, that is, saying one thing and doing another. Shared sovereignty or partnerships would allow political leaders to embrace sovereignty, because these arrangements would be legitimated by the target state's international legal sovereignty, even though they violate the core principle of Westphalian/Vatellian sovereignty: autonomy . . . Shared sovereignty or partnerships would *make no claim to being an explicit alternative to conventional sovereignty*. It would *allow actors to obfuscate* the fact that their behaviour would be inconsistent with their principles.
>
> (2004: 108, emphasis added)

It is this 'obfuscation', hiding the transformed nature of non-western state sovereignty while maintaining international legal sovereignty, which enables international institutions to present themselves as facilitating partners in a shared project rather than as coercive external powers. Robert Cooper, focusing particularly on the enlargement policies of the European Union, describes this as a new conflict-free 'postmodern' or 'voluntary' form of imperialism (Cooper 2003). Mark Leonard argues that unlike the old imperialism, based on conflict and overt subordination, the EU is completely transforming states from the inside, rather than ruling them from above, for example: 'Europe is changing all of Polish society, from its economic policies and property laws to its treatment of minorities and what gets served on the nation's tables' (Leonard 2005: 6).

The more sovereignty is 'voluntarily' shared between target states and international institutions, coercive external conditionality is exchanged for internal forms of 'enhanced surveillance' through the reporting mechanisms generated by the good governance requisites of openness and transparency enforced by international institutions (CfA 2005: 376). Policy-advisers can no doubt see the gains to be made in enabling western governments to talk about sovereignty and accountability in non-western states, while avoiding political responsibility for their actions and policy prescriptions. However, there is something more fundamental about the changing understanding of sovereignty than massaging policy proposals in disingenuous terms or attempting to dodge policy responsibilities.

The policy process of sovereignty production

Policy is actually shaped and guided and given meaning through the transformation of sovereignty as a goal of policy-making rather than being a natural assumption of statehood. International statebuilding is cohered on the basis of the critique of 'sovereignty' as a 'natural' or formal basis of statehood: a critique of the liberal framing of sovereignty as the right of autonomy explicit in being a recognized political subject. Within the post-liberal statebuilding paradigm, political autonomy is transformed from an unproblematic starting assumption into a problem which necessitates an interventionist agenda of relationship management in order to guarantee that this autonomy can be exercised in a capable and responsible way, according to the dictates of good governance.

While the goal of enhancing state sovereignty may sound like a liberal project, this is actually a fundamental critique and inversion of a liberal understanding of sovereignty as an expression of subject-hood or political subjectivity. In the post-liberal paradigm of international statebuilding, sovereignty becomes an aspiration which can never be fully or permanently achieved because safe autonomy can never be guaranteed. The capacity for sovereignty is understood to be a contingent one, dependent on managing policy in terms of equilibrium: in terms of responses to both internal and external pressures and threats.

In the redefinition of sovereignty, autonomy or self-governance does not apply to the capacity to be a self-directed interest-based actor. Sovereignty, in terms of autonomy and self-government, is reconstituted as the capacity to be able to manage the uncertainties of globalized problems and globalized responses to problems. Sovereignty becomes meaningful in terms of management capacities, implying an internationalized or globalized conception of what it means to manage policies at the level of a state. Sovereignty, autonomy and self-government are redefined in terms of capacities for good governance. In this sense, the post-liberal discourse of governance is central to the paradigm of international statebuilding and the set of policy practices which we call 'international statebuilding' could not be understood without this transformation of the content of these political concepts.

Returning to the subject matter of the previous chapter, on the liberal peace critique of international intervention; the international statebuilding paradigm has developed in response to the ad hoc approaches of the 1990s. The story of the pre-history of international statebuilding is constructed in terms of the two errors of not intervening enough and of intervening too much. This is commonly presented chronologically, with international statebuilding developing as a clear 'Third Way' response to the 'lessons learned'. The first way of intervening is generally described as 'the early exit': the early 1990s extensions of international peacekeeping which tended to respect the sovereignty of the states intervened in, establishing short-term assistance until post-conflict elections were held. This approach is, from the vantage point of today, understood as an attempt at international 'quick fixes', exiting after elections at low cost to the international community but with little in terms of lasting results. Technically, this is understood as placing unrealistic demands on post-conflict societies to be able to manage post-conflict peacebuilding in a sustainable way. The lesson from the early 1990s is that autonomy is not feasible.

The second way of intervening is generally described in opposite terms, as 'lacking an exit strategy'. In the late 1990s there was a shift in approach, with the extension of international mandates in Bosnia in 1997 and the establish-ment of protectorate powers by the UN in Kosovo and East Timor in 1999. This extension of international mandates was very much in line with UN and international thinking, highlighted by the Brahimi Report on peacekeeping reform in 2000. However, from the vantage point of today, this extension of international mandates is seen as technically mistaken, in putting too much emphasis on the capacity of international actors to manage and resolve the problems of post-conflict statebuilding. Without a realistic exit strategy it is now commonly asserted that there is the danger of dependency and reliance on international actors.

Much of the critical discourse of statebuilding as a liberal project (consid-ered in the previous chapter) reflects the attempt to articulate the problem as one of overambitious policy-interventions which mistakenly took direct responsibility for attempting to transform societies. Ghani and Lockhart, for example, compare international statebuilding interventions negatively with the US Marshall Plan of European assistance after the Second World War, suggesting that the 'US did not seek to impose any plan or project. . . . [and] made the recipient country the driver of strategy and policy as well as project manager' (2008: 87–88). They argue, along with many other com-mentators (for example, Fukuyama 2004: 53) that a host of external actors are sucking out institutional capacity though intervening rather than playing a constructive role (Ghani and Lockhart 2008: 98).

The 'Third Way' approach of the production of sovereignty as a process of relationship management has developed as a critique of the first two forms of external intervention. The response to the interventions of the 1990s has been that of international statebuilding, which rather than assuming the autonomy of the post-conflict state to be unproblematic or alternatively, denying the autonomy of the state, pursues the strategy of enabling autonomy to be exercised more safely or securely through interventions aimed at enhancing the institutional capacities of the post-colonial state. While setting the autonomy, sovereignty or governance capacity of the state being intervened in as the object of policy-intervention, the post-liberal paradigm asserts that those intervening are not operating out of their own self-interest and, more importantly, that the legitimacy of their policy-intervention stems from their goal of strengthening sovereignty rather than a 'right of intervention' or from their own power or authority. Thus external intervention has no limits other than the needs of the post-colonial state. The aspiration or goal of sovereignty becomes both legitimizing means and ends of the post-liberal framing of external intervention.

In this framework, the sovereignty of the post-colonial state is the object of intervention as well as legitimizing this intervention. For the post-liberal discourse, anything that is not shaped by this framework of sovereignty-building lacks legitimacy and the centrality of this goal is understood to be capable of giving coherence to the policy-interventions of international actors. Ghani and Lockhart argue that understanding sovereignty as a collective goal for all external and domestic actors enables the development of 'sovereignty strategies' which 'offer a common language for the different stakeholder groups' which need to be aligned around 'the goal of sovereignty' (2008: 171). While the production of sovereignty is the task of all those with a 'stake' in the process, they argue that these need to be cohered at the national level of the state intervened in, with the governing elites responsible for policy outcomes and ensuring the correct policy equilibrium or balance: 'National programs work because they support sovereignty, enhance government capacity to perform functions, balance priorities, and are accountable to the people' (2008: 211). These programs are not 'national' in the liberal sense of projecting a collective 'national' interest, but in the administrative sense of management responsibility.

The UK Department for International Development approach is clear in its assertion of the need to 'support policy leadership by developing countries without imposing our own views' (DFID 2005: iii):

> In recent years the UK has been moving away from traditional approaches to conditionality. We believe that it is inappropriate and has proven to be ineffective for donors to impose policies on developing countries. Instead, we believe that successful aid relationships must be based on mutual commitment and dialogue, transparency and accountability.
>
> (DFID 2005: 4)

This approach is echoed in the Commission for Africa report, which claims in its introduction:

> Our starting point was the recognition that Africa must drive its own development. Rich nations should support that, because it is our common interest to make the world a more prosperous and secure place . . . But what is clear is that if Africa does not create the right conditions for development, then any amount of outside support will fail.
>
> (CfA 2005: 1)

This paradigm has evolved through a critique of policy practices which have been seen to be either too interventionist or not interventionist enough. The goal of international statebuilding is to build governance capacity through external intervention, which is articulated in terms of negotiating a fine line between not doing enough and doing too much; this optimum is described as a policy-making 'sweet spot' by Paris and Sisk (2009c: 311). It is important to understand that this line to be negotiated or policy direction is not shaped by an understanding of what policy areas should be covered or ignored or in terms of how interventionist or coercive policy interventions are or necessarily how much these might cost. The key aspect of managing is the style of policy intervention.

This was captured well by Lord Paddy Ashdown who, as the first European Special Representative to take over administrative powers in Bosnia, was keen to distance his rule from that of the imposition of power, which had been the case under previous international High Representatives. Here the imposition of EU policy proposals was reposed as a voluntary choice deriving from the desire to 'join' Europe, rather than from the imposed external oversight of the Dayton settlement. This simulation now meant that Bosnian politicians were forced to 'freely' choose to implement EU programmes rather than having them imposed by edict. In 2006, Ashdown was interviewed on whether the shift in styles made any difference from the point of view of Bosnian representatives and citizens:

> Yes, it makes a huge difference. If it is imposed with a stick then the consequence is dependency . . . It takes a great deal of strength to be able to say: 'No, we are not going to do this. You have to do it yourself.' We have to be patient enough for the country to set back a bit when this happens . . . They have more independence because they are no longer supported by the use of the High Representative's powers. Europe has said that if reforms are imposed via the High Representative's powers then Bosnia cannot join . . .
>
> Is Europe acting in a quasi-imperialist fashion? Yes, but the difference

is that it is up to people to say no if they want to. This is still persuasion, it is not coercion. I think it is perfectly legitimate for Brussels to say: 'Guys here are the rules, if you want to join the club you have to conform to the standards. If you conform to them fine, but if you do not want to you do not have to join.' It was very difficult for the Republika Srpska parliamentary assembly to agree to abolish their army and put it at the disposal of state institutions, but *they did it, not me.* It was a free vote in the Bosnian Serb parliament, I did not impose it. I may have told them it would be a good thing and that if you want to get into NATO you have to, but it was they who took the final decision.

(Ashdown 2007: 113; 115, emphasis in original)

Here, Ashdown forwards a subtle distinction between direct imposition, where the EU potentially bears direct policy-responsibility, and the policy of indirect imposition, where Bosnia's elected representatives are held to be freely choosing certain policy prescriptions. The difference between these approaches is of fundamental importance for the EU and is the *sine qua non* of the statebuilding 'Third Way' approach. It is somewhat secondary that this shift in how international policy-making is constructed makes little difference to Bosnian representatives or to the Bosnian public who are still confronted with proposals drawn up by external actors. In the process of the production of sovereignty rather than its undermining, there is much less clarity in the relationship between external and internal actors. In the post-liberal framing of the discourse, autonomy or sovereignty or peace-building capacity are enhanced by international intervention, rather than undermined, as was the case in the late 1990s extensions of international power.

Conclusion

This framework of post-liberal governance operates through removing sovereign autonomy from the political agenda both domestically and internationally. It makes little sense to critique international statebuilding as an attack on state sovereignty or for undermining state sovereignty in terms of a classic liberal framing of rights and autonomy. In the post-liberal framework of international statebuilding, it is precisely the problematic nature of state autonomy and the hollow content of the assumed or 'natural' rights of the post-colonial state and its subjects which legitimizes international statebuilding policies and practices.

This 'Third Way' approach develops the 1990s view of the incapacity of the non-western subject, which reflected the lack of barriers to external intervention, but no longer works on the 'rights-based' liberal discourse of a denial or limiting of sovereignty as a reflection of this new relationship of inequality. Instead, at the formal level, sovereignty becomes the object of intervention: it is the lack of sovereignty that is being rectified. In this way, there is no intervention (in terms of a denial or over-riding of sovereignty) and no exit (in terms of the restoration of sovereign autonomy). There is no intervention and no exit because these terms derive meaning from a 'rights-based' framework of international relations, operating at the formal level of politics and law.

The paradigm of international statebuilding presupposes a different and non-rights-based framing of international regulation of the post-colonial state. Rather than the 1990s clash of rights, intervention is understood in the functionalist terms of managing an equilibrium of shared responsibilities (discussed at greater length in the next chapter). This technical or function-alist framing sees sovereignty as the product of international intervention rather than a pre-existing right of autonomy or of formal statehood. In this framing, the production of sovereignty is a shared goal by both domestic and international actors who together attempt to institutionalize a frame-work in which the needs of both domestic and international 'stakeholders' are secured through the inculcation of the methods and approaches of good governance. Here, the co-production of sovereignty is an ongoing process; it makes no sense to talk about sovereignty as a claim to autonomy, remov-ing the conceptual basis upon which non-intervention or intervention can be meaningfully discussed.

4 Post-liberal governance

Introduction

Post-liberal governance is a concept that best describes the paradigm of international statebuilding. This book is concerned with highlighting an ever clearer distinction between a traditional liberal-democratic conception of government rule and the conception of the role of government which appears to inform the policies and practices of international statebuilding. Therefore the prefix 'post' serves to emphasize the fundamental nature of this break and the shift in meaning of many of the concepts used in the statebuilding discourse, often resulting in a complete inversion of their meaning in the paradigm of classical liberalism. The changed nature of this paradigm has already been highlighted in Chapter 3, concerning the critique of the nation state and sovereignty. I call this post-liberal governance but it is quite possible that the same paradigm could be referred to when some commentators use the term institutionalism (which we will explore at some depth later in this chapter) or 'The Third Way' (Giddens 1998). As we shall see, nearer the end of this chapter, Foucault also facilitates the understanding of post-liberal governance in his use of the concepts of neoliberalism and of biopolitics; however, as the popular usage of these terms is somewhat different to that of Foucault, it makes more sense to use Foucault's work to help inform this analysis without relying directly on the use of these concepts themselves. The key point that needs to be borne in mind is that the exact terms used matters much less than the conceptual understanding of the distinctiveness of the paradigm of international statebuilding. It is this conceptual understanding that is the subject of this chapter.

The key point which this chapter seeks to highlight is that the paradigm of international statebuilding is dependent upon a framing of international regulation in terms of governance rather than government. This shift from government to governance is understood as having less to do with the actors engaged in the regulation or management of the international order than with the way in which this order is regulated or managed. It is quite possible to have an international order based on the nation state as the key actor and policy-making focus – and the construction or reconstruction of the nation state as the policy goal of international statebuilding – but still have a shift from government to governance. This is because post-liberal governance is not so much about replacing the nation state with other actors – whether they are trans-national companies or non-governmental organizations – but about how the nation state is understood to develop and implement policy. Governance concerns the way that governments govern: the rationality of government, its goals and objectives and its methods of relating to domestic society and to the international sphere.

The first section expands upon the concept of post-liberal and explains the distinction between this conception and the use of the terms liberal or neoliberal. The following section draws out how this distinction impacts upon our understanding of the differences between the concept of government and that of governance. We then turn to the paradigmatic shift which international statebuilding highlights and the critique and inversion of liberal categories. This section briefly analyses the critique of the liberal subject from within the disciplines of economics and sociology and how both these critiques have impacted on the post-Cold War discipline of international relations. In the final sections, we consider two fundamentally important turning points in the development of post-liberal governance as a coherent bundle of ideas and policy practices: first, in response to the crisis of legitimacy of the post-war West German state, which was to serve as a template for the development of the European Union (as treated by Foucault in the *Birth of Biopolitics*); and, second, as a response to the failure of post-colonial development, which was to become paradigmatic to an institutionalist understanding of the problems of international development today (through the influential policy work of Douglass C. North).

Liberal, neoliberal or post-liberal?

Few commentators apply the terminology of post-liberal governance; while, for many (as considered in Chapter 2), liberal or neoliberal governance seems to be the best way to critically describe and analyse the world and the policy framework of international statebuilding. For some commentators, international statebuilding appears as a liberal project, focusing on reconstructing the sovereign state and promoting the framework of market-based democracy, replete with the liberal assumptions of democracy, the rule of law and human rights protection. For other commentators, it appears that the shift from concerns of government (understood as making possible nation-state control and policy-making) to governance (understood as the globalization or internationalization of problems and policy-solutions without a sovereign or global government able to direct solutions and impose laws or regulations), has gone hand in hand with the rise of neoliberal policy doctrines of rolling back the state and allowing the free play of market forces. This book differs from both these dominant framings of the shift in policy approaches in a number of fundamental ways.

For the purposes of the analysis of the statebuilding paradigm, it is important to understand the developments in economic, political and social theory since the end of the Second World War. The shift from government to governance can be seen as a series of developments in the framing of governmental rationality which have resulted in both a critique of the state and the critique of the market. This shift takes us from the high-point of the liberal consensus in the 1950s and 1960s and early 1970s, through the breakdown of this consensus, expressed through the critique of the state in the late 1970s and 1980s, to the 'Third Way' critique of both state direction and market laissez-faire approaches in the 1990s and 2000s (Giddens 1998). This critique of both the state and the market – the two sides of the liberal framing of state intervention in the external economic and social sphere – constitutes what is described here as the post-liberal paradigm. Surprisingly few commentators, focusing on international relations and statebuilding, consider the policy paradigms and practices of international statebuilding to be new or to pose novel questions of the political and policy world. While most academic and policy commentators tend to be critical of the limited success of the policies and practices of international statebuilding, the nature of the critiques has tended to be based on the fact that international statebuilding is problematic on the basis of universalizing dominant western frameworks of government and policy-making.

Many commentators focus on the problems of international statebuilding as a traditional liberal problematic, and therefore call into question alleged assumptions about the universalization of liberal claims for the sovereign state (alleged to be being built or reconstructed) as well as liberal assumptions about the natural or unproblematic workings of market processes or formally democratic political competition (see, for example, Paris 2004; Richmond 2005; Barnett 2006; see also, Chapter 2 on the liberal peace critique). For other commentators, the focus is on what is called neoliberal governance, where the analytical concern is economic policy-making (for example, De Angelis 2003; Weiner 2001; Pugh *et al.* 2008). In this analysis, international statebuilding is understood to be driven by the desire to roll back the post-colonial or post-conflict state and to open ever larger areas of policy to the influence of market forces. This approach of neoliberal critique focuses on international statebuilding policies as a critique of the post-colonial state, and of its role in directing or controlling the economy, but is one-sided or narrow in presenting these international policy-practices as being mainly driven by economic needs.

Here, Foucault's discussion of the rise of neoliberal frameworks of thought in the post-war period is highly germane to our discussion. Foucault made the important point that the dynamic behind neoliberal framings may not be an economic one but rather a political one of the legitimization 'of government rule:

> And what is important and decisive in current neo-liberalism can, I think, be situated here. For we should not be under any illusion that today's neo-liberalism, is, as is often said, the resurgence or recurrence of old forms of liberal economics which were formulated in the eighteenth or nineteenth centuries and are now being reactivated by capitalism for a variety of reasons to do with its impotence and crises as well as with some more or less local and determinate political objectives. In actual fact, something much more important is at stake in modern neo-liberalism . . . What is at issue is whether a market economy can in fact serve as the principle, form, and model for a state which, because of its defects, is mistrusted by everyone on both the right and the left, for one reason or another.
>
> (2008: 117)

Nevertheless, the critics of statebuilding as a neo-liberal project usefully highlight that the language of economic theorizing is extremely important to understanding the changes that have taken place in the political conception of problems and policy solutions. The paradigm shift, from classic liberal assumptions to post-liberal framings, which problematize autonomy and legitimize the external interventions of international statebuilding, depends upon the extension into the political sphere of economic theorizing, particularly rational choice, behaviouralist approaches which have informed the growth and development of institutionalist economics (which we will deal with later in this chapter). As Foucault states:

> In short, through political economy there is the simultaneous entry into the art of government of, first, the possibility of self-limitation, that is, of governmental action limiting itself by reference to the nature of what it does and of that on which it is brought to bear, and second, the question of truth. The possibility of limitation and the question of truth are both introduced into governmental reason through political economy.
>
> (2008: 17)

For Foucault, the discussion about the economy is not one which is primarily addressing economic problems through advocating 'freeing the economy', but rather one of legitimizing governmental power on a new basis. It is only when neoliberalism is understood as a defensive project of attempting to legitimize political power that the shift to the post-liberal paradigm and its consequences can be fully comprehended. Neoliberalism for most critical commentators is merely about rolling back the state and freeing the market, for Foucault, its importance lay in the fact that it 'carried out a number of shifts, transformations, and inversions in traditional liberal doctrine' and it was these shifts which he held to be of fundamental importance (2008: 118).

Foucault went to some lengths to challenge the critical consensus that neoliberalism was really just a return to traditional laissez-faire market-led economic policies or a cover for state power in the attack on workers' rights and benefits. For Foucault, these critics missed the radical shift taking place:

> . . . [radical critics] ultimately make neo-liberalism out to be nothing at all, or anyway, nothing but always the same thing, and always the same thing but worse. Now what I would like to show you is precisely that neo-liberalism is really something else . . . Neo-liberalism is not Adam Smith; neo-liberalism is not market society; neo-liberalism is not the Gulag on the insidious scale of capitalism . . . This, I think, is what is at stake . . . to discover how far and to what extent the formal principles of a market economy can index a general art of government, the neo-liberals had to subject classical liberalism to a number of transformations.
>
> (2008: 130–31)

For Foucault, the radical critique of the Marxist left remained limited by the failure to understand the shift in the discursive framework of regulatory power away from a liberal discourse of the balance between state direction and market freedom. Foucault argued that this critique fundamentally missed the point and attempted to highlight the 'specific features of this neoliberalism which absolutely oppose them to everything one generally thinks one is criticizing when one criticizes the liberal policy of neo-liberalism' (2008: 134). Rather than promoting laissez-faire and the rolling back of the state to allow the free play of market forces, Foucault understood neoliberalism in the very different terms 'of dissociating the market economy from the principle of laissez-faire' and the 'uncoupling of the market economy and laissez-faire policies' on the basis of challenging the idea of the natural foundation of the market (2008: 131). Foucault correctly highlighted that rather than rolling back the state, this framework transformed the role of the state and the relationship between the state and the market.

Rather than intervention into the sphere of the market on the basis of correcting imbalances or directing the economy towards certain goals, neo-liberalism presupposed the state's intervention in constructing and creating the conditions for the market to work efficiently and effectively. This position effectively ruled out any sphere of division between the state and the market but without the relationship being cast in liberal terms of a sphere of autonomy of individuals or the sphere of collective autonomy in social direction of the economy. This framework removed the liberal assumptions of political autonomy in the pursuit of rational interests. In this framing, there is 'a market economy without laissez-faire', in other words, 'an active policy without state control': in order to promote the efficiency of the market, the state's role was that of 'permanent vigilance, activity, and intervention' (Foucault 2008: 132). The object of the state's intervention was to be society or the frameworks or institutions of social interaction itself, in order to remove the anti-competitive mechanisms or outcomes (2008: 160).

The developing paradigm of post-liberalism therefore inverts the traditional liberal rights-based framework which assumed autonomy to be the basis of government, informing the processes and ends of government. Post-liberalism instead assumes autonomy to be problematic and the fact that the economic and social sphere consists of autonomous actors is the reason for permanent intervention rather than non-intervention. This inversion of the conception of autonomy from a sign of 'no admittance' to a sign saying 'you have to come in' is of fundamental importance for our understanding of the statebuilding paradigm. The point about the paradigm shift to post-liberalism is not that there is a diminishing of state power or control but rather that this power and control should be exercised differently: that there is a different governmental rationality which gives policies and practices a different set of goals and frames of judgement.

In this framework, there are no rights-based limits to the power and control of government, either in terms of how to act in the domestic or in the international sphere. In fact, the traditional idea of liberal limits: the division between private and public or domestic and international is problematized on the basis that autonomy cannot exist without a regulatory framework. The construction of liberal binaries – for example, those of citizens and non-citizens, inside and outside, soldiers and civilians, intervention and non-intervention – makes no 'sense' from within a post-liberal framework. In this paradigm:

> [T]he problem is not whether there are things that you cannot touch and others that you are entitled to touch. The problem is how you touch them. The problem is the way of doing things, the problem, if you like, of governmental style.
>
> (Foucault 2008: 133)

Governance or government?

Much has been written about the shift from government to governance in the field of international relations. For the most part, this shift has been understood as deeply implicated in the process of globalization. As the world has become more interconnected, interdependent and globalized, the power and control of government is said to have diminished. In this respect, the shift from government to governance is held to be that of a shift from the power and control of the nation state to the sharing of power with other actors at the transnational or international level as well as at the subnational or substate level (see, for example, Rosenau 1995). This disaggregation of power is held to mean that the state is just one player, although a very important one, in the development of rules and regulations at the international or global level. The global or international level lacks a sovereign or a formally institutionalized government and is therefore understood to be a sphere of governance rather than government (see, for example, Finkelstein 1995).

For the purposes of understanding international statebuilding, within the paradigm of post-liberal governance, it is important to make a much more important distinction between government and governance than the one which is often made in the international relations literature. The distinction is not that the paradigm of governance lacks a hierarchy or a government but that, nevertheless, similar practices are facilitated. In which case, governance would be merely governing without the sovereign authority of government: governments can practice governance once they rule less as sovereign authorities and more as good administrators. In terms of governance, the key point is that it makes no difference whether there is a formally constituted government or not; what matters is the rationality of rule-making not the formal process of legitimizing the rules. Once the rationality, the way of rule-making, is understood to be the key to the distinction between government and governance, then: 'global governance is doing internationally what governments do at home' (Finkelstein 1995: 369). The distinction, in terms of rationality, is much more important than the sharing of the duties and aspects of government with other actors, especially with non-governmental organizations or businesses.

Governance means more than merely the technical absence of government or the making of policy, or regulatory guidelines, independently of the formally institutionalized authority of government. Governance implies and involves an entirely different relationship between the government and the governed. This shift in the relationships of government and the practices and rationales of government mean that governance is not at all restricted to non-governmental institutions. Governments can also practise governance because governance is a style of governing which operates within a different paradigm or governmental rationality to classical liberal government. Government implies command, control and direction; for this reason a hierarchical view is necessary. But governance does not imply any less of a role for governments, merely a transformed understanding of their role. States which practice good governance do not command, plan, control and direct, rather they are relationship managers: they help steer or pilot the state like a ship in a choppy sea. When they undertake the tasks of governance they are aware that they are not able to take the ship anywhere they like or in any direction that they may wish; they need to manage the external elements, such as the tides, rocks, other craft, the crew, resources, etc. In fact, even the analogy with steering or piloting, often made in the international relations literature, still lacks a full sense of the distinction.

Most importantly, governance is not about instrumental goals. Government presupposes an aim or a purpose which is striven for through a number of policy mechanisms which, for example, could be used to increase employment or increase the number of hospital beds, etc. The resources of society are mobilized around certain aims or goals which are collectively discussed and mandated through competitive elections. The essence of global governance is not so much the engagement of non-state actors as well as states in a policy or regulatory community with no fixed centre of power, but rather the lack of a clear set of goals and therefore the lack of any organization of resources around a goal. Massimo De Angelis (2003) makes this point quite well in highlighting that governance is a continual process of relationship management rather than the pursuit of discrete policy goals. He argues that governance is not linear in terms of instrumental goal orientation towards the achievement of external goals. The role of governance is not the formulation and implementation of policy but the promotion of frameworks through which problems can be addressed. Rather than discrete policies, governance is about the organizational principles through which relations must be managed, and therefore is a continuous process (2003: 3).

Governance is about the capacity for self direction in response to external variables rather than the capacity of government to decide autonomously on the goals and purposes of power. Therefore, governance is not at all about the lack of a sovereign or a formally constructed hierarchy but rather a recognition that the sovereign or government should govern in a different way: in a way that responds to external factors rather than one which seeks to set its own course despite them or attempts to change them. Governance, as a governmental rationality, thereby reduces the state to the status of any other social actor which needs to respond to external stimuli, whether they are interest rates, wage fluctuations or climate changes. How adept the state is at responding to these stimuli is held to be indicative of whether its governance is good or not so good.

Governance is different from government not merely in the style or ration-ale of governing. Of central importance to understanding the paradigm of international statebuilding is that governance is legitimized on very different terms; terms which are incommensurable with the classic liberal paradigm of popular sovereignty or of representative government. Whereas the legitimacy of government lies with the people – who are subject to the rule of govern-ment, and therefore is open to popular discussion and derives legitimacy from a popular mandate – the legitimacy of governance does not depend on the relationship between the government and the citizenry. Government refers to a process of goal orientation – of policy-making and implementa-tion – in this process, within the liberal paradigm, the government acts as the collective representative of a social collectivity of citizens: a separate and discrete territorial entity with its own interests. Governance, on the other hand, does not conceive of government as a discrete political subject or agent with distinctive self-interests which should inform the goals and implementa-tion of policy. Governance is blind to the origination of government or the political or representative legitimacy of policy-goals. Governance is a techni-cal or administrative understanding of the role of government, where policy goals and implementation are considered to be legitimate on the basis of their approach and understanding of the problem: the subject of governance – the active agent of governance – is not relevant.

This is why, in the literature on governance, the nation state (with its representational qualities, lacking in most other rule-setting collective asso-ciations) is not seen to be a qualitatively different actor from any other actor at any institutional level. As the Council of Rome stated:

> We use the term governance to denote the command mechanism of a social system and its actions . . . Taken broadly, the concept of govern-ance should not be restricted to the national and international systems but should be used in relation to regional, provincial and local governments as well as to other social systems such as education and the military, to private enterprises and even to the microcosm of the family.
>
> (King and Schneider 1991: 181–82)

Once government is no longer seen as having any qualitative difference from other formal and informal institutions which attempt to steer and guide human behaviour, the focus is on the quality of that steering rather than its representative legitimacy. This (as we shall see in Chapter 5 on the EU and export of good governance and in Chapter 8 on civil society) means that the political and legal institutional frameworks and the conception of the role of the citizen are very different under the framework of governance from that of government. Within the international statebuilding paradigm, the citizen is not the subject of the law or of policy but rather the object of policy-making. International statebuilding is concerned with the construction of the citizen or of civil society. This inverts the classic liberal conception of rights and law and the understanding of the relationship between the state and society. In this respect, the 'top-down' approach of governance reflects and is informed by the rise of institutionalist approaches, derived from both behavioural economics and sociological constructivism, which both see the individual subject as a secondary product of institutional frameworks, rather than as an originating rights- and interests-bearing actor.

The paradigm shift

While the classical framings of the liberal view of the subject were politically contested through the late eighteenth and the nineteenth century; the liberal paradigm did not become the dominant one in the US and Europe until the twentieth century. The problems of integrating the masses into politics, through the labour and trade union movements, was not fully completed until the post-Second World War period in which a liberal consensus was made possible on the basis of the political and social restructuring of the war and immediate post-war period and the social consensus of the long post-war boom. When we consider international statebuilding as a post-liberal paradigm, we are considering it in terms of policy framings or governmental rationality: how government and policy-making are understood and validated. Prior to the twentieth century, the classic ideas of liberalism operated as much as a challenge to power as a framework for legitimizing power. The idea of popular sovereignty was heavily restricted through elites' fear of the masses' engagement with politics and their potential hold on power. The economic and social divisions of society, reflected in the prevalence of class division, underlay and undermined any consensual frameworks based around the collective interests of a society conceived of as autonomous individuals. Differences in economic and social status and in political viewpoints seemed to be much more salient than liberal views of society which established the legitimacy of state power on the basis of a shared social consensus (mythologized in the social contract).

The liberal discourses of government policy-intervention, which presuppose the natural or autonomous workings of the market and the political process, assumed a level of social consensus which was not possible until the post-1945 era. In this period, politics and state power became contested within much more consensual terms. James March and Johan Olsen (1984) argue that it was the post-war period which saw the development of social and political science along lines which emphasized the positive nature of the autonomy of the liberal subject and in broad brush strokes describe,

what we will designate as the liberal paradigm of thinking about governmental rationality, as contextual, reductionist, utilitarian, functionalist and
instrumentalist:

Contextual: Politics was understood to be a process and the political institutions of a state were understood contextually, as integral to society rather
than separate and external to society. Political institutions were understood
to mirror or reflect society rather than as shaping or directing it and society
was understood as composed of competing (class interests) with the state
reflecting the balance and contestation of these forces. The causal links
ran from society to the polity rather than the other way around (March and
Olsen 1984: 735).

Reductionist: While society and class were important factors, social consensus facilitated aggregative approaches, understanding behaviour at both
individual and group levels. This behaviour was understood in a reductionist way, as the expression of preferences or interests which were formed
exogenously or external or prior to the establishment of the political process,
these positions and interests were understood to be shaped by the social and
economic position of the individual. Social and political phenomena were
understood as the aggregate of the pursuit of these reductionist interests, for
example, in the economic theory of markets or of voter preferences (1984:
735–36).

Utilitarian: The articulation of preferences and interests was understood as
utilitarian, as the product of rational calculation on behalf of individuals. The
dominant perspective was that of rational choice, with decisions being a matter of conscious and deliberative choice between options in the marketplace or
at the ballot box. With the assumption that preferences or interests were stable
it was assumed that both markets and political processes increasingly reflected
the needs and interests and choices of individuals (1984: 736–37).

Functionalist: Within this paradigm of rational choice it was assumed that
both markets and political systems became increasingly efficient, enabling
historical progress driven by individual autonomy as both markets and political
systems increasingly approached their optimal equilibrium (1984: 737).

Instrumentalist: Individual autonomy and the autonomy of both markets
and political systems was understood as purposive towards both individual
and societal ends. Behaviour and outcomes were understood as purposive
and instrumental, with the development of greater understanding (facilitated
by science and technology) relating means to ends (1984: 737–38).

In the liberal paradigm of the social sciences, the autonomous subject is central to understanding the operation of states and societies. It is the rational, instrumental pursuit of individual interests which forms the basis of the liberal polity and market economy. Individual autonomy both legitimizes government law-making as a collective representation of these interests and limits it through protecting the sphere of freedom and autonomy held to operate as civil society through market relations. Individual autonomy is seen to be the driving force for social, economic and political progress on the basis that individual self-interests are rationally constructed and collectively constitute the public good. It is on the basis of the pre-existing autonomy of individuals that institutions, such as those of politics and law are held to be established on the basis of ensuring the security and freedom of society as a whole.

The post-liberal paradigm transforms this liberal paradigm, problematizing individual autonomy and understanding the role of laws and of institutions as primary rather than secondary. In fact, the relationship between institutions and society is inversed. This inversion was undertaken theoretically at different points and in different contexts prior to the policy-consensus around post-liberal programmes of governance at the end of the 1990s. The post-liberal paradigm developed in response to the failures of the market and the political process in the twentieth century. In order to trace the theoretical grounding of the paradigm shift we will briefly consider this shift within the key disciplines of economic theory and sociological theory, both of which attempted to address the political crises of the twentieth century through the problematization of liberal assumptions of the rational autonomous political subject. Both these approaches posit the political subject as the product of formal and informal institutional frameworks which are held to be prior to and to construct the subject.

It could be argued that the starting point of the challenge to liberalism in both the economic and sociological spheres was Edmund Husserl's work on phenomenology. Walter Eucken, the founder of the Freiburg School of 'ordoliberalism' in the 1930s was heavily influenced by Husserl, who was based at Freiburg, as were other leading intellectuals in post-war Germany who developed the ideas of Husserl's *The Crisis of European Societies and Transcendental Phenomenology* (1970) in a challenge to the accepted doctrines of the market and state intervention (Foucault 2008: 103–4). Classic liberal assumptions about the market were considered to be 'naïve naturalism', in which perfect competition and the rational pursuit of self-interest were considered to be naturally given rather than intellectual constructs which required certain conditions to become effective. Rather than a starting point, the natural view of the market should instead be seen as a policy goal or objective of government policy-making (Foucault 2008: 120).

Husserl's overturning of empirical theories of objectivity, focusing on the inter-subjective construction of social reality was also the starting point for the Frankfurt School of critical theory, which emphasized the social nature of subjectivity rather than the naturalistic approach of positivism (Heartfield 2010; Foucault 2008: 15). Today, the critique of the liberal subject appears to be very similar, whether the behavioural economics approach, informing the institutionalist frameworks of World Bank advisors, such as Douglass North and Paul Collier, is considered or that of critical sociological perspectives, which similarly posit the importance of difference, in terms of both formal and informal institutional structures. In fact, Foucault highlights the importance of the shared intellectual origins of both institutionalism and critical theory, noting: 'the curious closeness and parallels between what we call the Freiburg School or ordoliberals and their neighbors, as it were, the Frankfurt School' (Foucault 2008: 105).

Economic theory

Arguments which challenged the classic liberal assumptions about autonomy and progress developed in a cohered way in the discipline of economics, in response to the crises of the market in the 1920s and 1930s and later in response to the failures of post-colonial development in the 1970s. In both cases, the critique of the liberal paradigm serves as apologia (an attempt to explain and justify the status quo as inevitable) rather than as critique (an attempt to explain through positing potential alternative ways of thinking or acting). Whereas the liberal paradigm was universalist, the post-liberal paradigm relies upon complexity and differentiation. It is complexity which is the key to challenging classic liberal assumptions about perfect competition or perfect information. For the developers of institutionalist approaches, the apologia goes further to assert that there is no such thing as capitalism with a capital 'C', rather, there are many capitalisms. There is no universalist logic of capital; no grand narrative, in the words of the critical sociologists (which we consider in the following section).

The key aspect which economic theory brings in, which is shared by critical sociologists, is subjectivity: the importance of superstition, culture, and irrationality to decision-making. As John R. Commons described institutional economics back in 1936, it is based on understanding the importance of 'man's relationship to man' which is ignored in classical liberal economic theory which, to him, appeared to be 'based on man's relation to nature' (1936: 242). For Commons, the intangibles, such as good will, conceptions of rights and duties, etc., all influenced the 'reasonable' price that the buyer was willing to pay. These intangibles were understood to be shaped by collective institutions and collective norms and controls which meant that the classic liberal assumptions of perfect competition did not exist. Commons suggested that there was a 'nationalistic theory of value': that these national collective institutions meant that it was a fiction to think of the market as universalist in its operation; as much of a fiction as the belief in the universal individual subject of classical liberal political and economic theory:

> Even the individual of economic theory is not the natural individual of biology and psychology: he is that artificial bundle of institutes known as a legal person, or citizen. He is made such by sovereignty which grants to him the rights and liberties to buy and sell, borrow and lend, hire and hire out, work and not work, on his own free will. Merely as an individual of classical and hedonistic theory he is a factor of production and consumption like a cow or slave. Economic theory should make him a citizen, or member of the institution under whose rule he acts.
>
> (Commons 1936: 247–48)

The preceding paragraph sums up the essence of post-liberalism, which frees the individual from the strictures of classic liberal assumptions, allowing autonomy of choices but only once the individual is understood as a product of an institutional framework. For Commons, this methodological focus on the volition or choice of the individual was described as behaviouralism, where the will of the agent could be objectively understood through observed behaviour (Forest and Mehier 2001: 592). Commons therefore stressed that rather than treating humans as automatic pursuers of fixed interests, real-life behaviour had to be understood as shaped by institutional forms, especially those of custom and social norms. Individuals freely and rationally chose but on the basis of their cultural contexts and understanding. Here the individual will is both an act of volition and conscious rational choice but also a product of historical and social context, shaped and constructed on the basis of existing or habitual norms and values (Forest and Mehier 2001: 593).

The work of Commons and other institutional economists was developed further by Herbert Simon, who directly challenged the assumptions of the rational decision-making capacity of the classical liberal subject, dethroning the autonomous rational subject – homo œconomicus – from economic rational choice theory. In his argument, there was no such thing as perfect information or perfect rationality, merely 'bounded rationality' where not all the facts can be known or all the possible options considered. This critique of rationality was based on maintaining the liberal assumptions of the rational and autonomous actor but questioning the extent to which the outcomes would be rational. The decisions made with 'bounded rationality' were still rational, i.e. made on the basis of a freely willed conscious choice but they no longer resulted in furthering the collective good or in optimal outcomes. This critique of the rationality of the classical liberal subject was to have immensely powerful consequences, in being the intellectual basis upon which the post-liberal paradigm could be built: that of the simultaneous recognition and problematization of autonomy.

The crucial facet of institutionalism is that differences in outcomes can be understood as conscious, subjective choices, rather than as structurally imposed outcomes. The important research focus is then the individual making the decisions or choices and the subjectively created institutional frameworks (formal and informal) determining or structuring these choices. This is a social perspective which starts from the individual as a decision-maker and then works outwards to understand why 'wrong' choices are made, rather than equipping the individual with a set of universal rational capacities and understanding the differences in outcomes as products of social and economic context and relationships. This perspective is much more individual-focused but the individual subject is understood in isolation from their social and economic context. 'Wrong' choices are understood first in terms of institutional blockages at the level of custom, ideology and ideas and then in terms of the formal institutional blockages which structure the incentives and opportunities available to enable other choices. This problematization of the individual shares much with therapeutic approaches which also work at the level of the individual (attempting to remove psychological blockages to making better choices) rather than at the level of social or economic relations.

As Foucault notes, the work of these neoliberal or institutionalist theorists was not primarily concerned with economic theory; the institutionalist approach was closely tied to sociological framings and drew on legal and historical problematics, raising 'a whole series of problems that are more historical and institutional than specifically economic, but which opened the way for very interesting research on the political-institutional framework of the development of capitalism, and from which the American neo-liberals benefited' (Foucault 2008: 135). Of particular importance, as we shall see later in this chapter, is the impact of these ideas on World Bank policy-making in the 2000s, which can be clearly traced in the influence of Douglass North: 'The ideas of North on the development of capitalism . . . are directly in line with the opening made by the neo-liberals . . .' (Foucault 2008: 135).

Sociological theory

The sociological critique of the liberal paradigm can be clearly traced through the Frankfurt School and development of critical theory through to constructivist and post-structuralist approaches today (this section draws heavily on Heartfield 2010). The sociological critique of classical liberal assumptions of autonomy was much more far-reaching than that of the rational choice economic theorists. For this reason it has been important, not so much in the theoretical construction of the post-liberal paradigm, which enabled the categories of liberal rights-based approaches to be transformed and inverted, but in terms of understanding the popularizing and mainstreaming of the post-liberal paradigm, particularly in the post-Cold War period.

The Frankfurt Institute, directed by Max Horkheimer and Theodor Adorno, developed a critical sociology of knowledge as a challenge to the naturalism of classic liberal assumptions (paralleling the critique of the economic theorists considered earlier; see also, Foucault 2008; Meszaros 1989: 91–140). The classic liberal assumptions of the natural or spontaneous workings of the market and political processes were challenged for their conservative underpinnings, writing out of the question relations of power and domination, and establishing the possibility of fascism. The paradigm of classic liberalism was problematic in regard to the fact that it:

> . . . seeks to reduce society to the purely natural, it no longer aids in the liberation from the compulsion of institutions, but only furthers a new mythology, the glorification of the illusory primal qualities, to which is attributed what in fact only arises by virtue of society's institutions. The extreme model of rendering society 'natural' in such a false and ideological fashion is the racist insanity of national socialism.
>
> (Frankfurt Institute 1973: 23)

Rather than the autonomous subject having a 'natural' aspect, the liberal paradigm was seen to be a fictional discourse designed merely to regulate and control society. Where the liberal paradigm assumed universal, 'natural', characteristics of autonomy, the sociological critique contraposed the deconstruction of these universals, opposing itself to the 'grand narrative' or 'metadiscourse' of liberal autonomy (see, for example, Lyotard 1989; Derrida 1989).

In the post-liberal approach, preferences and interests are not pre-given or exogenous to the political system or the institutional framework, but rather are products of these frameworks and of social interaction. The work of sociologist Ulrich Beck probably best encapsulates the shift to a post-liberal paradigm of resilience rather than agency, in highlighting that, in a complex and globalized world, the unintentional outcomes of human agency are of greater importance than the intentional ones. In this framework, the liberal subject no longer exists. While individuals and collectivities still possess the formal capacities of the subject, the ability to make choices and decisions, this capacity is a responsive and reactive one rather than a self-directed one, organized around perceived rational interests. For Beck, this is the state of 'reflexive modernity' where: 'one is no longer concerned with attaining something "good", but rather with preventing the worst: self-limitation is the goal which emerges' (Beck 1994: 48). The impossibility of overcoming the difference of individual political subjects is central to the post-liberal paradigm. There can be no capacity to determine a collective interest beyond the individual's pursuit of self-interest which is inevitably problematic in an interconnected and globalized world. Rather than the pursuit of self-interest but on a collective scale, the post-liberal paradigm presupposes the need to rein back individual interests in the interests of collective resilience or good governance. In this framework, the legitimacy of government stems from its ability to limit its own conception of rational and legitimate interests rather than developing and pursuing them.

International relations

Both the economic and the sociological critiques of the liberal paradigm have shaped thinking in international relations, with the US theorists tending to be more influenced by economic theory and the European approaches more influenced by sociological enquiry (Keohane 1984; 1988; Krasner 1983; Kratochwil and Ruggie 1986; Ruggie 1983; Wendt 1987; Young 1986). Whereas the rationalist approach of international relations started off from the liberal assumption of autonomous and self-interested state actors, it increasingly emphasized the importance of regimes and institutions in shaping behaviour and preferences through the late 1970s and 1980s as global interdependencies and complex interdependence became increasingly important as a backdrop to strategic interaction. Rationalist approaches increasingly stressed the importance of institutional context as an explanation for variations in outcomes. In an important article, Robert Keohane (1988) discussed the similarities and differences between both economic and sociological approaches to institutionalism. While the rationalist approaches start from the assumption of state actors as rational interest-bearing subjects and then refined those assumptions through the empirical study of institutional regimes, sociological approaches, which Keohane labels, 'interpretive' or 'reflectivist', started from the intersubjective shaping of institutional norms and rules, with less attention to pre-existing or exogenous interests (1988: 381–82).

In international relations, rationalist approaches still tended to dominate prior to the end of the Cold War. For the rationalists, institutions were seen in the liberal paradigm, as products of the interests and preferences of states – as largely reflections of the social relations of the international sphere – although it was increasingly argued that empirical context and historical path-dependencies needed to be brought in to develop the rationalist frameworks. As Keohane noted, this was a very different starting point from the sociological one, often more favored in European theorizing, where:

> Institutions do not merely reflect the preferences and power of the units constituting them; the institutions themselves shape these preferences and that power. Institutions are therefore constitutive of actors as well as vice versa. It is therefore not sufficient in this view to treat the preferences of individuals as given exogenously: they are affected by institutional arrangements, by prevailing norms, and by historically contingent discourse among people seeking to pursue their purposes and solve their self-defined problems.
>
> (Keohane 1988: 382)

In his 1988 paper, Keohane hoped for the future establishment of 'a synthesis between rationalist and reflective approaches' through competition and dialogue (1988: 393). Keohane was confident at that point that the rationalist approach was heuristically the most powerful because it forced the analyst to look beneath the surface for interests and rational instrumental intent rather than merely relying on self-justification for knowledge of actors' intentions. From today's vantage point, it seems that this assumption was misplaced; rather than the sociological approach becoming an add-on to the rationalist one of autonomous interest-bearing subjects, the relation between the two approaches has been inversed. In the post-liberal paradigm of post-Cold War international relations, there is little room for rationalism as the globalized world is increasingly understood to be non-amenable to instrumental attempts to order and direct events.

It is the reflectivist approaches which appear to give greater heuristic insights into the globalized world. For this reason, David Held is representative of sociological approaches to the international sphere, in arguing that realist approaches merely reify or naturalize the existing order through taking a positivist approach (1983: 161). The work of John Gerard Ruggie has been a good example in this regard, as he has shifted from his early 1980s concerns with the rationalist neoliberal institutionalist agenda towards a sociological constructivist focus on the postmodern condition of international relations (Ruggie 1993). For constructivist sociological approaches, the realist world of Westphalian reciprocal relations of sovereignty and non-intervention is not a natural product of the international order but a contingent one. The framework of sovereignty is an institutional framework open to change. In this regard, international law is not a product of natural relations but more like a set of subjective rules determining the game and the behaviour of the players.

The work of Alexander Wendt reflects the shift from rationalism to reflectivism even more clearly because, unlike Ruggie and Held, he does not shift his ontological focus from the nation state as the key actor of the international sphere. States are treated as subjects but the nature of their subjectivity inverts the liberal paradigm of rational autonomous action and gives a fuller framework to post-liberal institutionalism. (It should be noted that the conception of post-liberal institutionalism is clearly apposite when dealing with the discipline of international relations as the label of neoliberal institutionalism is given to those who were working within the rationalist framework of regime theory.)

For Wendt, international law and political and legal rights are prior to the political and legal subject and constitute the subject. Society exists prior to the subject. He argues that: 'Rights are social capacities that are conferred on actors by others' permission to do certain things. . . . Far from being an epiphenomenon of material forces, international law is actually a key part of the deep structure of contemporary international politics' (Wendt 1999: 280). Society comes first, but this is not the society of a liberal conception:

> This may all seem very arcane, but there is an important issue at stake: are the foreign policy identities and interests of states exogenous or endog-enous to the state system? The former is the answer of an individualistic or undersociologized systemic theory for which rationalism is appropri-ate; the latter is the answer of a fully socialized systemic theory.
>
> (Wendt 1992: 402)

There is no 'natural' or 'rational' engagement with the external world, only an engagement which is inter-subjectively shaped through certain institu-tional frameworks. In which case, it is the regulative norms and values which are determinant of the actions of political subjects rather than a reflection of rational or instrumental needs and interests.

In this way, the sociological approach to international relations facilitates a view of difference which is not based on rational or political clashes of interests but rather is based on inequalities in access to the correct or best institutional frameworks. If ideas and communicative processes are the key to flexibility and adaptation to changing global threats, the answer is to unblock the barriers to states and other actors being included. This construc-tivist framing reflected and facilitated the more interventionist approaches of the 1990s, suggesting that external pressure on governments could be under-stood as politically empowering and giving voice to the voiceless (Keck and Sikkink 1998; Risse *et al.* 1999).

The shift to the sociological approach of reflectivism rather than rational-ism, within the discipline of international relations, indicates the post-liberal paradigm shift, which posits political subjects as the product of institutional frameworks at both the international and domestic levels. This shift is paradigmatic as the shift away from the rationalist approach does not necessarily involve the rejection of states as key subjects or actors; the shift is fundamentally about how these actors are understood to act and the method of judging these actions and the diminished nature of political autonomy.

Statebuilding and post-liberal governance

The paradigm of international statebuilding fully reflects this shift away from rationalist approaches in international relations and the critique of the liberal subject, developed through both economic and sociological theory. Where international statebuilding, as a framework of post-liberal governance, is most distinct is in the clarity of the discussion on what the role of the state should be (in the context of post-conflict reconstruction or preventive interventionist measures taken to ensure the stability of the non-western state). While disillusion with the liberal subject is widespread in our post-political age it is only around concrete issues of policy-making concern that the impact of this disillusionment can be seen clearly and coherently. If we were constructing a genealogy of the paradigm of international statebuilding, it would be less likely to be one concerning international administrations of the past or one developed from the 'lessons learned' of post-Cold War international peacekeeping, rather, it seems more useful to focus upon key moments where international policy-makers have sought to defensively respond to challenges to the universalist assumptions of the liberal paradigm. Two such examples are, first, the need to reconstruct the post-war West German state, independently of liberal assumptions of popular sovereignty and collective representation, and second, the need to explain how the growing integration of post-colonial states within the world market increased economic inequalities rather than ameliorating them. How these concrete examples might help us to understand the framework of international statebuilding policies and practices is the subject of this section.

Foucault's birth of biopolitics

The post-liberal problematization of autonomy and with it the classic liberal assumptions of government rationality have their roots in the crises of the liberal paradigm which came to a head in the early twentieth century. The Bolshevik revolution of 1917 created a non-liberal alternative and the threat of revolution and market collapse encouraged the extreme responses of fascism and Nazism as well as the interventionist regimes of Keynesianism and Roosevelt's 'New Deal'. In response to the crises of liberal governmental rationality, Foucault argued that in the inter-war and post-war period there were a 'number of re-evaluations, re-appraisals, and new projects in the art of government', particularly in Germany and the US (Foucault 2008: 69). These reappraisals and reevaluations of the liberal paradigm have been crucial to the development of the post-liberal framework.

Foucault has highlighted how the shift away from the traditional liberal paradigm involves, at its heart, the reappraisal of the role of the state. In the *Birth of Biopolitics*, he traced how the critique of the role of the state and the reworking of the liberal problematic was worked through in post-war Germany in the wake of the discrediting of the German state – whose national institutions and population were discredited in the wake of the Nazi experience – and the need to find an alternative source of legitimacy. The nascent West German state could not be legitimized on the basis of its historical past or on the basis of popular sovereignty:

> It is not possible to claim juridical legitimacy inasmuch as no apparatus, no consensus, and no collective will can manifest itself in a situation in which Germany is on the one hand divided, and on the other occupied. So, there are no historical rights, there is no juridical legitimacy, on which to found a new German state.
>
> (Foucault 2008: 82)

In fact, under Allied occupation, the problem of the reconstruction of the German state was seen to be one of the limitation or moderation of German sovereignty and of popular autonomy, hence the constitutional restrictions on German policy actions internationally and the diminished powers of representative institutions and greater independence of the Constitutional Court and the Bundesbank. As Foucault noted: 'both Western and Eastern Europe were reassured by ensuring that the institutional embryo being formed presented absolutely none of the dangers of the strong or totalitarian state' (2008: 83). The crisis of legitimacy of the German state appeared to necessitate an institutional framework which was legitimized without relying on the classic liberal assumptions of autonomy and which, in fact, assumed that autonomy was the problem which needed to be addressed.

The nascent German state was legitimized in administrative and technical terms, rather than in the liberal paradigm of the collective autonomy of rights-bearing subjects. Rather than political rights, it was the efficiency of governance and administration which was seen to be central. Sovereignty was to be legitimized as the product of good governance rather than being a natural starting assumption. Neither the state nor the popular will were to be the legitimizing subject of public law but the utilitarian or functional needs of the economy and society. It was assumed that there was no source of autonomous or independent or natural legitimacy. Autonomy was not the grounding principle of legitimacy but rather the problem that needed to be regulated: it was on the basis of the need for prior regulatory intervention and for the restriction of autonomy that government was to be legitimized. Foucault suggests that the shift from classical liberal frameworks of state/society relations can be understood as the birth of biopolitics, which is dependent upon the inversion of classical liberal categories:

> . . . it seems to me that the analysis of biopolitics can only get under way when we have understood the general regime of this governmental reason . . . this general regime that we call the question of truth, of economic truth in the first place, within governmental reason. Consequently, it seems to me that it is only when we understand what is at stake in this regime of liberalism opposed to raison d'État – or rather, fundamentally modifying it without, perhaps, questioning its bases – only when we know what this governmental regime called liberalism was, will we be able to grasp what biopolitics is.
>
> (2008: 21–22)

Neoliberal or, in the terminology used here, post-liberal, governance is an approach which legitimizes policy-making (and the limits to policy-making) independently of rights-based representative politics. This approach is different from the liberal balance of too much and too little, of fine-tuning economic and social life around policy goals. The fundamental difference is in the articulation of the relationship between the state and society. In the post-liberal paradigm, the state does not have autonomous legitimacy derived from the liberal paradigm of representing a collective social will. The experience of Nazism in Germany enabled fascism to be used as a field of adversity through which post-liberal themes could develop. These themes understood Nazism not in terms of the dictates of capitalist needs to discipline and contain the workers movement in the face of the threat of communism but as a 'truth' of the dangers of state autonomy (Foucault 2008: 110). For the neoliberal theoreticians, Nazism illustrated the problem of the state and in this respect was little different to communism and was a warning that the extension of Keynesian and New Deal approaches needed to be resisted (Foucault 2008: 111).

For the neoliberal theorists, it was not the case that Nazism was the consequence of capitalism and its contradictions rather it was the consequence of not accepting the needs of the market and of attempting to impose a subjective or collective will in the form of protectionism and planning (Foucault 2008: 114). The neoliberal framing argued that intervention into the sphere of the economy and society on the basis of attempting to direct the outcomes of social and economic processes inevitably led to the imposition of a totalitarian order:

So, from Saint-Simon to Nazism there is a cycle of rationality entailing interventions which entail the growth of the state, which entails setting up an administration that itself functions according to technical types of rationality, and this constitutes precisely the genesis of Nazism over two centuries, or at any rate a century and a half, of the history of capitalism.

(Foucault 2008: 115)

Rather than legitimizing state intervention on the basis of curbing problematic outcomes of the market economy, it was argued that the role of the state should be to ensure that the market economy worked more effectively. Rather than intervention into a sphere of natural or organic order to fine tune or correct outcomes according to the liberal discourse of freedom and security, the state should act preventively, ensuring that the market is facilitated. The key conclusion is that the liberal assumptions of laissez-faire are mistaken and little more than 'naïve naturalism' (Foucault 2008: 120). Following Husserl – and illustrating the links between neoliberalism and critical sociology – the post-war German liberals argued that the logic of competition had to be respected and understood and in certain circumstances carefully and artificially constructed. Market competition became a policy goal – 'an objective thus presupposing an indefinitely active policy' – rather than a natural given to be respected and, if necessary, intervened in after the event (Foucault 2008: 120).

This meant that there was no longer a division between an economy of autonomous self-interested subjects and the state, which was interventionist in terms of the collective will. There was no longer the distinction between autonomy and intervention or the state and the economy, as if they were two distinctive and reciprocally delimited domains (as in the liberal paradigm). As Foucault noted, in this paradigm:

Government must accompany the market from start to finish. The market economy does not take something away from government . . . One must govern for the market, rather than because of the market. To that extent you can see that the relationship defined by eighteenth century liberalism is completely reversed.

(2008: 121)

Governing for the market was very different to governing the market. It was not a matter of state intervention or direction but of facilitation, of indirect or institutional intervention to facilitate the most efficient outcomes of individual choices.

Institutionalism and the failure of post-colonial development

Post-liberal governance developed as a way of legitimizing external intervention in the reconstruction of the post-war West German state and became a key approach to understanding government in the framework of governance, playing a crucial role in the development and integration of the European Union in the post-Cold War period (see Heartfield 2010). However, focusing on this side of post-liberal governance tells us more about how this paradigmatic approach might be applied within western states or to European enlargement (considered in the next chapter) but tells us little about how post-liberal governance can operate as the projection of power and policy frameworks where there is much less at stake, for example, in the post-colonial world. To get a fuller understanding of the paradigmatic nature of post-liberal approaches to the international sphere it is important to attempt to understand how developments internal to western government thinking (particularly in Europe) gelled or coalesced with the development of institutionalist approaches in relation to understanding the economic problems of the post-colonial world. Post-war Germany was an isolated example, in terms of post-liberalism as a project of governance, until the end of the Cold War. The area in which institutionalist approaches developed and were cohered intellectually was not that of legitimizing forms of governmental regulation but rather in the apologia for difference.

Of central importance to understanding post-liberal frameworks as apologia is the work of Douglass North. The understanding of post-liberal institutionalism in the framework of World Bank thinking originates in the crisis of economic development in the 1970s – in this context, the post-liberal paradigm develops not in order to justify external regulatory power and to legitimize external intervention but rather to explain why external policy interventions have failed. Here the non-western state enters the picture, not as an object of interventionist measures but merely negatively as an institutional blockage. In this framing of apologia, the state (as a bundle of formal institutions) is not necessarily seen as the main blockage, rather society or culture (the bundle of informal institutions held to shape attitudes and opinions) is seen to be central.

Post-liberal institutionalism develops as apologia in order to explain the failure of international development, or why 'the gap between rich and poor nations, between developed and undeveloped nations, is as wide today as it ever was and perhaps a great deal wider than ever before' (North 1990: 6). Institutionalism arises in the international sphere as a theory of differential development which challenges Marxist approaches which focused on the reproduction of market inequalities and the operation of imperialist power relations. Rather than looking outside the post-colonial state at the external context of development, the apologist focus shifted attention to the inside: to the institutions of the post-colonial state and society. According to Douglass North: 'institutions define and limit the set of choices of individuals' (1990: 4):

> Institutions are the rules of the game in a society or, more formally, are the humanly devised constraints that shape human interaction. In consequence they structure incentives in human exchange, whether political, social or economic. Institutional change shapes the way societies evolve through time and hence is the key to understanding historical change.
>
> (1990: 3)

The institutionalist approach, like that of critical sociological thinking, sought to remove the 'naturalist' or 'materialist' basis of non-sociological approaches, which derived interests and needs from structural contexts, and instead focused on the inter-subjective aspects of rules and norms: 'Separating the analysis of the underlying rules from the strategy of the players is a necessary prerequisite to building a theory of institutions' (North 1990: 5). The 'strategy' of the players, i.e. the articulation of political demands or the economic choices made, were not understood as 'natural' but as shaped and constructed by the prior and pre-existing institutional rules. If these rules or norms were poorly constructed or no longer adequate then these demands and choices would have problematic consequences.

What the institutionalist approach emphasizes is the fact that individuals may act 'rationally' but in an 'irrational' context – i.e. where the institutional constraints are poor – and therefore rational actions may perpetuate irrational and counterproductive outcomes. In other words, the market will not necessarily tend towards equalizing outcomes if the institutional context creates the wrong incentive structures (North 1990: 6–7). For the institutionalists, the western advocates of free market solutions were wrong in idealizing the capacities of both markets and independent interest-based individuals; what they ignored was the crucial role of institutions which enabled both markets and individuals to efficiently make decisions. In the institutionalist world, there is no liberal assumption that the pursuit of individual interest will contribute to the collective good. If both individual and collective interests are jointly served this is either the work of fortuitous accident or of good institutional frameworks.

One of the key reasons for the lack of conjunction between individual and collective interests in post-colonial states and societies was understood to be that of culture or ideology. Here (see also, Chapter 8 on civil society) culture and ideology serve as apologia to suggest that there is very little that western intervention can achieve, as even formal institutional changes may possibly not be enough or could be counterproductive as the deeper problem is at the informal institutional level (North 1990: 45). Institutionalists (as we saw with Commons and Simon, earlier) focus on the lack of knowledge of market individuals and the lack of capacity to interpret and objectively judge on the basis of even this limited knowledge. However, in the framework of applying this paradigm to the failure of the market in the post-colonial world, the problematization of subjectivity went further, with the decisions and 'choices' made by societies and elites understood to be irrational because the institutional norms and values were divisive, for example, accepting nepotism and patronage or promoting racial, ethnic, class or gender discrimination (see also, Chapter 8).

The work of North best illustrates the approach of the inversion of the liberal paradigm which is highlighted by Foucault. It is important to emphasize that the post-liberal paradigm is dependent on the liberal ontology of rational self-determining subjects (North 1990: 5). The problems – whether of development, democracy or of security – are understood as problems of freely-willed individual 'choices'. These choices are not rational in their outcomes (in terms of leading to progress and efficiency, as in the liberal paradigm) because the rationality of outcomes depends on the formal and informal institutional frameworks in place. Rather than autonomy being a natural, universal capacity for independence, it is on the basis of autonomy that institutionalists understand the existence of inequalities and differences in capacities for independence.

This enables the post-liberal paradigm of international statebuilding to be extremely flexible. There is no limit to the reinterpretation of the problems and difficulties of the post-colonial world in terms of the failings of individuals (either at the level of society or elites). Perhaps the best example of an institutionalist framing of problems of post-colonial states and societies is that of Amartya Sen's. Taking a traditional headline grabbing example of what could be seen as a problem of structural global inequalities of wealth and power: famine; Sen asserts that famines are not 'natural' in terms of being the product of a lack of food. Instead, he argues that famines are caused by bad governance: by poor institutional responses. Therefore the solution is that of good governance, which would enable the market to provide food for those who need it (Sen 1999: 160–88; 1981; Sen and Drèze 1989).

This framing passes responsibility for policy outcomes entirely on to the society and state being intervened in. This makes it possible for the condemnation of post-colonial states and societies to develop in line with the amount of 'concern' expressed for their welfare and development. When it comes to the policy consequences of intervention, there is no difficulty for international interveners to bridge the gap between promises and outcomes as this can be entirely explained at the level of the state and society concerned, which appears to be less and less adequate or capable, the higher the external expectations are. This is the dynamic which drives the apologetic discourse of international statebuilding (see Chapter 2 on the liberal peace critique): the more interventions fail to achieve their aims, the more clear it is to interveners that there is a larger gap between their own 'liberalism' and the 'illiberalism' of the societies and elites being intervened upon (which is the essence of the 'lessons learned' approaches). In this way, every external goal of interveners which fails to be achieved implies the need for more attention to matters of good governance. The gap between policy-expectations and outcomes drives the international statebuilding paradigm of post-liberal governance, swallowing up more and more areas of policy-making, from development to rights-protections to post-conflict security.

International statebuilding

North himself was not initially concerned with western policy-making towards the post-colonial state. In fact, the post-liberal paradigm is not open to clear policy-frameworks. As North suggests, the problem with institutional approaches is that of causation:

> Does constitutional structure cause a political condition and a state of public opinion or does the political condition and a state of public opinion cause the constitutional structure? . . . How does one create self-enforcing constraints? . . . [C]reating a system of effective enforcement and of moral constraints on behavior is a long, slow process that requires time to develop . . . a condition markedly absent in the rapid transformation of Africa from tribal societies to market economies.
>
> (North 1990: 60)

The concern was with apologia rather than intervention. It was only in the post-Cold War era, with the removal of barriers to external intervention and conditionalities that the post-liberal paradigm became a guide to international policy-framing. As we shall see, this framework provided a highly suitable understanding of the nature and intractability of the problems of the post-colonial world as well as legitimizing a framework of policy interventions in which western policy actors could express their concerns but avoid any accountability for outcomes.

In the paradigm of international statebuilding, this programme of apologia is adapted as a set of workable assumptions for a highly interventionist framework of policy-making. Once the institutional framework (at both formal and informal levels) is problematized, a large sphere of policy-making objectives is opened up at the same time as operating as apologia for the limited success in the past and future. This has been achieved through making the autonomy of the post-colonial state and society both the cause of the problem and the object of policy-intervention. The dynamic is that of the critique of the liberal framing of autonomous capacity at the level of the state, or sovereignty (as highlighted in Chapter 3), and also at the level of the individual or society.

International statebuilding as a policy paradigm is premised on the understanding of previous policy interventions as mistaken in assuming a liberal framework of state-society relations. As Ghani and Lockhart state, policy interventions failed as they 'assumed functioning states as its constituent units'; this assumption meant that institutions were ignored at the level of both state and society, resulting in paper successes and the undermining of state effectiveness because there was little recognition that 'informal rules dominate the formal, distort or subvert them' (2008: 86, 108). Similarly, Barnett and Zürcher note that: 'states emerging from war do not have the necessary institutional framework or civic culture to absorb [liberalizing pressures] . . . which means that liberal peacebuilding is more likely to reproduce than to transform existing state-society relations and patrimonial politics' (2009: 23, 36).

In the discursive language of intervention, international statebuilding lacks both a clear rationale and political legitimacy within the liberal paradigm. It is only through the capacity to legitimize a framework of rule independently of the originatory rights of the subjects of that rule that the project of international statebuilding is possible. The post-liberal paradigm legitimizes a framework of rule on the basis of its functional and administrative capacity rather than on the classical liberal rights paradigm. In the post-liberal paradigm, the rights of the state being intervened in are understood as conditional upon the state's capacity for good governance and the rights of the state's citizens are similarly conditional upon their capacity to support and enhance good governance.

For post-liberal institutionalists, the world of competition and the market resembles the constructivist vision of international relations, where institutions and path-dependencies shape interaction and the development of interests and identities. The domestic collective or community, mythologically constructed in liberal discourse through the social contract, is deconstructed and demonstrated to be a product of good governance: of good institutional management. Markets and societies need to be constructed through the functional responsibilities of the state in providing law and order, welfare, education, transparency, etc.

Where the post-liberal paradigm is most important in the sphere of international relations has been the overcoming of the barriers of the rights-based discourses of international law, sovereignty and non-intervention. Rather than posing intervention as problematic; the post-liberal framework inverses this traditional conception of limits, problematizing autonomy. This sets up a programme of intervention without a pre-established limit. The limit to external intervention is instead understood in terms of equilibrium between different concerns which need to be balanced; this discourse is a much more arbitrary one.

Conclusion

It now appears that the high point of liberal paradigms of social and political thought and of governmental rationality were only the precursors for today's paradigm of post-liberalism. Whereas economic and social theorizing were much more open to post-liberal perspectives, political theory and international relations were much less so. In the aftermath of the end of the Cold War, international relations rapidly caught up with the post-liberal trends of economic and sociological thinking, where autonomy was conceived to be the problem rather than the starting assumption. With the rise of post-liberalism, the discipline of international relations was transformed and rather than the poor relation of political theory, increasingly became central to theorizing a post-government or post-sovereign world of post-liberal governance (Chandler 2009b; 2010a; 2010b). The paradigm of post-liberal governance which drives the discourse of international statebuilding is one which presupposes the pluralism of the realist non-liberal world of Cold War international relations, where difference is the prior assumption rather than universality. Reconstructed in a post-liberal framework, this is a world where difference and inequality are seen to be inevitable on the basis of the autonomy of individuals and states. The fact that there is autonomy, rather than empire, is then held to require the permanent mobilizing of interventionist mechanisms of international statebuilding in order for the dangers posed by autonomy, both domestically and internationally, to be mitigated.

5 The EU's export of 'the rule of law' and 'good governance'

Introduction

One way of highlighting the connection between the paradigmatic framing of international statebuilding and its connection with the critique of autonomy from within the institutionalist approach of good governance is through a consideration of the European Union's policy interventions. The European Union is generally considered to be the statebuilding institution par excellence (see, for example, Trauner 2009; Grabbe 2006; Leonard 2005). In fact, it appears that it is difficult for the EU to act in the international sphere without acting within the paradigmatic framing of international statebuilding; virtually no external relations are inculcated without being discursively framed in terms of the export of the rule of law or good governance. Whereas it is common to see criticisms of post-Cold War interventions undertaken by individual EU member states, other leading western states (especially the US), or led by the United Nations, much less attention has been placed upon the EU's projection of its power within the framework of international statebuilding and the majority of academic and policy studies have been overwhelmingly positive. For the purposes of clarifying the discursive framing of statebuilding in post-liberal terms, the policy practices of the European Union in Southeastern Europe provide an almost text-book case study. An analysis of this framing also helps to see why the EU's extensive regulatory reach is rarely perceived to be problematic or understood as limited or counterproductive in the same way as the more ad hoc approaches to international intervention in the recent period.

This chapter suggests that EU governance in Southeastern Europe reproduces a post-liberal discourse in which the failures and problems which have emerged, especially in relation to the pace of integration and the sustainability of peace in candidate member states such as Bosnia-Herzegovina, have merely reinforced the EU's external governance agenda. On the one hand, the limitations of reform have reinforced the EU's projection of its power as a civilizing mission into what is perceived to be a dangerous vacuum in the region. On the other hand, through the discourse of post-liberal governance, the EU seeks to avoid the direct political responsibilities associated with this power. Rather than legitimize policy-making on the basis of representative legitimacy, post-liberal frameworks of governance problematize autonomy and self-government, inverting the liberal paradigm through establishing administrative and regulative frameworks as necessarily prior to democratic choices. This process tends to distance policy-making from representative accountability, weakening the legitimacy of governing institutions in Southeastern European states which have international legal sovereignty but lack genuine mechanisms for politically integrating society.

The EU's discourse of governance enables it to exercise a regulatory power over the pre-accession states in the region – Albania, Bosnia-Herzegovina, Croatia, Macedonia, Serbia, Montenegro and Kosovo – while evading any reflection on the EU's own management processes which are depoliticized in the framing of the technocratic or administrative conditions of enlargement. In this way, the responsibility for the integration process and any problems which might arise are seen to have their roots in the institutional frameworks (both formal and informal) which are held to reproduce non-rational, non-liberal, or politically 'immature' outcomes in the autonomous political processes of Southeastern European elites and their interactions with their societies. This is regularly expressed, for example, at the time of writing, by the UK Shadow Foreign Secretary, William Hague, in his view of the need to extend the EU's 'strong outside pressure' to overcome the political blockages to reform in Bosnia (Morris 2009). The discourse of governance reinterprets the limits to the EU's external attempts at social and political engineering its 'near abroad' as indications that the EU should try harder and be more 'hands on' in its external assistance for institutional change, the core policy framing of post-liberal international statebuilding. In this discourse, the problem is the autonomy or the sovereignty of candidate states, rather than their lack of independence to make and implement their own policies.

As we have highlighted in the preceding chapters, the post-liberal discourse of governance is very different from the modern liberal discourse of government. While government presupposes a liberal rights-based framing of political legitimacy, in terms of autonomy and self-determining state authority, the discourse of governance focuses on technical and administrative capacity, or the way of rule, rather than the representative legitimacy of policy-making or its derivational authority (EU 2001b; see also, WB 1989; 1992; 1997; 1998). This shift is vital to understanding the discursive framework in which the EU can export good governance and claim a legitimate authority to judge the capacities of new member and candidate states in Southeastern Europe. The discourse of governance is, in this respect, one in which the external engagement of the EU is seen as a prerequisite for policy progress rather than as an exception to the norm in need of special justification; and one where the legitimacy of this intervention, and of the policy prescriptions attached to this, is judged in technical or administrative terms rather than liberal democratic ones.

The EU governance discourse focuses on sovereignty, but not in the framework of a liberal discourse of external intervention, which justified the undermining of formal sovereign rights on the basis of securing the rights of individuals. In this post-liberal discourse, intervention is required but to strengthen sovereignty not to undermine it. There is no longer a potential clash of rights – or of the interests of interveners and intervened upon – once the goal of sovereign capacity is held to be privileged above all others. In the terminology of influential policy analysts Ashraf Ghani and Claire Lockhart (2008) this external governance assistance does not undermine sovereignty but rather it supports it through overcoming the 'sovereignty gap': the technical and administrative weaknesses of Southeastern European new members and candidate states (as considered in Chapter 3). The European Union has become the exporter of this framework of governance par excellence, through the enlargement process, in which candidate states have been member-state built.

The EU has been keen to promote itself as a policy-leader in the field of governance and this has been taken up supportively by many academic commentators, keen to emphasize that the EU is unique as a policy-actor, exercising 'soft power', 'normative power', or building a 'voluntary empire' (for example, Manners 2002; Sjursen 2006; Cooper 2003). In this way, the EU's exercise of power and influence is contrasted positively to the 'neo-colonial' or 'hard power' approaches of the US or of the individual member states. This chapter seeks to problematize some of these assumptions about the EU's governance discourse and its policy practices in relation to Southeastern Europe and suggests that the technocratic and administrative legitimization of external intervention is not beyond criticism in both normative and practical policy terms.

This chapter briefly reviews the EU's governance framework, both in terms of the institutionalist paradigm and the mechanisms of implementation in Southeastern Europe, operationalized through the rubric of member-state building, and traces their development since 1999, particularly in relation to the Stabilisation and Association Process. It seeks to highlight briefly how the EU has denied its power in the very processes of exercising it, through:

- presenting its policy framework in the language of 'partnership' and country 'ownership';

- internationalizing the mechanisms of its domination through engaging a multitude of external states and international organizations;
- internationalizing or Europeanizing the candidate state's core institutions of governance; and
- engaging with and attempting to create a policy-advocating 'civil society'.

It concludes by considering some of the limitations to the post-liberal governance discourse of member-state building.

The institutionalist paradigm

The West European states, collectively operating as the EU, could not avoid being the determining influence in the political and economic affairs of Southeastern Europe with the end of the Cold War. The problem that the EU faced was how to manage this position of power and influence. According to the report of the International Commission on the Balkans, chaired by Guiliano Amato, former Italian prime minister, *The Balkans in Europe's Future*:

> If the EU does not devise a bold strategy for accession that could encompass all Balkan countries as new members within the next decade, then it will become mired instead as a neo-colonial power in places like Kosovo, Bosnia and even Macedonia. Such an anachronism would be hard to manage and would be in contradiction with the very nature of the European Union. The real choice the EU is facing in the Balkans is: Enlargement or Empire.
>
> (ICB 2005: 11)

This quote sharply sums up the dilemma facing the EU, which appeared to face two unpalatable options: either to leave the Southeastern European states to manage their own affairs and problems or to take on an increasingly formalized responsibility of managing them themselves. The response of the EU has been to develop a 'Third Way', a method of intervention and regulation, but one that does not formally undermine the sovereignty and legal independence of Southeastern European states. This third way approach is that of the post-liberal discourse of governance: external regulation without the formal responsibility for governing and policy-making in the region. In this way, the governance discourse of enlargement has enabled discussion of EU engagement to be framed outside the traditional understandings of sovereignty-based international relations: the either/or of respecting sovereign autonomy or coercively intervening to undermine sovereignty. The discourse of governance asserts that it is supportive of sovereignty but on the basis that sovereignty is understood as a capacity to manage autonomy, rather than being a product of autonomy and co-determinate with it. This framework enables interventionist practices and conditionalities to be posed as capacity-building the Southeastern European candidate states rather than as impositions denying or undermining their sovereignty. The policy practices bound up with the discourse of governance are those of international state-building. Whereas traditional liberal discourses presupposed sovereignty and political autonomy as the condition of statehood, the governance discourse sees statehood as separate from sovereignty (seen as the capacity for good governance). The institutionalist approach of governance understands the problems at economic, social and political levels as a product of poor institutional frameworks, which have been unable to constrain actors' pursuit of self-interest in irrational or destabilizing ways. This discourse operates at the formal level of state institutions and at the informal level of civil society.

The formal level of state institutions

Institutionalist approaches to governance are legitimized on the basis that the autonomy of state-level political processes is potentially dangerous and destabilizing. The starting assumption with regard to member-state building in Southeastern Europe was that external engagement was necessary for both the interests of the European Union and for the citizens of Southeastern European states themselves. The European Commission asserted that:

> The lack of effective and accountable state institutions hampers the ability of each country to co-operate with its neighbours and to move towards the goal of closer integration with the EU. Without a solid institutional framework for the exercise of public power, free and fair elections will not lead to representative or accountable government. Without strong institutions to implement the rule of law, there is little prospect that states will either provide effective protection of human and minority rights or tackle international crime and corruption.
>
> (EU 2001a: 11)

The problems identified in the governance sphere were not with the formal mechanisms of democratic government or the electoral accountability of government representatives but were concerns that went beyond procedural questions of 'free and fair elections' to the administrative practices and policy choices of governments and the attitude, culture and participation-levels of their citizens. Where the traditional liberal agenda focused on processes rather than outcomes and free and fair elections were seen to be the main indicator of representative and accountable government, under the post-liberal framing of governance, institution-building was now held to be the key to democratic development. According to the Commission, strengthening state institutions was vital for 'assuring the region's future, being as relevant to human rights and social inclusion as it is to economic development and democratisation' (EU 2001a; see also, Storey 1995).

The EU's approach to institutional governance reform has been described as implying no less than the 'reforming and reinventing [of] the state in Southeastern Europe' (EWI 2001: 18). As the European Stability Initiative observed:

> A new consensus is emerging among both regional and international actors that the most fundamental obstacle to the advance of democracy and security in South Eastern Europe is the lack of effective and accountable state institutions. Strengthening domestic institutions is increasingly viewed as the key priority across the diverse sectors of international assistance, as relevant to human rights and social inclusion as it is to economic development and democratisation.
>
> (EWI 2001: 18)

The EU's process of governance regulation of Southeastern Europe has involved close integration with a large number of non-EU actors, such as the Organization for Security and Co-operation in Europe (OSCE), UN agencies, the international financial institutions and a variety of informal and ad hoc institutional experiments, with leading examples being the Contact Group, the EU-led Stability Pact, the Peace Implementation Council (for Bosnia) and the International Steering Group (for Kosovo). The international institutions involved in stabilizing and integrating the Southeastern European states within European structures have consistently viewed the governance agenda as their central concern in the region. Today, the argument is still often repeated that many states in the region lack sufficient capacity and suffer from historical 'path dependencies' which have undermined the relations between states and their societies. One typical expression of this framing was that of Valentin Inzko, the Austrian official serving as the EU's High Representative in Bosnia when, in August 2009, he put the lack of political progress down to the fact that he felt that Bosnia suffered 'from a "dependency syndrome" that dates back centuries, to when it was part of the Ottoman Empire' (Whitlock 2009).

The informal level of civil society

In the discourse of governance, the concept of civil society is used very differently from the conceptualization in traditional political discourses of liberal modernity. Whereas, for traditional conceptions of civil society, the autonomy of civil society as a sphere of association and citizenship was seen as a positive factor, for the EU, civil society is seen as problematic and in need of external intervention and regulation. Civil society discourse highlights the problematic nature of autonomy, understood as irreducible differences which risk conflict if they are not regulated via the correct institutional mechanisms. In the distinctive use of difference in this context of external engagement, the concept of civil society is used in ways which reflect and draw upon pre-modern concepts problematizing and essentializing difference, especially the pre-existing discourses of race and culture (considered at greater length in Chapter 8).

Regarding civil society, the European Commission was even more forthright in its condemnation of the aspiring Southeastern European members involved in the Stabilisation and Association Process:

> [N]one of the countries can yet claim to have the level of vibrant and critical media and civil society that is necessary to safeguard democratic advances. For example, public and media access to information, public participation in policy debate and accountability of government and its agencies are aspects of civil society which are still largely undeveloped in all five of the countries.
>
> (EU 2001a: 10–11)

In this case, the potential accession states from the region could apparently not even make a 'claim' that they could safeguard 'democracy' in their states without external assistance in the form of civil society capacity-building. In fact, the Commission was clearly concerned as much by society in the region as by government, arguing that the aim of its new programmatic development was necessarily broad in order 'to entrench a culture . . . which makes forward momentum towards the EU irreversible' (EU 2002: 8).

The way in which civil society relates to earlier framings of race and especially of cultural distinctions can be seen in the understanding of the problems of ethnic or regional divisions within Southeastern European societies. Here, civil society is seen as weak or problematic and as undermining external attempts to reform and improve governance. Education is often highlighted as especially important in terms of transforming societal informal institutional structures. For example, Claude Kiffer, who runs the OSCE education department in Bosnia, suggests that '[t]he absence of genuine education reform designed to bring future citizens together undermines all other reforms so far . . . The system is producing three sets of citizens who do not know anything about the others and have no intercultural skills' (Cerkez-Robinson 2009). David Skinner of Save the Children further argues that education systems are problematic in the region as they apparently fail to 'produce citizens with critical thinking skills' (Cerkez-Robinson 2009). The good governance agenda with its institutionalist emphasis on state-level institution-building and civil society development developed in the 1990s, reflecting the regulatory power which the EU had over the region, enabling external institutions to take an active interest in questions which were previously seen to be ones of domestic political responsibility. This transformation in relations of power and influence is a crucial determinant for the governance discourse and in explaining the post-liberal intervention-ist thrust of external policy-making. The Commission argued that its focus on building the capacity of state institutions and civil society development reflected not only the importance of this question and the clear needs it had identified, 'but also the comparative advantage of the European Community in providing *real added value* in this area' (EU 2001a: 9). It would appear that the Southeastern European states were fortunate in that their wealthy neighbours to the west had not only identified their central problems but also happened to have the solutions to them already at hand.

The rule of law and the export of governance

Central to the export of good governance under the EU is an understanding of the rule of law within the paradigm of post-liberal governance. It is this framing which enables the EU to export its regulatory regime in its dealings with other actors and potential members, such as the states of Southeastern Europe. In the paradigm of post-liberal governance, the rule of law is under-stood in terms which are not compatible with the conceptual frameworks of classical liberalism. Whereas in liberal modernity the rule of law was under-stood to derive from the legal subject, in post-liberal frameworks the rule of law is held to constitute the legal subject or citizen. This inversion of the classical liberal framing of law enables law to be understood and to be legiti-mized as something external to the state and society being intervened in and as something which can be exported as part of the statebuilding process.

The legitimacy of both the EU's export of good governance and the broader process of external regulation, which we call international statebuild-ing, depends upon the inversion of traditional understandings of how law derives its legitimacy. This understanding of law, as legitimized independ-ently of those who are subject to it can best be conceptualized as post-liberal because the law is legitimized on the basis of the incapacity of the autono-mous subject (both the state and the society) which is being statebuilt. In fact, it is the alleged incapacity of the object of international statebuilding intervention which is the basis for legitimizing the regulatory and administra-tive codes projected in the international statebuilding process. This inverts the classical liberal relation between the law and the legal subject: within the post-liberal paradigm of statebuilding, the legal subject of classical liberal frameworks is thereby transformed into an object of law rather than its legitimizing subject.

At the core of the inversion of the relationship between law and the legal subject is the understanding of the autonomy of the state and society being statebuilt as problematic. Thus autonomy becomes the object of interventionist policy rather than a reason which makes external statebuilding illegitimate. In the classical liberal framework the rule of law meant a legal framework which was consented to by those bound by it, any other framing of law would be alien and a tyranny rather than a freedom. It is this inversion of the classical meaning of the rule of law, which makes the export of good governance the *sine qua non* of the international statebuilding process. The rule of law can only play such a central role in international statebuilding policy discourses because its meaning has been changed in this way. As Ghani and Lockhart state:

> . . . the most crucial function performed by the state is law making (i.e., establishing the rules by which society operates . . . As a result of the rule of law, citizens understand a distinct set of rights and duties that guides their behavior toward other citizens, as well as toward the larger community.
>
> (2008: 125)

Here, it is clear that the rule of law does not derive from society in the sense of a pre-established consensus. The rule of law is understood as fundamental to the existence of society as the precondition for social consensus.

This post-liberal framing of the rule of law presupposes not a lack of autonomy but rather the problematic nature of the autonomy of the subject state and society being intervened in; making the subject of intervention incapable of legitimizing the rule of law (as discussed in the construction of the post-war West German state in Chapter 4). In this sense, the legitimacy of the international statebuilding project is an arbitrary and ad hoc or indeterminate one; it does not derive from a classical liberal framing in the relationship of representative or sovereign accountability. Even if the state concerned is held to freely invite the support of external statebuilding actors – for example, Bosnia, in the signing of the Dayton Peace Agreement, or Southeastern European states, in signing partnership agreements with the EU – the decision of when the statebuilding process is complete and autonomy is no longer considered to be problematic (and therefore membership of the EU held to be possible) is a matter of external decision rather than that of the objects of statebuilding.

In this framework, law is considered to be legitimate if it is cast in terms which limit the autonomy of the legal subject rather than in terms which express subject autonomy. It is the transformed understanding of autonomy, which enables a discussion about the rule of law in terms which could, literally, not make sense in a liberal paradigm. Here, law is understood as prior to the legal subject and in fact as constituting the legal subject. Law is prior to the legal subject because the post-liberal paradigm poses the autonomous subject as the problem at the heart of international statebuilding: the problem to which statebuilding is the solution. The rule of law is prioritized as the necessary circumscription of the autonomy of the subject. The legitimacy of the rule of law is derived from this circumscription of autonomy not from the subject's free will or autonomy itself.

The autonomy of the subject or the sovereign has, of course, been historically subject to limits within the discourse of modern liberal political theory. In the post-liberal discourse of governance, these limits and the forms in which they are legitimized differ from those of liberal discourse. In the post-liberal paradigm, limits to autonomy or the power of sovereign governments, are seen as legitimate in themselves (Bickerton 2009). In the international statebuilding literature, the sharing of sovereignty or the co-production of sovereignty is understood to be essential for the moderation of sovereign autonomy, with little consideration of the source of legitimacy for these externally-constructed limits.

The classic liberal conception of the limiting of popular sovereignty is often located in *The Federalist* (Hamilton *et al.* 1948), a collection of papers which informed and advocated for the ratification of the US constitution in the 1780s. The checks and balances advocated so eloquently by the founders of the US constitution differed radically from the regulatory frameworks established in the international statebuilding paradigm which seeks to tie the hands of governments in states alleged to be failing or at risk of failure, in order to ensure that they are bound by the rule of law. The checks and balances of international statebuilding are often posed in the functionalist terms of the need for external expertise in developing the adequate structures of good governance necessary for addressing the complexities of the globalizing world. Therefore, the role of the international financial institutions is considered necessary for assisting in poverty reduction and sustainable development, the role of external advisers in judicial reform or civil service training or educational development or military demobilization, are also considered necessary in terms of their own areas of technical expertise. In this way, a functional division of labour between international actors is held to constitute a number of checks and balances, which do not necessarily amount to a formal international administration but are nevertheless held to be essential to create the policy environment of good governance and the transparency necessary for accountability both domestically and internationally.

International institutions and international actors are increasingly understood as necessary in facilitating democratic accountability and ensuring the rule of law (see, for example, Buchanan 2007; Keohane *et al.* 2007). However, within international statebuilding, the rule of law is prioritized over democracy. Democracy is merely an internal check on state power and often seen as one which is inefficient, either due to the power of the state or the lack of capacity of civil society (see Chapter 8). It is important to emphasize that this view of the necessity for external constraints on autonomy and the prioritizing of the rule of law over democracy, or the freely chosen will of the state and society being intervened upon, cannot be legitimized within a liberal paradigm. For the classic liberal paradigm, the understanding of the derivation of law independently of those subject to it could only be tyranny: the constraints on sovereign autonomy can only be legitimate if they derive from those who are subject to the law: if they derive from the popular will (see, for example, Hamilton *et al.* 1948; Bickerton 2009).

For the classic liberal conception, it is not possible to conceive of law which is derived from external authorities as law which could be in the interests of those subject to it. The founders of the US constitution expressed the classic liberal assumptions of autonomy that, to be legitimate, rule and law had to be freely chosen and therefore an expression of the freedom and autonomy of the people. Rule and law could not legitimately limit autonomy as the liberal conception of law depends on law being an exercise of autonomy and freedom, not a restriction of it. This is why the US constitution is something which 'we the people' constitute for themselves (Hamilton *et al.* 1948: 464; Bickerton 2009). The framework of modern law is given by the French and US constitutions as the first examples of the self-rule of autonomous subjects.

In sum: in the liberal framework of law, law cannot be legitimized independently of those subject to it; this is why the paradigm of international statebuilding is explicitly post-liberal. It stands on the basis of the critique of the liberal subject and with it the liberal paradigm of governing rationality. As Lord Paddy Ashdown, the former European Union Special Representative with administrative powers over post-war Bosnia, has asserted: 'It is much more important to establish the rule of law quickly than to establish democracy quickly' (2003). The rule of law takes on a greater importance in international statebuilding than it has done in any domestic setting. This is because the statebuilding paradigm expresses the post-liberal framing of the relationship between law, democracy and rights in a much clearer form. The inversion of the liberal paradigm is clear in that the rule of law is no longer perceived as part of the superstructure, i.e. as determined by social forces and economic interests: law is understood as constitutive of the social and economic order. For it is the rule of law which is held to prevent the post-conflict state from falling back into collapse and social disintegration, not by imposing a strong state capable of suppressing opposition but by constraining the autonomy of the sovereign or governing powers.

The rule of law, as it has developed within the international statebuilding paradigm and as it is exported in the frameworks of good governance by the EU, is legitimized as a circumscription of autonomy. In a state under this framing of the rule of law, the public authorities can only act as servants of the law. Foucault argues that this framework can be seen as the opposite of traditional government, highlighted by Hayek's assertion that the rule of law can be best understood as 'quite simply the opposite of a plan' (Foucault 2008: 172). According to this reading, the rule of law can be understood as the opposite of traditional sovereign government in four key respects: first, a plan has an objective, a set of explicit aims or goals; second, a plan allows for corrections or rectifications; third, a plan depends on the public authorities having a decision-making role; finally, a plan presupposes that the government is in control of its resources. Good governance, on the other hand, according to Hayek, means that the state should never pursue particular aims or goals, should have fixed and stable laws binding the state as much as citizens and blindness towards outcomes: governance is about establishing the rules and norms which enable people to pursue their own goals not about directing society. The state which is subject to this framing of the rule of law is not one which is accountable to its citizens for outcomes or one which represents their collective interests but one which rules on the presumption that it cannot represent a collective interest distinct from that of other actors or institutions and that recognizes no interest beyond the administrative and technical needs of ensuring stability both domestically and internationally.

The export of the rule of law can therefore be understood as central to the production of good governance in that the assumption is that the problems of autonomy can be constrained through the subsumption of government under governance. Once autonomy is problematized external assistance in building sovereignty necessarily is seen to involve the strengthening of sovereignty through the constriction of government autonomy. In the post-liberal discourse this restriction of autonomy and the regulatory framing of institutionalism is not in need of justification but is the starting assumption of statebuilding intervention. It is only from within this paradigm of understanding that EU statebuilding can be framed as the 'co-production of sovereignty'.

The co-production of sovereignty

In the governance agenda, sovereignty is no longer understood as something that inheres to state institutions per se, but rather is understood to be a variable quality or capacity for good governance. For those tasked with building the 'sovereignty' or the governance capacity of other states, the traditional liberal discourse, which assumed sovereign autonomy to be a positive quality, has little purchase. Stephen Krasner (2005), Robert Keohane (2002), Ashraf Ghani and Clare Lockhart (2008) and other commentators have commented positively on the EU's approach to the 'co-production' of the sovereignty of Southeastern European states, or the EU model of 'shared sovereignty' or 'conditional sovereignty'. This post-liberal framing of sovereign rights and legitimacy has been shaped by the governance discourse of 'partnership' and 'country ownership'. These concepts have been central to the Stabilisation and Association Process (SAP) which was launched in May 1999, to cover Albania, Bosnia-Herzegovina, Croatia, Macedonia, Serbia and Montenegro.

The SAP is the cornerstone of EU policy of exporting its governance agenda through 'anchoring the region permanently to the development of the EU itself' (EU 2001c: 3). This 'anchoring' is seen as crucial to the encouragement of reforms in the governance sphere, relating to the rule of law and democratic and stable institutions. The legitimacy of the EU's relationship of regulation is based on two grounds, the recognition by Southeastern European elites of the need to reform to meet the governance prescriptions of the EU and the EU's offer to provide financial assistance with the promise of EU membership at some point in the future. The policy of aid in return for the EU's regulatory control over the reform process was underpinned by the CARDS (Community Assistance for Reconstruction, Development and Stabilisation) assistance programme providing €4.65 billion over 2000–2006. In 2007, this process was streamlined as the Pre-Accession Assistance Programme (available to candidate countries and potential candidates in the region) with €11.5 billion available from 2007 to 2013 (EU 2008). The legitimacy of this buying of external influence is bolstered by the promise of EU integration, i.e. 'on a credible prospect of membership once the relevant conditions have been met' (EU 2001c: 3).

In 2000, the EU Zagreb Summit endorsed the SAP objectives and conditions, namely the prospect of accession on the basis of the Treaty on European Union and the 1993 Copenhagen criteria, the CARDS assistance programme, and the countries undertaking to abide by the EU's conditionality and to participate fully in the SAP. Ahead of the EU-Western Balkans summit in Thessaloniki in 2003, the General Affairs and External Relations Council adopted the Thessaloniki agenda for moving towards European integration, strengthening the SAP by introducing new instruments to support reform and integration efforts, including European Partnerships, this time including Kosovo, as governed under the auspices of UN Security Council Resolution 1244, within its remit (see, for example, EU 2005). The European

Council argued that, for the Southeastern European states, the process of formulating the SAP contract would be 'both pedagogical and political' (EU 2001d). The 'pedagogical' aspect of the process highlights the relationship of subordination involved. As the EU reported, this process: 'has proved an effective means of focusing authorities' minds on essential reforms and of engaging with them *in a sustained way to secure implementation*' (EU 2001d: IIIc, emphasis added).

The European Commission stressed that there is 'a close *partnership* with SAP countries' (EU 2001c: 7, emphasis in original). This partnership was held to start by involving countries closely in the programming, including discussions on CARDS and Pre-Accession Assistance strategies; countries would also be involved in ongoing dialogue on developing annual action plans. The European Commission strongly emphasized the importance of country 'ownership':

> This partnership helps promote each country's sense of *ownership* over Community assistance that is crucial if it is to have the desired impact on the ground. This national commitment is all the more important for . . . institution building, which require the countries to undertake reforms if the assistance is to be effective.
>
> (EU 2001c: 7, emphasis in original)

Country ownership is clearly central to the EU SAP. However, it is clear that the promotion of 'ownership' was being pushed by the EU itself and does not involve any real equality of input over policy guidelines. While the formal regulatory mechanisms stress 'partnership' and 'country ownership', at the informal level, real ownership is exercised by the European Commission which guides donor coordination and works closely with the major international institutional actors, such as the World Bank (EU 2001c: 8). For example, once the Stabilisation and Association Agreements (SAAs) were signed the relationship of regulation became fully institutionalized (the SAAs are legally binding international agreements) (EU 2002: 4).

The first SAA agreement was signed with Macedonia in April 2001 and entered into force in 2004. The second, with Croatia, was signed in October 2001 and entered into force in 2005. Albania signed up to the formal process of negotiating the SAA in 2003 and Serbia and Montenegro and Bosnia-Herzegovina in November 2005. The agreements were 'the principal means to begin to prepare themselves for the demands that the perspective of accession to the EU naturally entails' (EU 2001c: 3). These demands were determined by the EU and considered to be so onerous that the Southeastern European states would need the additional encouragement of conditionality:

The Stabilisation and Association Agreements, then, are posited on respect for the conditionality of the Stabilisation and Association process agreed by the Council. But they also bring with them a dynamic means of operationalising that conditionality and give the EU the leverage necessary to get the countries to adopt genuine reforms with a view to achieving the immediate objectives of the agreements. The mechanisms of the Agreements themselves will enable the EU to prioritise reforms, shape them according to EU models, to address and solve problems, and to monitor implementation.

(EU 2001d: III)

The EU attains the necessary 'leverage' over states in the region through conditionality at three levels – the SAP, programme and project levels. At the SAP level, lack of progress in the reforms advocated by the EU in the economic, political and social spheres can lead to financial assistance being frozen or 'granted through other means' (EU 2001a: 24). If the EU chooses it can invoke 'programme conditionality', threatening to close certain aid programmes if the country concerned fails to satisfy the external administrators with regard to 'specific reform targets or adoption of sectoral policies' (EU 2001a: 25). 'Project level conditionality' can apply to ensure that the candidate state meets 'specific conditions' judged to be related to the project's success.

The SAP is a contractual relationship; but a contract made between two unequal parties, with only one party being the judge of whether the conditions of the contract are met and in a position to coerce the other. From the EU perspective, the political strategy towards the region 'relies on a realistic expectation that the contract it enters into with individual countries will be fulfilled satisfactorily' (EU 2001c: 3). The contracts commit the Southeastern European states to a relationship of subordination to EU mechanisms. They establish formal mechanisms and agreed benchmarks which enable the EU to work with each country towards meeting the required standards and focus attention on key areas of EU governance concern (EU 2001c: 3).

CARDS programmes of assistance, the major external aid associated with the SAP, focused clearly on EU-defined priorities. The first priority institution-building area in terms of overall CARDS support is:

Familiarisation of the *acquis communautaire* as countries start to move their legislation – especially on areas covered under the SAA – more into line with the approaches used inside the EU. This will focus on core *acquis* issues relating to the internal market.

(EU 2001a: 37)

This is followed by civil service reform to develop 'administrative procedures in conformity with EU standards', fiscal and financial management reforms, trade and customs regulation and reform of the legal and administrative framework of justice and home affairs (EU 2001a: 38).

The European Commission's desire to impose a pre-established governance agenda of institutional reform seems to assume that there is a 'one size fits all' method of strengthening Southeastern European government institutions as it enforces its 'leverage' over the region through a number of similar mechanisms of conditionality with the stress upon EU managerial control and 'co-ordination' of external directives, together leaving little doubt that the SAP is far from one of 'partnership'. Yet, the 'partnership' element has been central to keeping the EU's options open with regard to the membership process. As Christopher Bickerton notes, partnership does not just conceal the power inequalities involved in the process of integration, preventing candidate states from negotiating the transitional measures adopted by existing members. It also helps to mitigate tensions and uncertainties of existing member states about enlargement by creating a flexible framework in which the vicissitudes of internal EU institutional wrangling can be played out as problems with the pace of capacity-building and ownership in the applicant states (Bickerton 2005; see also, Heartfield 2007; Grabbe 2003).

The process of relationship management with the candidate countries in the region has been much more interventionist and regulatory than the enlargement process that involved the states of Central Eastern Europe. Allegedly, the Southeastern European states are too weak to be left to their own devices in meeting the conditions of the accession process. The more 'hands-on' approach of the SAP is held to be essential for the EU to replicate the success of the enlargement process in earlier rounds. Here, where states are weaker, statebuilding is part of the enlargement process itself. For the process of statebuilding, the EU needs to have much more leverage than in relation to the Central Eastern European states. From the perspective of the EU administration, the reforms being insisted upon are in Southeastern European states' own interests; they are held to be legitimate policy goals in their own right and so cannot be left to publics to decide upon. In these circumstances, EU conditionalities operate as a process of relationship management rather than merely establishing the end goals of membership of the EU club.

The centrality of conditionality in the Stabilisation and Association process in Southeastern Europe is rarely fully drawn out. There is an assumption that conditionality is explicitly projecting the EU's norms and values in a way which promotes democracy and strengthens state institutions. In fact, the reality is very different. Accession states have formally decided to accede to the EU and, in this respect, their decision is a voluntary and autonomous one. However, the decision to sign up to the Stabilisation and Association Process blurs the clarity of the relationship between the EU and aspirant states. This is because the accession states are signing up to a process where the conditionality is an ongoing one. The democratic and voluntary aspect of the process, in effect, ends with the signing of the agreement as the ongoing steps and conditions are managed through bypassing the democratic political process. From the position of the EU, the candidate countries only need to make one democratic decision, which is to subordinate themselves to the accession process. The process of aligning policy with the needs of the EU *acquis* then allows little room for democratic consideration as the policy process becomes an external one, where the external advisers state why policy reforms need to be made and when they need to be achieved, leaving the specific content up to the local authorities, albeit with external advice and support.

It is important to realize that the incremental use of conditionalities is not some technical process, it is entirely political. When the EU is considering which 'benchmarks' are important or what level of reforms are necessary for the next stage, a large number of factors come into play, including: 'enlargement fatigue' which tends to add further conditions to satisfy member states which are more hostile to enlargement; broader policy concerns with security or crime and corruption; and specific views with regard to the perceived needs of statebuilding in particular aspirant states. Incrementalized conditions are designed to ensure that the process of EU relationship management continues: this blurs the clarity of goals with a focus on the means; i.e. the process of external statebuilding takes centre stage.

Governance not government

In many ways, the relationship of inequality between elected representatives in the region and the external regulatory bodies, such as the EU, is highlighted in the international regulation of Bosnia and Kosovo. Rather than standing out as exceptions because of the restrictions on local sovereignty and self-government – thereby institutionalizing a relationship of inequality and external domination – Bosnia and Kosovo, in fact, indicate with greater clarity the problems of post-liberal governance, at the levels of institutional reform and civil society intervention, in the context of an unequal 'partnership'. In both Bosnia (under the administrative regulation of the international Office of the High Representative) and Kosovo (where the highest civilian power is the International Civilian Representative) – both these positions being 'double-hatted' with the position of EU Special Representative (EUSR) – there are elected governments at local, regional and state levels. In both cases the international administration is held to be part of a contractual process moving towards 'ownership', self-government and integration into European structures (see, for example, Meurs and Weiss 2005; Chandler 2006b).

In Bosnia, the EU is in the process of winding down the executive powers of the High Representative and the key question is how conditionality can be used to provide the leverage previously rendered by the threats of dismissals and direct imposition by the Office of the High Representative (OHR). The SAP is seen to be contractually tying-in and committing politicians to work on the EU road. Conditionality is not about final membership conditions, which are open-ended due to uncertainty over enlargement criteria – which depend on a number of political considerations not some abstract set of technical or administrative factors. Conditionality is a process of relationship management which aims at incremental progress to ensure that reforms happen without stand-offs between politicians and EU administrators. The conditionality of the SAP is seen to be about the day-to-day management of the accession and reform process, with the EU officials wary of conflict if they ask for 'too much too soon'. This delicate process of reform management transforms the political centre from the domestic sphere to the international one. The EU is not just deciding upon its own standards for new members; the EU policy engagement in the states of the region and the EU Special Representatives are important political factors in the societies which they seek to manage, attempting to make delicate political decisions on how to move the reform process forwards.

Here, the distinction between 'hard' and 'soft' powers in the context of the EU's relationship with Southeastern European states is not of fundamental importance. Once tied into the SAP, the alleged 'pull of Brussels' (EU conditionality) is no different from, for example, the 'push from Bonn' (the executive powers of the OHR). The EUSR does not need to use executive powers once the policy process is institutionalized and incremental conditionality is used to oversee the policy process, setting the timetable for reforms and the policy content. While the fact that Bosnian politicians themselves vote for the requirements of EU accession is vital for the EU's own credibility, the fact that policy is presented to the legislature as a *fait accompli* makes the policy process little different when viewed from the domestic perspective (Ashdown 2007). Whether the policy is brought with the 'hard' threat of dismissals or with the 'soft' threat of funding withdrawals and the stalling of the accession process, there is still little opportunity for political parties to debate upon policy alternatives. The external framework of policy-making means that political parties negotiate with the international administrator behind closed doors rather than with each other in public (Farrell 2008).

This process of political management under the auspices of the SAP, or the 'soft power' pull of Brussels, results in not just an externally-driven political process but one that is openly manipulative. Rather than clarifying what EU membership will involve, the pressure is for elites to evade open or public discussion and instead to attempt to buy social acquiescence. The strategic use of conditionalities also means that the EU openly seeks to turn political issues into technical ones in order to massage and facilitate the reform process (Venneri 2008). This was clear in Bosnia, when police reform was billed as a technical necessity and conditional for signing the SAA, at a time when there was no agreed EU framework for centralized policing (ESI 2007; Muehlmann 2008). This was an attempt to reshape the Dayton framework and weaken the powers of the Bosnian-Serb entity but framed as a technical necessity. This instrumental and manipulative use of conditionality can also be seen in ongoing discussions to use human rights requirements to reform the tri-partite voting for the Bosnian Presidency. Rather than openly state policy goals, which would be controversial, the dynamic is to push controversial reforms under the guise of technical or administrative necessity. The political shaping of Southeastern European society by external managers tends to degrade the entire political process, highlighted by the hollowing out of the opportunities for domestic debate and engagement, encouraging the collaboration of political elites and external administrators against the wishes and aspirations of citizens of these states.

It is in this context that the post-liberal conception of the role of civil society becomes important. The EU argues that it is more democratic than elected representatives and has shared interests with the citizens of Southeastern European states. For example, opinion polls in Bosnia show that the overwhelming majority of the population support joining the EU; this is the case for each of the three main ethnic constituencies (see, for example, ORI 2007). For the EU, its interests are therefore the same as those of the Balkan peoples: there is a mutual interest in a better future of peace, stability and prosperity. The claim is that the EU is therefore not forcing anything on anyone.

However, the passive opinion poll support for the EU is not reflected in major political party positions. The national question still plays a defining role for many Southeastern European states for fairly obvious reasons. Rather than take on board the realities of the region, EU officials argue that the EU needs to 'help bridge the gap' between political elites and the people. This 'gap-bridging' is held to be the task of an improved, more capable, civil society. To this end, civil society groups are funded and encouraged to talk about single issues which the EU is keen to promote – from the importance of small and medium enterprises to issues of jobs, crime, corruption and healthcare. The EU argues that its missions and Special Representatives listen to the people and engage civil society, while the elected politicians do not.

This 'democratic' discourse, which portrays the EU as the genuine representative of the people against the illegitimate or immature politicians, fits well with the allegations that politicians do not have the citizens' public interests at heart and therefore must be motivated by private concerns of greed and self-interest. It also tends to discount the votes expressed in elections as being the product of elite manipulation or electoral immaturity. The process of conditionality around an external agenda is then seen to be stymied or blocked by the processes of domestic representation (much as the Irish electorate were seen to be irrationally blocking the Lisbon treaty), implying that the votes of the public should count for less than the consensus of international experts.

This elitist discourse then results in a manipulative view of conditionality, where political decision-making seeks to evade public accountability. In Bosnia, EU experts and political elites talk about a 'window of opportunity' for reforms; this window is alleged to be after the last municipal elections in October 2008 and before the next state-level elections in 2010. A process of manipulation develops where politics is actively excluded from the public sphere and decision-making is a matter of elite negotiation with Brussels. In short, the EU is reproducing itself in Southeastern Europe. EU member state-building in the region is a good example of the new relationships cohered and reproduced through the post-liberal governance discourse. Where states have a tenuous relationship to their societies the relationship management of the EU sucks the political life from societies, institutionalizing existing political divisions between ethnic or national groups through undermining the need for public negotiation and compromise between domestic elites.

The externally-driven nature of the policy process means that political elites seek to lobby external EU actors rather than engage in domestic constituency-building. Even more problematically, the fact that it is in political elite and EU officials' interests to keep the process of relationship management going means that local political elites are increasingly drawn away from engaging with their citizens (in a similar way to political elites in member states). Rather than exporting democracy and legitimizing new state structures, the process of EU member statebuilding in Southeastern Europe is leading to a political process in which the voters and the processes of electoral representation are seen to be barriers to reform rather than crucial to it.

The post-liberal state

States that are not designed to be independent political subjects in anything but name can easily become a facade without content. States without political autonomy may have technically sound governance and administrative structures on paper but the atrophied political sphere hinders attempts to reconstruct post-conflict societies and overcome social and political divisions. The states created, which have international legal sovereignty but have ceded policy-making control to external officials in Brussels, lack organic mechanisms of political legitimization as embodiments of a collective expression of the will of their societies. Their relationship of external dependency upon the EU means that the domestic political sphere cannot serve to legitimize the political authorities or reconstruct their societies.

Bosnia is the clearest case of a new type of post-liberal state being built through the EU enlargement process of distancing power and political responsibility. To all intents and purposes Bosnia is a member of the European Union; in fact more than this, Bosnia is the first genuine EU state where sovereignty has in effect been transferred to Brussels. The EU provides its government; the international High Representative is an EU employee and the EU's Special Representative in Bosnia. This EU administrator has the power to directly impose legislation and to dismiss elected government officials and civil servants. EU policy and 'European Partnership' priorities are imposed directly through the European Directorate for Integration (see, for example, the 280-page document outlining the timetable for implementing the EU's medium priorities, BH EDI n.d.). The EU also runs the police force, taken over from the United Nations at the end of 2002, and the military, taken over from NATO at the end of 2004, and manages Bosnia's negotiations with the World Bank. One look at the Bosnian flag – with the stars of the EU on a yellow and blue background chosen to be in exactly the same colours as used in the EU flag – demonstrates that Bosnia is more EU-orientated than any current member state (Poels 1998). However, the EU has distanced itself from any responsibility for the power it exercises over Bosnia; formally Bosnia is an independent state and member of the United Nations and a long way off meeting the requirements of EU membership.

After 15 years of statebuilding in Bosnia there is now a complete separation between power and accountability (see Chandler 2006a; 2006b). This clearly suits the EU which is in a position of exercising its influence over the tiny state without either admitting it into the EU or presenting its policy regime in strict terms of external conditionality. Bosnia is neither an EU member nor does it appear to be a colonial protectorate. Bosnia's formal international legal sovereignty gives the appearance that it is an independent entity, voluntarily engaged in hosting its state capacity-building guests. Questions of aligning domestic law with the large raft of regulations forming the EU *aquis* appear as ones of domestic politics. There is no international forum in which the contradictions between Bosnian social and economic demands and the external pressures of Brussels' policy prescriptions can be raised.

However, these questions are not ones of domestic politics. The Bosnian state has no independent or autonomous existence outside of the EU 'partnership'. There are no independent structures capable of articulating alternative policies. Politicians are subordinate to international institutions through the mechanisms of governance established which give EU bureaucrats and administrators the final say over policy-making. The Bosnian state is an artificial one; but it is not a fictional creation. The Bosnian state plays a central role in the transmission of EU policy priorities in their most intricate detail. The state here is an inversion of the sovereign state central to liberal modernity. Rather than representing a collective political expression of Bosnian interests – expressing self-government and autonomy, 'Westphalian sovereignty' in the terminology of statebuilders – the Bosnian state is an expression of an externally-driven agenda.

The more Bosnia has been the subject of external statebuilding, the less it has taken on the features of the traditional liberal state form. Here, the state is a mediating link between the 'inside' of domestic politics and the 'outside' of international relations, but rather than clarifying the distinction it removes the distinction completely. The imposition of an international agenda of capacity-building and good governance appears internationally as a domestic question and appears domestically as an external, international matter. Where the liberal paradigm of sovereign autonomy clearly demarcated lines of policy accountability, the post-liberal paradigm of international governance and statebuilding blurs them. In this context, domestic politics has no real content. There is very little at stake in the political process. In fact, political responsibility for policy-making disappears with the removal of the liberal rights-based framework of political legitimacy (see FES 2005).

For external statebuilders, the subordination of politics to bureaucratic and administrative procedures of good governance is a positive development. In functional terms they argue that sovereignty, and the political competition for control of state power that comes with it, is a luxury that Southeastern European states often cannot afford. Robert Keohane, for example, argues that many states, now negotiating EU ties, are 'troubled societies' plagued by economic, social and ethnic divisions, which mean that elections can be highly problematic 'winner-take-all' situations. In these states, unconditional sovereign independence is a curse rather than a blessing and conflict can be prevented by enabling 'external constraints' on autonomy in exchange for institutional capacity-building (see Keohane 2002: 755–56; Paris 2004: 187–94).

Post-conflict states, such as Bosnia, stand in desperate need of a statebuilding project which can engage with and cohere society around a shared future-orientated perspective (see also, Bickerton 2005, who expands this argument to Eastern European accession states more generally). What Bosnia has received is external regulation which has, in effect, prevented the building of genuine state institutions which can engage with and represent social interests. These weak states are an inevitable product of the technical, bureaucratic and administrative approach exported under the paradigm of post-liberal governance.

Conclusion

The EU as a policy actor is the most advanced proponent of post-liberal governance as a way of understanding the rationality of its policy-making. While, within the EU itself, the shift from representational to administrative frameworks of legitimacy has been relatively uncontested, the logic of this process appears much more clearly when it is articulated as a coherent framing for the EU's engagement with other actors, particularly in the enlargement process. Here it is possible to much more clearly draw out the governing rationality of the EU as one which is based on the problematization of autonomy. As a leading actor in the field of international statebuilding, the EU is explicit in projecting an understanding that autonomy cannot be reinstated as an end goal of the international statebuilding process and that the sovereignty which is co-produced can no longer be understood in classical terms of autonomy. This is because, within the international statebuilding paradigm, autonomy is considered to be problematic per se.

It is this permanent problematization of autonomy which marks the international statebuilding paradigm, as exemplified by the EU, as post-liberal rather than comprehensible as a set of policy practices and meanings within a liberal paradigm. However, the presupposition of this critique is that the problem is not just the failure of the state or the failure of the state or society to autonomously rule safely but also that the aspiration to autonomy itself is problematic (as discussed in Chapter 3 on post-liberal governance). It is on this basis that limits to autonomy are seen to be necessary and legitimate, and the goal of international statebuilding can be understood not so much in terms of the restoration of autonomy but in terms of the limitation of autonomy: making statehood safe for the society intervened in (safe for itself) and for the international community.

It is as a limitation on autonomy that the EU's concern with the export of the rule of law should be understood. Through the internationalization of the rule of law – and not merely its reduction to a technical or administrative code, but also its deep imbrication in the form of governance as a rationale or way of policy-making itself – it becomes possible to export a set of regulatory practices independently of traditional concerns of liberal framings of law and politics. The EU has developed this approach as its own and in its promotion of good governance asserts a relationship of management which does not just invert an understanding of liberal conceptions of rights and sovereignty but also produces and reproduces an understanding of state–society relations which understands autonomy itself as problematic and in need of external regulatory constraints. In this way, the EU reproduces its own framework of legitimacy and governing rationality, which is posed in contradistinction to that of its member states which are held to have 'learned the lessons' of autonomy in the two world wars and to have recognized that only the voluntary acceptance of limits to their autonomy can help mitigate the problems of their own sovereign status.

6   Security and statebuilding

From intervention to prevention

Introduction

As touched upon in Chapter 4 (on the development of the paradigm of post-liberal governance), the disciplinary subject matter of international relations is not amenable to full appropriation within the framework of classical liberal assumptions about rights and political subjects. International relations' resistance to liberal framings has been central to the discipline's centrality in the working through of what is described in this book as the post-liberal paradigm of understanding the political sphere and policy-formation. This chapter is concerned with how this is reflected in the shifting understanding of security at the international level, particularly how the classical subject-based approach of international relations and political theory – the understanding of security in relation to the autonomy and freedom of the political subject – has been rearticulated from the assumptions of the rationalist approach of realism, via the 1990s debates on the 'right of intervention', through to the post-liberal framings of the Responsibility to Protect and international statebuilding.

In the heuristic terms of paradigm shifts, this chapter will draw out three stages: first, the subject-based framing of security as a product of self-help in the anarchical sphere of international relations, which dominated the traditional discipline of international relations; second, the shift towards a liberal discursive framework of intervention posed in terms of the weighing of competing concerns of security and freedom, reflected in debate on the alleged clash of rights of individuals and states, which was dominant in the 1990s; and third, what we describe in this book as the post-liberal paradigm, cohered in the 2000s, which moved beyond the liberal security/freedom problematic, reformulating the political subject in relation to security in terms of resilience (the capacity to manage internal and external security threats) rather than autonomy (the capacity to strategically project interests). In this framework, international security is no longer concerned with the problematic of securing autonomy but with the problematic of a preventive securing against the dangers of autonomy. This post-liberal paradigm shift will then be drawn out through a consideration of the discursive framing of the Responsibility to Protect (R2P). The doctrine of R2P was initially developed in response to the destabilizing consequences of the 'liberal turn' of the 1990s, which appeared to remove the limits to the use of unilateral force and restrictions of international law. As it has developed, R2P has reflected the shift away from the liberal framing of international intervention as enhancing autonomy, towards the post-liberal framing of resilience through limiting autonomy; in the phraseology of R2P this can be understood as the shift from intervention to prevention.

The relationship between freedom and security

The non-liberal problematic

The traditional discipline of international relations conceived its subject matter in terms of a world of nation state subjects existing or coexisting in a relationship of anarchy or a state of nature. Modern liberal political theorizing assumes both a society and a sovereign, mythically constructed in terms of a social contract, whereby individuals agree to give up some of their original rights to autonomy to have their freedom and autonomy secured by the state. By contrast, the world of international relations was understood to be one in which there was no social contract, constituting a sovereign hierarchy on the basis of securing individual freedoms. The reason for the non-liberal nature of international relations was articulated clearly by Thomas Hobbes in his classic work of political theory, *Leviathan* (1978). Individuals in the state of nature are equally vulnerable to attack and concerns of individual security undermine the capacity for industry; in the international sphere, states are much less equal, less vulnerable and capable of sustaining both industry and defensive security. The key point which flows from this and enables us to explain the non-liberal nature of international relations is that of inequality: states are not equally vulnerable and therefore are less likely to submit to sovereign power. While the constitution of a global or world sovereign might appear to be in the interests of lesser powers, as a framework for defending their security, for major powers there is no incentive to give up sovereign rights to a higher power. Where classic liberal theory presupposed the equality and autonomy of political subjects as the basis of the social contract and as a precondition for the guarantee of equal rights in the political and legal sphere, these presuppositions were absent in the international sphere.

The lack of equality between political subjects does not just explain the lack of a sovereign in the international sphere, it was also held to explain why international law was understood as much more contingent than domestic law. In the international sphere, law was based on the contractual agreement of subjects rather than the consensual creation of a higher power with the capacity for compulsion; therefore law and international institutions did not have an independent existence from the will of autonomous states – the political and legal subjects of the international sphere. Security was understood to be achieved in the international sphere purely through the process of self-help. The international sphere was one of strategic interaction in which security was achieved through the practice of autonomy: strategically deciding whether to act defensively or aggressively, to make or break alliances. The autonomy of political subjects was the goal of security, with the balance of power and the making or breaking of alliances given its organizational rationale by the need to prevent any one power becoming dominant over others. The freedom and autonomy of nation states was understood as the central means through which they could secure themselves and as the end or goal of security policy.

In this framework, there were no collective interests beyond those that reinforced the autonomy of the subjects of the international sphere. For this reason, the basis of international law or inter-state consensus was that of opposing the hierarchical use of power and aggression of powerful states against the less powerful. Freedom and security were understood to be synonymous on the basis of the sovereignty of nation states: freedom and security were both the means and the ends of sovereign autonomy. Here the goal of freedom and security is equilibrium, the balancing of interests between autonomous subjects. The problem of equilibrium is at the heart of the non-liberal security problematic, or 'security dilemma' (coined by John Herz [1951]; see also, Butterfield 1951: 19; Wheeler and Booth 1992: 29). Equilibrium is the guide to policy-making for the non-liberal state of international relations theory: if states arm themselves for reasons of defense or attack then other states will take similar precautions, similarly if a state becomes too powerful relative to others, then other states will make alliances against them. The doctrine of the balance of power reflects the traditional international relations understanding of the problematic of maintaining an equilibrium of forces.

The problem of equilibrium was central to the traditional non-liberal sphere of the international and to what we will describe here as a developing post-liberal paradigm. Importantly, it should be borne in mind that the problem of equilibrium was one that was understood to be open to resolution or amelioration by nation states as active political subjects. The problem of equilibrium was a geo-strategic one in which rational actions were presupposed on behalf of all actors. This enabled strategic balancing, negotiations, alliances and the whole range of international diplomacy. While the equilibrium was one which was constantly shifting (or open to change) this was understood as a problematic that was open to statesmanship and rational calculation. Of course, there was always an important element of contingency and indeterminacy, but the discipline of international relations was based on the capacity to structure and model the contingent effects of the rational choices of state actors. This was very different to a classic liberal problematic of security where the autonomy of the rights-bearing individual was enhanced by removing the problem of equilibrium and the construction of a hierarchy or sovereign power and the reason why international relations was held to be merely a sub-branch of political theory.

The liberal problematic

The non-liberal framing of the international sphere assumed that freedom and security were indivisible at the level of the individual subject – the nation state. This stood in stark contrast to liberal political theory – to the understanding of domestic politics – in which the constitution of a sovereign meant that freedom and security were a matter of balancing the interests of the individual and the collective interests of the public. However, there is no fundamental clash of freedoms as it is held to be in the individual's interest that the freedom and autonomy of society is protected (in the same way as it is in the individual's interest that they should be bound by the law). The liberal conception of a freely constructed social contract presupposes that the individual consents to be bound by the collective will and held to account legally and politically.

The relationship between freedom and security within the liberal paradigm is that of a collective understanding of freedom and security rather than an individual one. In this paradigm, the axiomatic assumption is that the individual is free and autonomous – then on the basis of these natural or original 'rights of man', liberal political theory constructs a framework upon which these rights become the basis upon which sovereign rule is both legitimated and limited as a product of the individual's will. In terms of political theory, the liberal problematic is that of intervention: the discussion of when the sovereign should intervene and act to limit the freedom and autonomy of the individual on the basis of that individual's own will.

In the 1990s, the reframing of the international sphere as amenable to liberal discourses of intervention posited the emergence of a global sovereign capable of weighing a balance of security and freedom in terms of a liberal framing, in which the rights of states – of sovereignty – were weighed against the collective interests of international society. This liberal framing of security and freedom was articulated on the basis of the constitution of a new legal subject: the individual subject of human rights, in whose name intervention for the purposes of collective security was held to be justified.

Foucault described the liberal paradigm of the discursive framing of freedom and security in terms of intervention as the 'liberal economy of power' sustained by the constant 'interplay of freedom and security' (2008: 65). The classic liberal view, presupposing the autonomy of the political subject, understood government intervention in society as legitimized by the need to produce and reproduce the freedom and autonomy of political subjects:

> The new [liberal] governmental reason needs freedom therefore, the new art of government consumes freedom. It consumes freedom, which means that it must produce it. It must produce it, it must organize it. The new art of government therefore appears as the management of freedom, not in the sense of the imperative 'be free', with the immediate contradiction that this imperative may contain. The formula of liberalism is not 'be free'. Liberalism formulates simply the following: I am going to produce what you need to be free. I am going to see to it that you are free to be free . . . [A]t the heart of this liberal practice is an always different and mobile problematic relationship between the production of freedom and that which in the production of freedom risks limiting and destroying it.
>
> (Foucault 2008: 63–64)

The liberal paradigm of government intervention is not that of empowering or capacity-building the citizen, for it is assumed that the liberal political subject is already free and capable of exercising rational autonomy. Intervention (government policy-making) is legitimized on the basis that it removes barriers to the freedom of action of individuals, for example, in regulating monopolies or ensuring welfare benefits and so forth. The problematic of intervention to secure freedom is that too much intervention risks undermining these freedoms – restricting the freedoms of employers and workers to freely trade and contract with others or citizens from speaking and organizing freely. For Foucault:

> What, then, will be the principle of calculation for this cost of manufacturing freedom? The principle of calculation is what is called security. That is to say, liberalism, the liberal art of government, is forced to determine the precise extent to which and up to what point individual interest, that is to say individual interests insofar as they are different and possibly opposed to each other, constitute a danger for the interest of all.
>
> (2008: 65)

The liberal paradigm of freedom and security is very different from that of equilibrium of non-liberal subjects operating without a sovereign in a state of nature. In the 1990s, in the wake of the end of the Cold War, discourses of intervention emerged in regard to international relations on the presupposition that the international sphere was now open to a liberal appropriation, with the immanent emergence of an international or global consensus capable of generating the legitimacy for collective security in which an interventionist discourse was possible. This presupposed that interventionist states were capable of assuming the mantle of a global sovereign (representing the interests of international society as a whole) and that their actions, in restricting or overriding sovereign autonomy, could be legitimized on the basis of the freedom and autonomy which was to be secured.

The post-liberal problematic

The earlier paradigms grasped the international political sphere in two distinct ways: first, as a sphere of international relations, of sovereign states without a government; in which case, the only mechanism of securing the subject is by autonomously determined equilibrium; second, as a domestic sphere of government, of sovereign rule, in which intervention can secure and protect the freedom and autonomy of political subjects. In both these frameworks it is suggested that freedom and security are mutually reproducing: they are two sides of the same coin. It is not possible to have freedom without security or security without freedom. In fact, it is not possible to understand the meaning of either freedom or security without the starting assumption of the pre-given or natural autonomous political subject. The non-liberal paradigm of international relations shared the same starting point as that of liberal political theory: that of the autonomous political subject.

What this book describes as the post-liberal paradigm of international statebuilding departs from this shared starting point of the autonomous political subject. Without the rationalist assumptions of originatory autonomy, the connection between freedom and security is broken and both terms lose their meaning. Without the centrality of autonomy as both the means and end of security, freedom merely means the ability to make rational choices or decisions and security has no goal apart from maintaining the status quo. In this paradigm, there is a return to the traditional problematic of international relations – that of equilibrium – but it is a problematic constructed without rational agency or rational subjects which are the subjects of geo-political contestation. Equilibrium refers to the problematic of 'global security' or of collective security threats. These threats are understood to derive independently of conscious or rational human agency. Whether the threats are understood in terms of environmental warming, global economic downturn, resource depletion, refugees, crime, poverty, conflict or terrorism, they are understood to elude the capacity of autonomous states: they are conceived as global problems with necessarily global solutions.

The security threats of the post-liberal problematic are not open to traditional strategic engagement as they lack rational agency: it is believed that terrorists cannot be negotiated with any more than carbon emissions and also that these global security threats cannot be overcome: the war on terror cannot be 'won' anymore than the war on global warming or poverty. Security becomes a process of management, in which autonomy and freedom are seen as problematic rather than as the grounding basis for policy-making and strategy. The fact that these threats cannot be secured against successfully means that the problem is not just that states acting individually cannot resolve the security threats, but that states acting collectively cannot resolve them, merely collectively act to bring a security equilibrium. The governmental rationale of achieving this post-liberal security equilibrium is that of attempting to manage risk and to act preventively, seeking to adapt to threats – whether from terrorists or the environment. This framework has much less political or subjective agency, the task of security is an ongoing one of relationship management and of adaptation to external forces or threats which cannot be precisely known or secured against.

In the post-liberal discourse of global security the problematic of adaptation and equilibrium is one of resilience: of the capacity to adapt to and balance external pressures. In this discursive framing, the weak link in the development of collective mechanisms of balance and equilibrium are those states least able to implement the governmental framework of adaptation and resilience: those that lack good governance. This is the reason why, in the post-liberal security paradigm, weak or failing states are considered to be the most important security threat. This is not because they themselves are literally a threat – in the way that 'rogue states' were in the past – but rather because they can become the vehicles of these threats. This is well described by Ghani and Lockhart (as noted in the introductory chapter of this book):

> A number of contemporary global crises have their roots in forty to sixty fragile countries. As these states have experienced prolonged conflict or misrule, networks of criminality, violence, and terror have solidified, providing an ever expanding platform that threatens the entire globe.
> (2008: 23)

Weak or failing states are understood to undermine the security of international society as a whole in that they are held to provide 'an ever expanding platform' for global security threats to gain a foothold, develop and then expand at the risk of 'the entire globe'.

Dealing with the problem of weak or failing states in the post-liberal paradigm of international statebuilding does not rely on a liberal discourse of intervention, as there is no rationalist assumption of the positive nature of their autonomy. There is no assumption of the power of sovereign autonomy either as a means to achieve security or as an end to be achieved through security. The post-liberal paradigm does not operate within the discourse of originatory rights or that of the separation or distinction between state and society or between the domestic and the international (as considered in Chapter 4 on post-liberal governance).

This blurring of the domestic and the international can be understood as an inevitable consequence of the liberal framing of the international sphere in the 1990s. The difference is that the post-liberal framing denies the capacity of sovereign intervention (by the 'international community') in securing the subject. The security of the collectively conceived global subject of global security and of its component parts (in our case, the failing state and society) depends upon the institutional frameworks through which it is influenced (in the case of the weak or failing state, both domestically and internationally). It is held to be the task or responsibility of the failing state and society to ensure that institutional blockages are overcome and if the failing state is unable or unwilling to address the question of institutional frameworks then it is the task of other actors to assist in this process.

In this paradigm, freedom and security are both problematized as ends in themselves and as means to an end. Freedom is redefined as the capacity to make the right decisions and responses to external problems. In this respect, there is a return to the non-liberal discourse of equilibrium; the task of good governance is to find the equilibrium point between different interests and different potential threats and dilemmas. In this sense, in a world held to be rapidly changing and where globalized threats are not easy to recognize and respond to, security is no longer the goal of state policy, but rather resilience: the capacity to respond and adapt to new threats and to manage a world of complexity and uncertainty. In this paradigm, autonomy is no longer understood with reference to the capacity to generate policy-direction and goals internally. Security is gained through the development of resilience and the recognition that security has to be global to deal with global threats and global problems; therefore the precondition for security is the interdependence of states within international institutions and networks. Equilibrium is the watchword for securing the post-liberal subject, but this is not a matter of self-direction as in the non-liberal world of traditional conceptions of the international sphere, but achieved through resilience: through understanding the complex balance of threats and needs generated through global interdependencies.

The responsibility to protect

In the post-liberal paradigm, failing or weak states require international state-building intervention in order to secure themselves and prevent them from being a security threat to the international community. In this framework, the task of international actors is not one of liberal 'intervention' in order to adjust shortcomings or to respond to state collapse or conflict, but one of post-liberal 'prevention', to ensure that states are included in international institutional frameworks capable of ameliorating the dangers of their sovereign autonomy. This shift from the interventionist discourse of the 1990s to the statebuilding discourse of prevention can be highlighted through an analysis of the development of the conception of the Responsibility to Protect (R2P). This is a particularly useful case study as few commentators engaged with R2P, either as advocates or as critics, have sought to explain how the understanding of R2P has changed from the framework of intervention to that of prevention. In fact, the dominant understanding is that it is a framework for intervention but one that has somehow failed in this regard; therefore the predominant tendency has been to discuss R2P in terms of the gap between the promise of intervention and the reality, where it appears that intervention is no longer a central concern. In analysing this 'gap' between the R2P's alleged 'promise' and its 'reality', the shift from a liberal to a post-liberal framing of policy-practices becomes clear.

In 2001, when the International Commission on Intervention and State Sovereignty (ICISS) published its report 'The Responsibility to Protect', there was little doubt that, as stated in the 'Foreword', the concept of R2P was

> about the so-called 'right of humanitarian intervention' – the question of when, if ever, it is appropriate for states to take coercive – and in particular military – action, against another state for the purpose of protecting people at risk in that other state.
>
> (ICISS 2001: vii)

The ICISS was tasked with trying to develop a global political consensus on the question of humanitarian intervention, which it believed it had achieved through reformulating the problem in terms of the 'responsibility to protect'. For the advocates of R2P, its endorsement at the UN General Assembly 2005 World Summit was taken as a fundamental turning point. For Gareth Evans, former Australian foreign minister and primary architect and leading authority on R2P, the summit marked 'the really big step forward in terms of formal acceptance of R2P' (Evans 2008: 44). For Alex Bellamy, the summit heralded a transformation of R2P from a 'concept' – an idea – to a 'principle' – a 'fundamental truth' based upon a 'shared understanding' and a 'sufficient consensus' – making the right of intervention no longer subordinate to the other key international principle: the right of sovereignty (Bellamy 2009: 6). Yet, even its advocates argue that the summit 'achieved much less than had been envisaged', with leading proponents of the cause expressing a 'deep disappointment' with what had been achieved, and many stating a need for the Summit Outcome to be 'reaffirmed', to be 'operationalised', and for the 'shaky consensus' to be hardened (Bellamy 2009: 91–93).

Gareth Evans argues that the work of establishing R2P is still to come and involves taking on 'three big challenges' (2008: 54). The first challenge is conceptual: defining the concept – the meaning – of R2P. One would have thought that this was pretty fundamental. In fact, it is strange to talk about R2P as if it had some real existence despite the fact that there is no clarity about what it might actually entail. The second challenge is the institutional one: what institutions are necessary or have the task of carrying 'it' out (whatever the 'it' of R2P might be). The third challenge is the political one: mobilizing the political will for the institutions (as yet undecided) to act on R2P (once it is clear what that might mean). This chapter suggests that, once the underlying shift from intervention to prevention is highlighted, the apparent gap between claims of the importance of R2P as an interventionist regime and the lack of certainty of what the R2P might mean, let alone how the R2P as an interventionist project might be turned from an 'idea' into established policy 'practice', can be better understood.

The problems of relating its advocates' liberal ideal of R2P with the post-liberal policy framings which have been its outcome will be addressed, first, through a consideration of the R2P on its own terms. It will be argued that the ICISS report should be understood as recognition of the deeper problems of building consensus around the concept of 'humanitarian intervention' rather than as a solution to the problem. In fact, it was the ICISS report itself which sowed the seeds of confusion and evasion which seem to have dogged the concept of R2P. Second, this chapter will put R2P in the broader context of international disengagement and the desire to shift political responsibility away from leading western states. The gap between the liberal 'promise' and the post-liberal 'reality' of today's R2P consensus will be located in the fact that it implies less responsibility for western states to act and to intervene and reflects the broader context of post-Cold War lack of strategic concern with large areas of the world, such as sub-Saharan Africa (and in this context fits well with the institutionalist apologia developed by Douglass North and others, considered in Chapter 4).

R2P and the ICISS report

In terms of the contrast between the international consensus for R2P at the United Nations Summit and the lack of practical clarity or political obligations, unravelling the gap between rhetoric and reality is made easier when we understand the concept in the context of post-Cold War international relations. The advocates of R2P tend to take R2P out of context and believe that R2P only starts with the ICISS report, without which it is alleged, the idea 'would never have been given birth' (Evans 2008: xiiii). These advocates understand R2P as born in the wake of the UN failure to agree on military intervention for humanitarian purposes and therefore as inspired by the failures of Rwanda and Srebrenica and therefore as about saying 'never again' in the face of mass atrocities.

In fact, this view of R2P – understood as the establishment of an international consensus on humanitarian intervention – was a fiction in the heads of a few ICISS commissioners and activists. As Gareth Evans himself states, when the ICISS report was published, shortly after 11 September 2001, international policy and academic focus was elsewhere and 'the report seemed likely to disappear without a trace' (Evans 2008: 5). Bellamy goes further to argue that it was the unpopular US-led invasion of Iraq which killed off the desire for discussion of humanitarian intervention and that the war in Iraq was wrongly associated with the R2P (Bellamy 2009: 70). This exaggerates the links being made and conflates the ICISS report opinions with those of international society more broadly: as a reflection of the desire for humanitarian intervention post-Kosovo which is then allegedly muted by Iraq.

In fact, it was international disarray over Kosovo which heralded the first steps away from the 1990s liberal problematic of security, which informed declarations of western mission and humanitarian responsibility. The ICISS report itself reflected the problems of humanitarian intervention, recasting the 'right of intervention' accruing to western military actors, as the 'Responsibility to Protect' and shifting the focus away from the interveners to the objects of intervention. The difficulty of justifying western military intervention was also reflected in the report's shift of focus away from non-consensual military intervention, in its argument for a continuum of responsibility: 'to prevent'; 'to react'; and 'to rebuild'.

While a small group of liberal interventionists saw the ICISS report as a resolution to the problems of gaining international consensus for coercive intervention in the cause of human rights, there is no evidence that this was actually achieved. As Bellamy notes, little consensus was achieved for the argument for giving institutional backing to the concept of humanitarian intervention, outside the Canadian government and a few prominent ICISS commissioners themselves (2009: 70, 95). What the report did do was set up a moral case for more engaged regulation and consensual intervention in the domestic policy processes of non-western states: a framework which the US was keen to promote, especially in relation to sub-Saharan Africa and the newly reconstituted African Union. The R2P continuum implied that few areas of domestic policy-making were now 'out of bounds' once it was established that the international community had a duty to assist potentially 'weak' or 'failing' states in carrying out their responsibility to prevent 'mass atrocity crimes'. The desire to take the edge off the focus on western-led military intervention and to focus on more indirect mechanisms of 'conflict prevention' was further encouraged by the international policy problems of western responsibility in the Global War on Terror; most specifically, the war and occupation of Iraq.

In fact, rather than seeing the invasion and occupation of Iraq as nearly ending the R2P discussion, it should be seen as clarifying the dynamic behind R2P. The R2P which emerged post-Iraq reflected more acutely the crisis of confidence about western intervention which began to emerge with the ICISS report itself. Where the ICISS report begins to restore the credibility of the UN – highlighting the difficulties western states faced in mustering the legitimacy for non-consensual intervention if the UN Security Council failed to agree strict criteria – today's framework of R2P is even less confident in a non-bureaucratic and non-legalistic justification for intervention. Where the inability to win a consensus around the Kosovo intervention enabled the UN to regain ground, the discrediting of unilateral action in the international sphere after the Iraq invasion strengthened the UN's hand further and encouraged successive Secretary-Generals to regain the upper hand over the moral agenda of ending mass atrocity crimes (Evans 2008: 69).

R2P beyond ICISS

In September 2003, the UN Secretary-General Kofi Annan gave new life to R2P by selecting Gareth Evans to be on the High Level Panel on Threats, Challenges and Change, charged with preparing the ground for the 2005 World Summit declaration. The panel's report, *A More Secure World: Our Shared Responsibility* (UN 2004), released in December 2004, was then used as a basis for the Secretary-General's report to the summit, *In Larger Freedom: Towards Development, Security and Human Rights for All* (UN 2005a), published in March 2005. Annan took over the R2P language of the ICISS report but distanced it from the use of coercive force, putting the recommendations in different sections of the report. While the discussion on the criteria for coercive intervention was to be a subject for the Security Council and the potential reform of their decision-making powers, the R2P was clarified as a matter of state capacity, as a normative moral principle requiring a state to protect its own citizens (Bellamy 2009: 76).

The separation between the R2P and the use of coercive force continued the shift of focus of the ICISS report; moving further from an emphasis on western state responsibilities of intervention and towards an emphasis on the responsibilities of the 'failing' state. For the advocates of humanitarian intervention, this was a major shift which, as Evans notes, 'resulted in them being seen as quite separate, rather than inherently linked, proposals when they came to be debated at the World Summit' (Evans 2008: 46). Evans was clearly 'unhappy' that Annan's delinking of coercive intervention and R2P had resulted in the failure of the World Summit to adopt any criteria which could legitimize the use of force independently of a Security Council decision (Evans 2008: 140).

If we take R2P at face value as 'ending mass atrocities once and for all' (Evans 2008) then it appears paradoxical that the one thing that did not occur was any international commitment on this precise point. Despite the reproduction of the language of the International Criminal Court, in the construction of mass atrocities as justiciable crimes – 'Each individual State has the responsibility to protect its populations from genocide, war crimes, ethnic cleansing, and crimes against humanity' (UN 2005b: Art. 138) – there are no institutional obligations which flow from this, other than those which pre-existed the declaration.

Article 138 of the World Summit Outcome declaration asserted that individual states accepted their responsibility to prevent such crimes. Article 139 asserted that the UN General Assembly members were committed 'to helping States build capacity to protect their populations . . . and to assisting those which are under stress before crises and conflicts break out'. The same article went further in declaring that 'the international community, through the United Nations' has the responsibility to protect populations through 'appropriate diplomatic, humanitarian, and other peaceful means, in accordance with Chapters VI and VIII of the Charter'.

Article 139 clarifies that the international community is

> prepared to take collective action, in a timely and decisive manner, through the Security Council, in accordance with the Charter, including Chapter VII, on a case-by-case basis . . . should peaceful means be inadequate and national authorities are manifestly failing to protect their populations from genocide, war crimes, ethnic cleansing, and crimes against humanity.
>
> (UN 2005b)

There is no discussion here of any ICISS-inspired independent criteria which could justify the use of military force independently of the Security Council and the UN Charter framework. The Secretary-General's follow-up report, in January 2009, *Implementing the Responsibility to Protect* (UN 2009), confirms this, asserting that: 'the responsibility to protect does not alter, indeed it reinforces, the legal obligations of Member States to refrain from the use of force except in conformity with the Charter' (2009: §3).

In this context, the application of R2P seems little different from a non-R2P response to international crisis situations where mass atrocities are occurring or seem possible. This was highlighted in Kenya, at the end of 2007, where disputed elections led to ethnic-related violence, with 1,000 people killed and 300,000 displaced. UN Secretary-General Ban Ki-moon publicly characterized this as an R2P situation (Evans 2008: 51). Here, R2P was seen to facilitate international pressure on the Kenyan government and to provide a discursive framework for international diplomatic involvement. Even, in the case of Darfur, it was alleged that becoming classed as an R2P situation did not mean that non-consensual force would be used, or that R2P had 'failed' because military coercion was not deployed (Evans 2008: 61).

In fact, it appears that the more that R2P has been disassociated from the ICISS focus on justifying military intervention the more confusing the pronouncements of its leading advocates have become. Under ICISS, R2P could justifiably be seen as a concept designed to make humanitarian intervention more acceptable (Bellamy 2009: 52). Yet, in 2008, Gareth Evans was seemingly right to assert that the biggest misunderstanding about R2P was the belief that 'R2P is just another name for humanitarian intervention' (2008: 56). As Alex Bellamy states, counter-intuitively perhaps, the World Summit Outcome position 'is seemingly at odds with the concerns which animated those most closely associated with the ICISS and with the concerns which have animated most of the commission's commentators' (2009: 4).

R2P 'lite'?

It would appear that all that remains of the R2P's liberal discursive formulation of intervention is the moral focus on the centrality of the potential victims of 'mass atrocity crimes'. As Gareth Evans states, without the R2P focus on potential atrocity victims, the legitimacy of external intervention in the domestic affairs of 'vulnerable' states would be much more disputed:

> The whole point of embracing the new language of 'the responsibility to protect' is that it is capable of generating an effective, consensual response to extreme, conscience-shocking cases in a way that 'right to intervene' language simply could not. We need to preserve the focus and bite of 'R2P' as a rallying cry in the face of mass atrocities.
>
> (Evans 2008: 65)

Evans seeks to resist the apparent watering-down of the R2P concept, arguing that without the focus on the potential victims of mass atrocities it will

not be possible to garner international support for external intervention.
Diplomatically, rather than challenge the UN Summit Outcome from a more
open position – asserting that the UN has retreated from the assertive military
interventionism of the ICISS report – Evans seeks to argue that – in broaden-
ing the conception of R2P too far, 'to embrace what might be described as
the whole human security agenda' – the UN risks inviting opposition from
many states and commentators

> who see it as the thin end of a totally interventionist wedge – as giv-
> ing an open invitation for the countries of the North to engage to their
> hearts' content in the *missions civilisatrices* (civilizing missions) that so
> understandably anger those in the global South, who have experienced
> it all before.
>
> (Evans 2008: 65)

He raises the concern that, in this way, the possibility of military intervention would be opened up in a 'whole variety of policy contexts', such
as that of the Burmese/Myanmar government's failure to react adequately
to Cyclone Nargis; inevitably giving the concept of R2P a bad name. Here,
Evans' argument that R2P should be primarily about 'prevention' but also
strictly limited in application to 'atrocity situations' becomes a contradiction
in terms. Evans himself admits that: 'of course, it is true that some full-
fledged R2P mass atrocity situations evolve out of less extreme human rights
violations, or out of general conflict environments' (Evans 2008: 69). This
makes it difficult to understand Evans' determination to have his cake and
eat it, concerning prevention (which only makes sense at a general level) and
the focus on mass atrocities (where reaction or 'humanitarian intervention'
only occurs in specific isolated cases).

At this level, the lack of clarity over R2P, both in conceptual and institutional terms, is an inevitable consequence of its development out of the ICISS
report which attempted to muddy the waters over the right of intervention.
It is not conceptually possible to consider R2P, in its original conception,
in terms of prevention, no matter how often the advocates of R2P repeat
the mantra that 'prevention is the single most important dimension of the
responsibility to protect' (Evans 2008: 79). It is not possible to draw the line
that makes R2P a tenable concept once it is no longer about legitimizing coercive military intervention. Even the language used by Evans to describe the
conundrum is contradictory. For example, in relation to Mynamar/Burma,
is the situation 'best characterized and responded to as a human rights and
democracy problem, requiring whatever mix of pressure and persuasion will
best work, or as an R2P situation in the making?' (2008: 73). Here, the inti-
mation is that 'an R2P situation' involves the need for military intervention

if necessary, but Evans has already stated that not all 'R2P situations' require military intervention; some can be dealt with by international 'pressure and persuasion'. How can a judgement be made in advance about the potential for mass atrocities, in order to enable R2P prevention to take place as some discreet set of practices, separate from international responses to 'a human rights and democracy problem'?

The contradictions multiply as Evans tries to dig himself out of the hole which he has created here. For Evans, the solution to the conundrum is 'the need for some further criteria to be developed and properly applied if any kind of credible "R2P watch list" is to be prepared' (2008: 74). On the basis of a set of indicators, which Evans admits are 'an art rather than a science' and 'essentially seat of the pants judgements', he suggests we can draw up a list of countries which, without mass atrocities 'obviously occurring', are nevertheless of 'R2P concern' (2008: 74). The poverty of the argument is clear, for Evans asserts: first, that these indicators, yet to be properly thought through – such as history of mass atrocities, persistent tensions, poor coping mechanisms, receptivity to external influence and poor leadership – can clearly distinguish a select list of countries; that, second, any such list and labelling could generate a consensus around this classification; and, third, that, once clarified and consented to, some set of discrete policy measures could be set in place to prevent 'mass atrocities' as a distinct sphere of policy intervention.

There is no possibility that a discrete range of prevention, intervention and rebuilding mechanisms can be instituted which address such limited concerns. Mass atrocities do not arise *de novo*, but in a context of inequalities and conflict. Some R2P advocates, such as Alex Bellamy, are more aware of this problem. However, even Bellamy tends to underestimate the potential conceptual vacuum created by shifting the focus of R2P to prevention rather than intervention. He argues that:

> Much work needs to be done on clarifying the responsibility to prevent and identifying the measures required . . . The first, and perhaps most important, task is to identify precisely what it is that the responsibility to prevent is seeking to prevent and what measures are necessary to achieve that goal.
>
> (Bellamy 2009: 130)

It appears inevitable that, in shifting the emphasis from intervention to prevention, rather than establishing an international consensus on coercive action, we are left merely with a set of questions as to what R2P could mean or how it could be 'operationalized' in terms of its original liberal framing as a guide to intervention.

The R2P is dead. Long live R2P

The UN Secretary-General's 2009 follow-up report seeks to evade the problems with the ICISS view of a continuum of responsibility beginning with prevention. Despite the declarations of Gareth Evans, it is clear that in the ICISS formulation, the idea of a continuum of intervention, the '3Rs' – the responsibility to prevent', 'the responsibility to react', and 'the responsibility to rebuild' – is conceptually problematic, merely developed as an 'add-on', tactically designed to win greater support for the core concern of enabling military intervention (Bellamy 2009: 52). The Secretary-General's report substitutes the ICISS report's 'three pillars' with its own post-liberal framing of a 'three pillar strategy', summarizing the World Summit Outcome: pillar one is 'the protection responsibilities of the State'; pillar two is 'international assistance and capacity-building' for the State; pillar three is 'timely and decisive response' by the international community.

Rather than focusing on the responsibilities of western states to prevent, react and to rebuild, the reshaped R2P is focused on the responsibilities and capacities of the 'weak' or 'failing' state, held to be in need of assistance. It is the non-western state which is at the centre of today's R2P. This is clear in the UN Secretary-General's report's reinterpretation of the fundamental cause of mass atrocities: taking the emphasis away from the context of war and conflict and shifting an understanding of causation towards the institutional framework of the state concerned:

> The twentieth century was marred by the Holocaust, the killing fields of Cambodia, the genocide of Rwanda and the mass killings of Srebrenica . . . the brutal legacy of the twentieth century speaks bitterly and graphically of the profound failure of individual States to live up to their most basic and compelling responsibilities.
>
> (UN 2009: §5)

This shift is of fundamental significance for the 'operationalization' of R2P today within the post-liberal paradigm of international security. Framing mass atrocities as occurring as the result of failings at the level of the 'individual state' concerned, implicitly takes these abuses out of any international context of war and conflict and is a crude institutionalist (see Chapter 4) re-reading of the history of these events, which all occurred in the context of war and intervention and a question over the nature and borders of the state.

The focus on the responsibility of the non-western state, while having a shaky basis in any socio-political understanding of the context of mass atrocities, distances the discussion from overt and coercive western intervention. The R2P of the 2009 follow-up to the World Summit inverses the problematic at the heart of the 2001 ICISS report – the problem is seen to be the weak institutional capacity of some sovereign states not the legal barrier of sovereignty itself:

> As the assembled Heads of State and Government made absolutely clear, the responsibility to protect is an ally of sovereignty not an adversary. It grows from the positive and affirmative notion of sovereignty as responsibility, rather than from the narrower idea of humanitarian intervention. By helping States to meet their core protection responsibilities, the responsibility to protect seeks to strengthen sovereignty, not weaken it.
>
> (UN 2009: §10a)

Where 'humanitarian intervention' put the emphasis on leading western states overtly intervening to take responsibility for stopping mass atrocities, the new-look R2P argues that western responsibility is much more limited. Essentially the role for western powers is an indirect one, providing support to the 'weak' and 'failing' state in enhancing its 'sovereignty'. Rather than the R2P being a coda for direct humanitarian intervention it has become the key normative justification for the more indirect forms of intervention associated with the post-liberal framing of international statebuilding.

Beyond the rhetoric of its advocates, the R2P appears to be no more about a focus on mass atrocities than it is about establishing a right of humanitarian intervention. Something else would appear to be going on in the gradual transformation from the 'right of humanitarian intervention' of the 1999 Kosovo war, to the R2P of the 2001 ICISS report, and the R2P of the 2005 World Summit. It seems that successive Secretary-Generals have sought to use the ethical or moral consensus around mass atrocities to facilitate a broader strengthening of UN institutions and mandates. For the UN, and for R2P as it exists today, it is not the intervention (or reaction) aspect which is central but the institutionalization of international cooperation coordinated through the UN. The UN has turned the issue of humanitarian intervention, which in the 1990s threatened to undermine its authority – by questioning the sovereign rights of member states and UN Security Council authority over intervention – into an issue of international governance which asserts the UN's moral authority over major western powers and post-colonial states. Key to this has been the UN's assertion of an administrative and technocratic agenda of 'good governance' as the solution to a range of problems from development to conflict prevention.

Good governance, bad governments

Today's framework of R2P shifts responsibility away from direct western solutions, whether economic, political or military, and towards indirect western engagement which is held to be able to ameliorate problems but cannot be expected to prevent them:

> The responsibility to protect first and foremost, is a matter of State responsibility, because prevention begins at home and the protection of population is a defining attribute of sovereignty and statehood . . . the international community can at best play a supplemental role.
>
> (UN 2009: §14)

'Pillar one' of the Secretary-General's 2009 Report therefore foregrounds the non-western state as the bearer of responsibility for mass atrocities.

'Pillar two' asserts that the problems of scarcity and conflict in the non-western world can be understood through the framework of state institutional capacity. The 2009 Report asks the question 'why one society plunges into mass violence while its neighbours remain relatively stable'? The answer it provides is the post-liberal framing of the extension of rational choice perspectives, in the understanding that the institutional framework of the state is the key to paths of development or conflict, asserting that this abstract schema is one based on principles which 'hold across political and economic systems' and hold 'regardless of a country's level of economic development' (UN 2009: §15).

This post-liberal institutionalist approach understands mass atrocities outside of any concern with economic and social relations, focusing merely on the institutional structures which are held to shape the behaviour of individuals, either providing opportunities and incentives for mass atrocities or limiting the possibility of these occurring:

> Genocide and other crimes relating to the responsibility to protect do not just happen. They are, more often than not, the result of a deliberate and calculated political choice, and of the decisions and actions of political leaders who are all too ready to take advantage of existing social divisions and institutional failures.
>
> (UN 2009: §21)

The understanding of mass atrocities as a product of institutional shortcomings then sets the agenda for international preventive engagement to assist in institutional capacity-building that would make states 'less likely to travel the path to crimes relating to the responsibility to protect' (UN 2009: §44):

> Experience and common sense suggest that many of the elements of what is commonly accepted as good governance – the rule of law, a competent and independent judiciary, human rights, security sector

reform, a robust civil society, an independent press and a political culture that favours tolerance, dialogue and mobility over the rigidities of identity politics – tend to serve objectives relating to the responsibility to protect as well.

(UN 2009: §44)

These policies flow less from evidence linking institutional frameworks to mass atrocities (UN 2009: §44), than from the desire to lower expectations about both western willingness and capacity to make a substantial difference to ongoing conflicts and instability. Here, the best that the international community can do is to indirectly work to facilitate good governance mechanisms and capacity-build state institutions and civil societies, which are the ultimate solution, rather than the direct provision of expensive social, economic and military resources.

The R2P concept depends upon the conceit that non-political, technical and administrative experts, coordinated through the UN, can understand, prevent and resolve conflict. This conceit only works through reducing social, economic and political problems to technical and administrative questions of institutional governance. At the core of R2P is the assertion that: 'Achieving good governance in all its manifestations – representative, responsive, accountable, and capable – is at the heart of effective long-term conflict and mass atrocity prevention' (Evans 2008: 88). The R2P's reinterpretation of 'mass atrocities' in the institutionalist framework of post-liberal governance is explained by Gareth Evans in this way:

Some conflicts that may appear at first sight to be clear-cut examples of loot seeking or a contest over resources – in Sierra Leone and the Democratic Republic of the Congo, for example – were more fundamentally driven by the failures of basic governance: decades of misrule and corruption by parasitic state elites and associated socioeconomic deterioration and institutional decay. These made their ruling regimes extremely vulnerable to both general popular discontent and the specific ambitions of rebels and various external actors, with poor governance not only fuelling political and economic grievances but reducing the risk and cost of mounting violent challenges to it.

(Evans 2008: 88)

However we might understand the proximate causes of conflict – rebel groups or exploitative rulers or external actors seeking to gain resources – the structural causes of conflict and therefore the possibilities of 'mass atrocities' are located in the failing institutions of the state and the lack of good governance.

Post-liberal institutionalism provides a convenient framework of understanding for the UN, for the answers are not to be found in large-scale measures of economic and social transformation nor merely in the prosecution of individuals (as with the ICC), but in the institutional framework of states held to be at risk of 'failing' or of failing to take on 'their most basic and compelling responsibilities'. If the cause of 'R2P situations' is at heart the lack of 'good governance' the solution would appear to be the inculcation of the practices and norms of 'good governance' which are seen to be open to understanding and export, through either the 'carrot' of aid, loans and membership of international institutions or the 'stick' of sanctions and the threat of more coercive forms of intervention (see also, the previous chapter on the EU). Through marshalling these 'carrots' and 'sticks' with the cooperation of the international financial institutions, regional organizations and associations and the UN's own institutions, the UN is seen to be the key to the coordination of the necessary tasks of prevention and the similar 'good governance' responsibilities of post-conflict rebuilding.

The underlying assumption is that the more that the institutions of the 'failing' or the 'post-conflict' state are engaged with by international institutional actors, the more secure their sovereignty and their capacity to take up their 'responsibilities' will be. In the words of the UN Secretary-General's follow up report: 'The State . . . remains the bedrock of the responsibility to protect, the purpose of which is to build responsible sovereignty, not to undermine it' (UN 2009: §13). Far from a discourse of military intervention – undermining sovereignty – the revamped R2P is understood to be a framework of state capacity-building. As Alex Bellamy notes, the R2P, as endorsed by the World Summit and subsequently by the UN Security Council, is essentially about 'international assistance to help build responsible sovereigns with appropriate capacity' (2009: 4).

While the post-liberal institutionalist perspective provides a coherent framework for understanding the problems of the post-colonial world and for limiting expectations of any external solutions or ideas of western 'responsibility', it is a paradigm which lends itself as much to apologia and non-intervention as to intervention. The post-liberal framing of problems and solutions is not fully cohered as long as there are expectations that the west will, in fact, take responsibility. The criticisms of international intervention in the literature on international statebuilding (as considered in Chapter 2) have assisted in this lowering of expectations, questioning the assumption that greater external engagement can strengthen and cohere states, either in terms of prevention or rebuilding (for example, Chesterman *et al.* 2005; Paris and Sisk 2009a). Many experts argue that international support for states is just as likely to have unintended consequences, whether it is the risk of preventive intervention encouraging conflict or of post-conflict intervention undermining country ownership and creating dependencies. While the best institutional frameworks may well ensure that conflicts can be mitigated or prevented, it is widely recognized that there is no clear framework of policy which can ensure that these necessary institutions take root (Paris and Sisk 2009a; North 1990).

Nevertheless, the post-liberal reposing of economic, social and political problems at the level of institutional frameworks and the solutions at the level of external mechanisms of prevention to assist in creating viable institutions, achieves one important benefit: taking the responsibility for social, economic and political crisis away from both international power inequalities and from western states as policy actors. All that external actors can do is attempt to assist institutional reform: there is no 'illusion' that greater levels of economic aid will work or that military interventions could be a magic solution. The focus on state institutions of the 'failing state' shifts the policy and coordination responsibility away from western states and international institutions (see also Ghani and Lockhart 2008; Chandler 2009a).

R2P: divesting western responsibility

While the R2P was certainly resuscitated by the disastrous invasion and occupation of Iraq, the policy discourse is not one of intervention but of recasting the framework of international regulation. The ICISS report itself could be seen, as mentioned earlier, as less about seeking to ensure that western powers had a blank cheque for intervention and more as a way of evading the focus on western responsibility. In the post-Cold War world, it appeared that the more the west declared its responsibility for dealing with conflict and crises, the more western governments were stuck in the cleft stick of either standing on the sidelines or sending in the marines and coping with body-bags returning home as well as being saddled with responsibilities for outcomes, often in parts of the world where they had little long-term strategic interests. While Kosovo clearly exposed the awkwardness of the 'damned if we do and damned if we don't' dilemma for western politicians (Thakur and Schnabel 2000: 497) it was the earlier failure of intervention in Somalia which should be signalled as heralding the start of the policy discussion of R2P.

At the heart of the discourse of the Responsibility to Protect appears to be the desire to divest western responsibility rather than to take it on. As Francis Deng *et al.* noted in the mid-1990s, when the concept of 'sovereignty as responsibility' was first developed, it was necessary as a response to superpower withdrawal from Africa:

> It is important to explore the implications of this shift in great power roles for the management of conflict in Africa. In the changing world

context of the 1990s, Africa has little choice but to confront a wide variety of clashes on the continent and to do so increasingly on its own ... [T]he 'aggravating external factor' had been removed, but so had 'the moderating role of the superpowers both as third parties and as mutually neutralizing allies'. Given Africa's resource constraints, who can assume the mantle of peacemaker when state actors fail to govern responsibly?

(Deng *et al.* 1996: 168)

In the wake of US disengagement from Africa, understood to have been hastened by the disastrous direct military intervention in Somalia, the question for international policy-makers was how to develop a new set of relations emphasizing the need for strengthened regional institutions in enforcing stability, with western states playing a much less directly interventionist role: 'With the great powers reducing their involvement in Africa, further US peacemaking initiatives will most likely emphasize the leading role of local actors and take an indirect form' (Deng *et al.* 1996: 189). At the end of the 1990s, only around 25 per cent of UN peacekeeping troops were contributed by major western powers, by the beginning of 2008 this figure was down to 10 per cent (Bellamy 2009: 161). As Bellamy notes: 'there is a vast difference between the states which mandate peace operations and advocate R2P, robust doctrines and civilian protection, and the states which actually contribute most of the troops to UN peace operations' (2009: 161; see also, Cunliffe 2007).

In fact, rather than juxtaposing intervention and withdrawal, it would be better to see R2P as a process of relationship management where regulatory frameworks are reshaped under a desire to internationalize regulation in areas which are no longer considered to be of vital security interest. The central area of R2P concern is the regulation of sub-Saharan Africa and in this guise, the policy practice has not lagged behind the declarations of R2P intent. In 2003, the African Union was formally established as a replacement for the Organization of African Unity, reflecting the changing nature of African security. Rather than an organization expressing solidarity between African states against external intervention, the AU was established as a mechanism for external intervention. In this context, the power and authority of the AU was drastically enlarged, with a right of intervention in cases of war crimes, genocide and crimes against humanity (Bellamy 2009: 78).

Bellamy notes that the organizational capacity behind R2P is being built not by western states or international institutions, like the UN, directly but indirectly through institutions such as the African Union. The AU's African Standby Force (ASF) is being given international funding to build five regional brigades capable of deploying 20,000 troops by 2010. The US aims to train 75,000 African peacekeepers by 2020 through its Global Peace Operations Initiative and Britain and France are also both heavily involved in training African troops for peacekeeping operations (Bellamy 2009: 161). Bellamy asserts that far from a licence for western states to take interventionist responsibility for

> 'ending mass atrocity crimes' in sub-Saharan Africa, it appears that the emphasis on 'African solutions to African problems' permits the [Security Council] P5 to defer its responsibilities to the AU in cases where the former lacks the political will to act.
>
> (Bellamy 2009: 79)

The R2P of the 2005 World Summit Outcome and the Secretary-General's follow up report in 2009 can only be understood in the wake of the broader post-liberal shift in the framework of international regulation and intervention since the end of the Cold War. Rather than seeing the mass atrocities of Rwanda and Srebrenica as marking the birth and transformation of R2P, it would therefore make more sense to see Somalia, Kosovo and Iraq as the turning points in the problematization of western responsibility and the mutual desire on behalf of both the UN and leading western states to internationalize responsibility for relationship management with the post-colonial world on the basis of indirect forms of regulation: through intervention at the level of the institutions of the non-western state and, failing that, at the level of regional organizations. Ironically, this R2P is a far cry from the liberal interventionist fantasy which claimed that western leaders and western states would take direct responsibility for intervening in the cause of protecting human rights.

Conclusion

The retreat from the interventionist discourse of the 1990s has been couched in the post-liberal framework of prevention rather than that of intervention. Here, there is no longer an immanent global sovereign capable of intervening, but rather a project to establish institutional frameworks capable of preventing insecurity from becoming too problematic. Good governance is held to be the solution to security problems which cannot be predicted in advance. What we are seeing in the shift to institutionalist perspectives, highlighted by the shifting discourse of R2P, is, in fact, a shift away from earlier paradigmatic framings of security. In effect, security and freedom are no longer relevant categories and lack their symbiotic relationship of the past. In this framing there is neither freedom nor security as political subjects are removed from post-liberal framings.

While the ICC approach of laying responsibility at the feet of individual government leaders and army officials is clearly inadequate as a way of grasping the causes of conflict or of preventing it, the R2P approach suggests even less political accountability. For the R2P, implicitly – as long as state institutions fail to create a framework which enables conflicts to be ameliorated and the rule of law and human rights to be enforced – it is inevitable that political actors will attempt to take advantage and that the incentive, to assume state responsibilities of protection, will be lacking. In this framework, actors in 'failing' states have less responsibility for outcomes, as they are seen to be shaped by their institutional context, with little capacity to overcome these structural constraints.

Even more counter-intuitively, international institutions have less responsibility. The emphasis on 'good governance' as prevention and on institutional reform takes the emphasis away from any broader transformative vision of social, economic and political change. In this context, external western actors appear to be powerless to influence events and can only 'at best play a supplemental role' (UN 2009: §14). In effect, any external responsibilities are removed once 'mass atrocities' are understood to be structured by institutional frameworks. The blame for recurring crises is located narrowly at the level of post-colonial state societies and political elites rather than in any policy interventions (intended or unintended) by external actors.

The institutionalist perspective of the R2P is both conceptually and institutionally a reflection of the evasion of western responsibility under the post-liberal framing of capacity-building and empowering the post-colonial state as the subject/object of security. Conceptually, it denies the economic, social and political frameworks which would inculcate western powers in the problems and underdevelopment of post-colonial regimes. Institutionally, it seeks to relieve western states of direct responsibility to respond to crises, through establishing indirect mechanisms of policing and military intervention, as illustrated with the development and training of the African Union. The gap between the promise and the practice of R2P becomes narrowed once the intention to evade western responsibility is clarified. This makes the calls from R2P advocates for a struggle to muster the political will to turn the R2P from an idea into a practice particularly misleading. It would appear that it is not so much the political will to complete a liberal project of intervention which is lacking here but a political understanding of the post-liberal framing of intervention in the regulatory terminology of the ongoing need for prevention.

7   Development as freedom?

From colonialism to climate change

Introduction

In the post-liberal statebuilding paradigm, individual autonomy or freedom is the central motif for understanding the problematic of development in the post-colonial context. Rather than a material view of development, human agency has been placed at the centre and is increasingly seen to be the measure of development, in terms of individual capabilities. In the words of Amartya Sen, the winner of the 1998 Nobel Prize for Economic Science, freedom is seen to be both the primary end and principal means of development: 'Development consists of the removal of various types of unfreedoms that leave people with little choice and little opportunity of exercising their reasoned agency' (Sen 1999: xii). In this post-liberal discourse, of 'human development', freedom and autonomy are foregrounded but development lacks a transformative or modernizing material content. In this discourse, development is taken out of an economic context of GNP growth or industrialization, or a social and political context in which development policies are shaped by social and political pressures or state-led policies. The individualized understanding of development takes a rational choice perspective of the individual or 'the agent-orientated view' (Sen 1999: 11), in which development focuses upon ways of enabling individuals to make more effective choices by increasing their capabilities.

In this paradigm, change does not come from above but through the agency of individuals, who act and make choices according to their own values and objectives (Sen 1999: 19). The outcome of development can therefore not be measured by any universal framework; different individuals have different development priorities and aspirations and live in differing social and economic contexts. While a critique of top-down state-led approaches to development, the post-liberal framing should not be confused with neoliberal advocacy of the free market. Markets are not understood as being capable of finding solutions or leading to development themselves but are seen to depend on the formal institutional framework and also the informal institutional framework of social culture, ideas and 'behavioral ethics' (Sen 1999: 262). Although the individual in need of empowerment and capability- or capacity-building is at the centre, both the post-colonial state and the society are understood to have secondary and important supporting roles in developing the institutional and cultural frameworks to enable individuals to free themselves or to develop themselves (Sen 1999: 53).

The discursive framing of development, in terms of empowerment and capacity-building centres on the individual responsibility of the post-colonial or post-conflict subject, and has rightly been critiqued for its emphasis on 'non-material development', which has tended to reinforce global inequalities of wealth (Duffield 2007: 101–5), and as marking 'the demise of the developing state' (Pupavac 2007), as the poor are increasingly seen to be the agents of change and poverty reduction, bearing policy responsibility rather than external actors. Vanessa Pupavac, for example, highlights that, as development has come to the forefront of international agendas for statebuilding and conflict prevention, there has been a distancing of western powers and international institutions from taking responsibility for development, with a consensus that the poor need 'to find their own solutions to the problems they face' (2007: 96).

This chapter draws out the changing nature of western discourses of development and the understanding of policy practices as promoting the empowerment of the post-colonial other. The paradigm of development as freedom, central to discourses of development within the international statebuilding paradigm, will be traced out in relation to two earlier framings of the problematic of development and autonomy. These three framings of the problem of development will be considered from the viewpoint of western policy-makers or international interveners and in their differing relationships to the object of intervention – the colonial or post-colonial state. In this way, we will draw out the different rationales in which development fitted into the paradigms within which this relationship of domination or influence was conceived.

Background

The problem of development has been one of the most sensitive questions raised in the external intervention in and regulation of the colonial and the post-colonial state. The framing of development has been a sensitive question as it has arisen defensively, in the context of the need for apologia: originally, in the negotiation of the ending of formal colonial rule and, subsequently, as a way of rationalizing support for one-party rule in post-colonial Africa and of rationalizing the limited aspirations of external powers in the post-Cold

War era. It should be emphasized that, in the days when colonial hierarchies were unquestioned, development was not a question of concern, regardless of the nature of economic crisis. For example, in response to the Irish potato famines of the 1840s, British administrators did not reconsider or reflect defensively upon colonial economic policy but saw Irish habits and life-styles as the cause of their poverty and of the famine. Questions of poverty and development were discussed less in economic policy terms than as racial or cultural problems connected to diet, overpopulation, laziness and indifference. In this context, Britain's mission' in Ireland 'was seen not as one to alleviate Irish distress but to civilize her people' (Sen 1999: 174).

The discourse of development arose only as colonialism became problematized, in the context of the need to justify and rationalize inequalities, which critics alleged were being reproduced and reinforced through the hierarchies of colonial power relations or the pressures of the world market. It is for this reason that the problematic of development has often tended to be closely bound up with policy framings alleged to be concerned with empowering or capacity-building post-colonial societies themselves. The post-liberal paradigm of international statebuilding builds on earlier discursive framings of development (analogous to that of civil society, discussed in the following chapter), stressing the need for ownership; but is distinct from these approaches in that it inverts and transforms the traditional liberal paradigm which understood economic development and political autonomy as mutually supportive aspects of liberal modernity.

Earlier discourses rationalizing unequal treatment sought to adapt liberal approaches to the colonial or post-colonial world through the emphasis on the problems of material development, understood to be the precondition for equality. The statebuilding paradigm inverses the problematic – the framing of the relationship between development and autonomy: posing the autonomy of the post-colonial or post-conflict subject as a problem for development rather than the lack of development as a problem for political autonomy. This means that development, in relation to state failure or state fragility, becomes a process of external relationship management on the basis of the barriers of autonomy to development and autonomy itself becomes an explanation for inequality and intermittent crisis rather than an end goal, in which these problems are seen to be alleviated.

The historically defensive and limiting nature of discourses of development is drawn out here through an initial focus upon the rise of the development problematic in the colonial era. In fact, it first arose with the problematization of colonialism in the wake of the First World War: development as a set of policy practices was used both to defensively legitimize colonial rule and to help further secure it. The classic example of discussion of development under the period of late colonialism was that most clearly articulated by Lord Lugard, under the rubric of the 'Dual Mandate', where development discourse operated to reveal the different and distinct development needs of colonial societies and therefore to indicate the need for a different set of political relations and rights than those of liberal democracies. The dual nature of the development discourse helped to shift the focus of policy-making away from the export of western norms, such as representative democracy, and towards support for traditional elites, empowering more conservative sections of society in the attempt to negotiate imperial decline through preventing the political dominance of pro-independence elites.

The second period, where development discourse comes to the fore in international debates, is that of negotiating relations with the post-colonial world. Here, too, the discourse was a defensive one, with an awareness of the lack of direct interventionist capacity and a need to respond to the perceived threat of the Soviet Union gaining influence in many states which were no longer formally dependent on western power. From the late 1950s to the early 1970s, development was presented as necessitating a centralizing state role as western governments sought to bargain with post-colonial elites, facilitating a strong state to prevent rebellions led by movements potentially sympathetic to the Soviet cause. The division of the world geo-politically, and the competitive balance of power, made the post-colonial state an important subject in its own right, with the possibility of choosing (and playing-off) competing external patrons. The western approach to development was one that argued that western standards of democracy and governance were not applicable for the management of post-colonial development needs.

From the late 1970s until the end of the 1990s, development was largely off the agenda as models of state-led development failed and the Soviet model became discredited. In this period, the international financial institutions were much less defensive and, under the 'Washington Consensus' framework of structural adjustment, sought to increasingly assert regulatory control over the post-colonial state, gradually extending the reach and focus of economic policy conditionality, with a programmatic focus on financial and monetary controls and neoliberal claims regarding the necessity of 'rolling back the state'. The lack of defensiveness meant that there was little focus on development as a precondition for political equality – either in terms of independence or liberal democratic frameworks of domestic rule. In this period, therefore, there was also little concern with the ownership of development. Rather than focusing on the empowerment of the post-colonial state and society, the international financial institutions openly claimed the mantle of development expertise and had little concern regarding the social impact of their financial stringency or about advocating the market as the framework which would provide solutions.

Today, the development and empowerment of the post-colonial state and society has made a comeback as a central discursive concern of international institutions and leading western states and is at the heart of the post-liberal paradigm of international statebuilding. The precondition for development becoming more central to western discourses has been the deprioritizing of the post-colonial world with the attenuation of super power competition. Consequently, western powers have sought to withdraw from direct policy responsibility (see the discussion of R2P in the previous chapter): this discourse of withdrawal has taken place within the rubric of anti-modernization frameworks, shaped by concerns over the environment and global warming and also reflected in the shifting policy focus – away from the open dominance of international financial institutions and from the market as a means of resolving the problems of development. Instead, development discourse focuses on empowering and capacity-building post-colonial states and societies in similar ways to the earlier discourses of the colonial and post-colonial periods. Once again post-colonial states and societies are held to be the owners of their own development, but in the very different context of western regulation and intervention in the twenty-first century.

Today's development discourse, of the importance of empowering the post-colonial subject, was well described by Gordon Brown, in 2006, when UK finance minister: 'A century ago people talked of "What can we do to Africa?" Last century, it was "What can we do for Africa?" Now in 2006, we must ask what the developing world, empowered, can do for itself' (Brown 2006). In the post-liberal discourse of development, it is often asserted that what is novel about current approaches is that of empowering the post-colonial world in relation to the needs of development. Many critiques of this approach have suggested that the discourse of empowerment and ownership is a misleading one, considering the influence of western powers and international financial institutions (for example, Harrison 2001, 2004; Rowden and Irama 2004; Gould and Ojanen 2003; Craig and Porter 2002; Fraser 2005; Cammack 2002; Chandler 2006a); this is no doubt the case. The focus of this chapter, however, is upon how the discourses of ownership and development have been historically linked and how, in the paradigm of international statebuilding, this discourse transforms and inverts the earlier attempts to explain differential policy frameworks, which understood development to be a precondition for autonomy; asserting a post-liberal claim that it is autonomy which is problematic for development. It is this distinctive framing, emphasizing the autonomy of the post-colonial subject, which facilitates development interventions aimed at indirectly influencing the autonomous choices of the poorest and most marginal sections of post-colonial societies.

Indirect rule in Africa

British colonization of Africa was not a gradual process, flowing from an existing relationship of regulation and intervention, but a rapid process, covering huge swathes of the hinterland of the Nile, Niger and Zambesi, as inter-imperialist competition in the 'scramble for Africa' (from the 1885 Berlin Conference onwards) meant that jurisdiction over a territory could not be claimed merely through extra-territorial treaties with the 'voluntary consent' of the natives. Increasingly, it became necessary to assume direct sovereignty: direct jurisdiction over the subject peoples rather than just over the business and activities of British subjects (see Lugard 1923: 9–47). The colonial claim to be safeguarding the 'interests' and 'advancement' of the natives was an inevitable by-product of these inter-imperialist rivalries, which forced the territorial partition of Africa. Without this pressure there would have been little need to emphasize development or to make economic policy, beyond the extra-territorial treaties needed to safeguard strategic and commercial interests.

Although, in 1865, a Royal Commission had recommended abandoning Britain's older settlements on the West Coast, by the end of the century Britain was responsible for a vast empire in Africa. Ironically, the political powers and responsibilities acquired bore little relationship to the political importance that these areas held. Britain had been forced to declare sovereign power over vast African hinterlands, but had little desire to take on the governing responsibility. Initially, as Lord Lugard noted, the British government passed responsibility for acquiring territory to chartered companies, such as the Royal Niger Company, the Imperial British East Africa Company and the British South African Company, which unlike those in the Dominions (which were commercial companies that gradually acquired administrative powers) were formed to do the work of administration, with a commercial arm to fund it. This privatization of the colonial project was the first step towards distancing colonial power from the legal responsibility for governing these new territories.

In the British case, the African protectorates were already, in effect, a postscript to the glory of Empire. The African states were classed as Protectorates not Crown Colonies. Lord Lugard quotes Sir C. Ilbert, a leading authority of the day, that 'for purposes of municipal law an African Protectorate is not, but for purposes of international law must be treated as if it were, a part of the British dominions' (Lugard 1923: 34). The African states were 'protectorates' not colonies, which already highlighted a defensive, contradictory and problematic approach to the assumption of colonial power over them. The distinction lay not so much in the power that the British government could exercise but in the responsibilities that it accepted. According to the rulings of the British courts:

East Africa, being a protectorate in which the Crown has jurisdiction, is in relation to the Crown a foreign country under its protection, and its native inhabitants are not subjects owing allegiance to the Crown, but protected foreigners, who, in return for that protection, owe obedience.

(cited in Lugard 1923: 36)

The growth of empire was now perceived increasingly as a problem rather than as an opportunity. Unlike in India and the Far East, in Africa there was a high turnover of colonial staff and few administrators took their families with them or would have thought of their stay as more than temporary. It was clear that Britain had no interest in devoting the resources necessary to exercise direct sovereignty over its African territories. Colonial administrators were much more conscious of the fragility of their rule than in the pre-war era, and nowhere more so than in sub-Saharan Africa. It was in order to address this problem that the discourse of development and the policy-making frameworks associated with it, particularly in the administrative conception of indirect rule, developed in an attempt to shore up external administrative authority through talking-up the autonomy and independence of native chiefs, who they sought to rule through and to develop and to capacity-build.

Pre-figured by the 'scramble for Africa', the First World War highlighted the end of the confident imperial project of universalism under the Victorian banners of empire and free trade. It is important to recognize that the rise of Japan as an Asian 'Great Power' (Schmitt 2003: 231), the impact of inter-European war and the use of colonial troops to fight (Furedi 1998: 38–40) and the post-1917 withdrawal of Russia from the imperialist club, meant that by the 1920s the world could no longer be easily understood in terms of racial hierarchies (see also, Chapter 8):

> Most serious were the loss in prestige and the intrusion of gnawing doubts as to the supremacy and even the validity of western civilization itself. The west's decline of faith in itself coincided with the east's growing confidence in its right and ability to assert its equal claims.
>
> (Emerson 1960: 17)

As Rupert Emerson describes it, with the focus on the distinct and separate development needs of the colonial societies a new framework of indirect rule was experimented with, based on giving traditional authorities official recognition. This meant that 'Europeans regularly attributed to the chief a greater measure of royal omnipotence than was traditionally accorded to him by native custom' (1960: 250). While the chief's substantive power may have passed to the colonial power, his formal authority was often enhanced and, as long as he was compliant, he would receive the protection of the external power. Emerson argues that this process corrupted both chiefs and colonial officials:

> For the chief it meant subservience to the alien authority . . . In the case of the colonial official it meant that he tended to align himself with reactionary elements in the society just at the time when the forces for change were beginning to come into prominence . . . For some, prisoners of the dogma of indirect rule, the maintenance of an increasingly anachronistic traditional society tended to become an end in itself.
>
> (1960: 251–52)

David Laitin describes the process through which British colonizers revived the status of the Yoruba kings, creating administrative mechanisms of indirect rule through reifying tribal associations and encouraging claims based on the invention of traditional and historic rights (Laitin 1985). The legacy of the colonial focus on development through indirect rule was that of 'divide and rule' mechanisms, which undermined a cohesive national polity, reconstituting chiefly rule as a barrier to independence:

> In West Africa, up to the end of the 1940s, they redoubled their efforts to launch their colonies down the same slipway of chiefly rule which their own colonialism had previously done its best to undermine. Titled honors were duly handed around to suitable chiefly recipients . . . Hard-pressed district officers were urged to invent new ways in which the authority of chiefs, now that Britain was to withdraw, could be reinforced by prudent measures of administrative devolution, notably in the matter of 'native tax' and 'native treasuries'.
>
> (Davidson 1992: 104)

There is little doubt that the development discourse evolved out of a concern over the weakness of the colonial administrative power and the fear that open rule would encourage resistance. As Lugard noted, in contrast to territories such as Hong Kong where direct rule was 'thoroughly efficient', in Africa there were few British staff and if there was direct rule without tribal authority: 'There could only be one end . . . eventual conflict with the rabble' (1923: 216). The insight that Lugard had was to make a virtue out of development differentials as an argument for recasting British policy requirements in ostensibly neutral terms. Rather than an overt act of external domination, Lugard's attempt to stave-off the end of colonial rule through the empowerment of native institutions was portrayed to be in the development interests of the poor and marginal in colonial society. Through the rubric of interventionist administrative 'good governance', native institutions were to be built and, simultaneously, external control was to be enhanced. As Lugard describes:

> The Resident [colonial official] acts as sympathetic adviser and counsellor to the native chief, being careful not to interfere so as to lower his prestige, or cause him to lose interest in his work. His advice on matters of general policy must be followed, but the native ruler issues his own instructions to subordinate chiefs and district heads – not as the orders of the Resident but as his own – and he is encouraged to work through them, instead of centralising everything in himself . . .
>
> (Lugard 1923: 201)

For Lugard, 'the native authority is thus *de facto* and *de jure* ruler over his own people', there are not 'two sets of rulers – British and native – working either separately or in co-operation, but a single Government' (1923: 203). Lugard states: 'It is the consistent aim of the British staff to maintain and increase the prestige of the native ruler, to encourage his initiative, and to support his authority' (1923: 204). Development was key to legitimating Lugard's strategy of indirect rule, with the reinvention of native authorities with modern administrative techniques, which could assist in developing trade through introducing a wider use of money, rather than barter, and could expand the scope of political identification beyond personal social connections. The introduction of direct taxation, for example, was seen not in narrow functionalist revenue raising terms, but as a mechanism of strengthening the links between the colonial administration and native rulers and, through them, the links to the rural mass.

Not only would colonial oversight encourage good governance and transparency in tax assessment, collection and accounting, but it would hopefully play a political role in giving the masses a greater sense of identity with the traditional administering authorities, heading off anti-British protest and support for pro-independence elites:

> . . . the Suzerain power imposes the taxes . . . and the general rate . . . the actual assessment is in the hands of the native ruler and his representatives . . . guided and assisted by the British staff. It therefore appears to the taxpayer as a tax imposed by his own native ruler, though he knows that the vigilant eye of the District Officer will see that no unauthorised extractions are made . . . Since the salaries of the ruler and the officials of the 'Native Administration' are paid out of their native treasury funds, they cannot be regarded by him as officials paid by the Government.
>
> (Lugard 1923: 207)

In Lugard's view, the problems of external rule were to be resolved through the discursive framing of development as a set of technical and administrative skills necessary for the gradual assumption of self-rule. There was no necessary contradiction between strengthening the capacity of local native administrations for 'self-government', increasing and extending the social and political bonds between the masses and the native administration, and enhancing the power and authority of colonial rule. The discussion of development and its link with the mechanisms of indirect rule was the first attempt made to extend the policy framework of intervention with the goal of empowering and capacity-building the colonial other. This framing of empowerment developed in response to the negotiation of colonial withdrawal and the desire to use development as a discourse to undermine the legitimacy of the nationalist elites through external administrators posing as the representatives of the poor and marginal, in whose interest it was alleged that development had to be managed through the maintenance of traditional institutions.

Lugard criticized attempts to export British methods of administration and political institutional forms to less developed societies, such as India, on the basis that this merely destroyed organic native structures of social and political mediation without creating any new ones in its place. He therefore attempted to use development and the focus on the poor as a way to challenge the liberal focus on the development of representative institutions on the western model, which was being followed in India at that time. In language that would not be out of place in 'lessons from Iraq' policy documents, concerning the disbanding of the army, he notes:

> To overthrow an organisation, however faulty, which has the sanction of long usage, and is acquiesced in by the people, before any system could be created to take its place . . . would have been an act of folly which no sane administrator could attempt.
>
> (Lugard 1923: 224)

He argued that – while the jury was still out with regard to India, and that anyway it was too late to revive alternative traditional models of rule – African development was less advanced and had clearly not reached the stage where the representational model could be successful rooted in existing social relations. He stated that it was not yet the case that 'a comparatively small educated class shall be recognized as the natural spokesmen for the many' (Lugard 1923: 194). Lugard posed indirect rule as necessary in opposition to those who sought to mould a compliant native political professional elite and focused on the qualities of native administrators through civil service training in the values of good governance. While the dominant framework was a liberal one of training a colonial elite in western values, Lugard suggested that a non-liberal, differential, approach was necessary, providing African owner-ship of development rather than creating a professional class of 'Europeanized' Africans who would soon challenge colonial rule. For Lugard:

> The fundamental essential, however, in such a form of Government is that the educated few shall at least be representative of the feelings and desires of the many – well known to them, speaking their language, and versed in their customs and prejudices . . . In present conditions in Africa the numerous separate tribes, speaking different languages, and in different stages of evolution, cannot produce representative men of education.
>
> (1923: 195)

Lugard argued that Europeanized or westernized educated professional Africans would be antagonistic towards the native rulers and councils estab-lished under indirect rule and would judge colonial policy in terms of western mechanisms of liberal democracy. This approach reflected the framework of aristocratic prejudice of British colonialism, asserting that the lack of material equality required differential development aims to those aspired to under liberal modernity:

> This pattern rests essentially upon the two assumptions, familiar to aristocracies everywhere, that the backward masses, incapable of admin-istering themselves and misgoverned by their own regimes, will receive a far better deal at the hands of their advanced overlords, and that they are primarily interested only in living their lives in peace and quiet with rising standards of welfare to be provided for them from above.
>
> (Emerson 1960: 38)

The colonial discussions of development thereby questioned the existence of organic links of political interest between the educated native elites and the masses, seeking to demonstrate that external actors were more capable of looking after their interests. From its inception, the discourse of international development was thereby closely linked to the naturalization or essen-tialization of difference and presented as a critique of liberal assumptions of universality. In this case, operating to privilege the voice of the peasant over the voice of the middle-class professional agitating for national independence and self-government:

> The proper focus of colonial attention is the 'real' people, the simple peasant mass, which gratefully accepts benevolent paternalism . . . The occasional outbursts of political agitation reflect, not the demands

of the 'real' people, but only the self-interested machinations of an untrustworthy few.

(Emerson 1960: 38)

It was from within this framing that, for example, Winston Churchill condemned the Indian National Congress, in 1931, for its inability to represent the interests of the people of India: 'They [Congress] merely represent those Indians who have acquired a veneer of western civilization . . . To transfer that responsibility to this highly artificial and restricted oligarchy of Indian politicians . . . would be an act of cowardice, desertion and dishonour' (Emerson 1960: 42).

The question of development and its relationship to empowerment and local ownership was revived in terms of content, but in a very different form, in the post-colonial era. Here, as considered in the next section, similar arguments to those put by Lugard, about the need for separate and distinct political forms to overcome the problem of development, were forwarded, while arguments which insisted on measuring the post-colonial state according to the standards of western liberal democracy were seen to be problematic in relation to development needs. Here, the critique of liberal universalism was rationalized in the context of the threat of the Soviet block and resistance to western influence per se, rather than merely to western rule in its most direct colonial form.

Post-colonial development

In the 1960s, there was a general awareness of the weakness and fragility of the post-colonial state and development discourse focused upon distancing the problems of the post-colonial state from the history of colonial rule. This defensive concern deepened with the perception that development might lead to the growth of influence of social forces which would be more sympathetic to Soviet rule. Whereas earlier the discourse of development and local ownership focused on the poor in an attempt to undermine the legitimacy of ruling elites, in the 1960s, development discourse focused on ownership at the level of state elites in order to prevent the masses from becoming a destabilizing force capable of aligning the regimes to the Soviet sphere of influence.

Taking over many of the development themes of the period of late-colonial rule, the rolling back of colonial power was initially seen as a matter of unfortunate timing. It was alleged that just when colonialism had undermined traditional structures of power and traditional relationships, thereby generating new social forces and social upheaval, the colonial powers had been forced to retreat, leaving behind new states which were ill-equipped to handle the problems of 'transition':

Everywhere in the world, this process of social mobilization makes the developing countries harder to govern by their own traditional elites, but still harder to govern from abroad. Everywhere the trend is toward rising costs of foreign intervention . . . The actual capacities of many of the new countries for self-government and for the maintenance of political cohesion have been quite limited. From the Congo to Laos and Viet Nam, political instability in many of the new countries has been extreme. In such countries only one form of rule seems even harder and more costly to maintain: government by foreigners.

(Deutsch 1966: viii)

The cause of the problem was initially seen as the fact that post-colonial states were external creations, not reflecting a social reality. In sub-Saharan Africa, states 'were not brought into being because of the cultural homogeneity and traditional unity of the people composing them; each was made up, in varying degrees, of disparate ethnic groups forced into a single political form by the imperial power' (Emerson 1966: 96). Even the struggle against colonialism, which was held to be the essential mechanism for forging national identity, was seen to have had little chance to develop before the withdrawal of colonial power, the only exceptions being the white settler states, such as Algeria, Rhodesia and Kenya (Wallerstein 1961; Emerson 1960). It was often alleged that the nationalist parties gained power too easily, before forging a close relationship with society, often having come into being only shortly before independence (Huntington 1968: 425). The rapid withdrawal of colonial power was asserted to mean that most African states were 'cheated of their revolution' (Emerson 1966: 110). Without a shared history or a shared language other than that of the former colonial power, it was feared that many sub-Saharan states would face a long and arduous task in the creation of social cohesion and developmental stability.

In recognition of the developmental problems of the post-colonial state, in the 1960s, development was increasingly understood to be a highly interventionist project, much more than 'just the establishment of that most complex of modern organizations, the machinery of state' (Pye 1962: 39). The problem of development was implicitly and explicitly seen as not merely the transfer of technical capacity and skills but also the changing of cultural attitudes and values. It was also understood that the process of 'transition' created many possibilities for conflict and instability before development could be assured. The problem of development was especially highlighted with regard to sub-Saharan Africa; in Lucian Pye's words, for the new states: 'the great objective is to achieve impressive elements of organization that characterize the modern nation-state; and the almost universal problem is that they have the form but not the substance of nationhood' (1962: 3).

Initially, in terms of presentation at least, it was their pre-modern social relations and cultures that were seen to be the central problems facing the security and legitimacy of these post-colonial states. Traditional patterns of social life meant that the state could not play the same developmental role as in modern western states. There was understood to be very little prior theorization of development, in terms of the different circumstances faced by post-colonial states in bridging the gap between the state and society – generally addressed under the rubric of 'nation-building'. As Pye noted, leaders of new states were 'provided with glowing expositions of the virtues of democratic values and republican constitutions' or they received 'extensive advice on limited technical matters of applied administration':

> But they are not offered any systematic guide to the nature of national development which can provide a sound basis for judging progress and for determining priorities for action. We seem to have neither the theoretical nor the applied knowledge to provide the basis for strategies for nation building.
>
> (Pye 1962: 6)

In terms of policy responses, the problem of development was seen to be a unique dilemma which had only arisen in the post-colonial period. It was clear that while democracy was a central motif of the Cold War divide, the west was in no position to break from supporting post-colonial states on this basis if it wished to keep them outside of the Soviet sphere of influence. In post-colonial 'transition' societies, western Cold War norms of judgement needed to be rethought. This need for a different set of policy judgements was well expressed by Pye:

> Is the emergence of army rule a sign of anti-democratic tendencies? Or is it a process that can be readily expected at particular stages of national development? Must the central government try to obliterate all traditional communal differences, or can the unfettered organization and representation of conflicting interests produce ultimately a stronger sense of national unity? Should the new governments strive to maintain the same levels of administrative efficiency as the former colonial authorities did, or is it possible that . . . because the new governments have other claims of legitimacy, this is no longer as crucial a problem? The questions mount, and we are not sure what trends are dangerous and what are only temporary phases with little significance.
>
> (Pye 1962: 7)

Samuel Huntington argued that, in so far as the American policy establishment was concerned, the lack of attention to the specific differences of the post-colonial state, despite its policy importance, was a major problem (1968: 5). He saw two reasons for this, linked to American historical experience. First, the US experience of economic plenty and political stability had led social scientists to believe that the problem of development would be automatically overcome by market forces. The understanding of development in the post-colonial state as a process that needed a strong regulatory state was therefore one which necessitated a policy strategy which was very different from that accepted domestically and which was not easy to openly articulate in policy terms. Pye argued that 'our policy is in search of purpose' (1962: 297), suggesting that: 'We have not been creative in exploring the prerequisites of successful assistance programs, and we have tended to vacillate between a narrow-minded economic approach and a diffuse desire for uncritical and "friendly" relations with the underdeveloped countries' (Pye 1962: 295–96). For Pye, it appeared that technical considerations dominated the presentation of US aid programmes to evade the difficulties of articulating strategic and pragmatic development goals: 'such considerations seem to provide us with objective and neutral standards that protect us from appearing to be unduly arbitrary' (1962: 297):

> Economic criteria are not unimportant and certainly should not be casually disregarded, but they are not adequate for policy in one of the most important matters of our time. The fundamental framework for our policy toward the underdeveloped areas must be defined by the entire range of our associations and our interactions with them, and it would be a gross if not insulting reversal of priorities to place at the heart of our relations with other societies such limited matters as our technical and economic assistance programs.
>
> (Pye 1962: 297)

Second, the US had imported its political framework from seventeenth-century England; it had been 'born with a government' and had 'never had to worry about creating a government' (Huntington 1968: 7). The US experience was of concern to limit government, 'confronted with the need to design a political system which will maximize power and authority' there was no answer except 'free and fair elections' (Huntington 1968: 7). The international policy advisors faced a difficult task in articulating why democracy in the west could only allegedly be preserved by limiting democracy in the post-colonial world. This was done through asserting the difference and distinctiveness of the post-colonial state and society in order to justify differential treatment:

> What we are witnessing is the failure of a series of experiments in grafting an alien form of government on peoples whose background

and circumstances are totally dissimilar . . . The first phase of the post-colonial reaction to colonialism involved the copying of the institutions of the imperial west. The failure of those institutions and its aftermath constitute a second phase . . . What the inarticulate masses wanted from the revolutions . . . was presumably not constitutional democracy or parliamentary government, but economic and social advance under their own leaders within a framework of national unity and strength.

(Emerson 1960: 289)

It is ironic that post-colonial commentators, such as Emerson, were happy to repeat similar arguments about local ownership and development to those which they condemned as aristocratic prejudice when they were formulated by the British colonial administrators to argue that advance under native administrations was key rather than democracy and parliamentary rule. In this context, however, development was to be undertaken by a very different framework of institutional innovation, through the military or under one-party systems. In the post-colonial context, the mass party was seen as playing a crucial role of integrating the masses into the political process and of marginalizing more radical alternatives (Foltz 1966: 120). A national project and national goal were seen as crucial to the integration of new elites, the problem being whether this cohesion could withstand the social pressures associated with mass mobilization.

Samuel Huntington's 1968 book, *Political Order in Changing Societies*, concretized the post-colonial perception of the problem of development and post-colonial order and stands as the classic text for this period. Whereas previous analysts had suggested that instability and authoritarian rule could be inevitable, Huntington proposed a much more coherent rationalization for a state-led interventionist approach to prevent instability and maintain order. He also inversed the late-colonial understanding of the problem being that the state institutions were in advance of society, suggesting that the issue should be seen from a new angle. Rather than seeing the lack of economic development as causing the state–society gap, he argued that it was the development process itself which was destabilizing:

It is not the absence of modernity but the efforts to achieve it which produce political disorder. If poor countries appear to be unstable, it is not because they are poor, but because they are trying to become rich. A purely traditional society would be ignorant, poor, and stable.

(Huntington 1968: 41)

This approach was later to directly inform the post-liberal, institutionalist, framing of 'Institutionalization before Liberalization'(see, for example, Paris 2004).

Rather than being the potential solution, rapid economic progress was held to be the problem facing non-western states, creating an increasingly destabilized world, wracked by social and political conflict:

> What was responsible for this violence and instability? The primary thesis . . . is that it was in large part the product of rapid social change and the rapid mobilization of new groups into politics coupled with the slow development of political institutions.
>
> (Huntington 1968: 4)

It was not the case that the political institutions of the post-colonial state were ahead of their societies (in terms of representing a national collectivity which was yet to become fully socially and economically integrated). The problem was alleged to lie with the institutions of the state rather than with society. Huntington's statebuilding thesis consciously sought to privilege order over economic progress, as both a policy means and a political end.

In many ways, the post-colonial thesis of development and local ownership repeats the core themes of the late-colonial problematic. In both frameworks, development is seen as a crucial precondition for political freedoms, either of self-government or of liberal democratic frameworks. The reason why development is privileged is as a rationalization for colonial or western support for non-liberal frameworks of representation. Development is raised as a technical problem but behind this framing is a clear political motivation, first to slow the withdrawal of colonial power and delegitimize anti-colonial protest and second to prevent the rise of pro-communist movements in post-colonial states. Huntington's work on development reflected his involvement in US policy-making in the Vietnam War. From 1966 to 1969 he was chairman of the Council on Vietnamese Studies of the US Agency for International Development's South-East Asia Advisory Group, and visited Saigon in 1967 on behalf of the State Department 'to investigate ways in which political power could be developed in Vietnam' (Leys 1996: 75).

It was his experience in Vietnam which convinced him of the urgency of the task. His concern was that instability in weak post-colonial states would favour the communists:

> The real challenge which the communists pose to modernizing countries is not that they are so good at overthrowing governments (which is easy), but that they are so good at making governments (which is a far more difficult task). They may not provide liberty, but they do provide authority; they do create governments that can govern. While Americans laboriously strive to narrow the economic gap, communists

offer modernizing countries a tested and proven method of bridging the political gap.

(Huntington 1968: 8)

Huntington's concern was that if the west complacently waited for economic development to bring democracy and security to the post-colonial world they would find the process being short-cut by communist takeovers which promised development and threatened to politically galvanize the newly created urban classes. Huntington's concerns were in many respects similar to those of the late-colonial theorists and, similarly to Lord Lugard, he attempted to develop methods through which governments could maintain non-communist order by marginalizing the power of urban groups, especially through the repression of middle class radicalism (seen as the greatest threat) (Huntington 1968: 373) and ensuring that the peasantry were satisfied through land reform and the promotion of individual land ownership (1968: 377) and could act as a counterbalancing conservative social force (1968: 72–78, 443).

Huntington was clear in his critique of the export of universal western norms, asserting that the promotion of democracy was not the best way to bring development or to withstand the threat of communist takeover. The barrier to communism was a strong state, capable of galvanizing society, possibly through the undemocratic framework of one-party or authoritarian rule: 'the non-western countries of today can have political modernization or they can have democratic pluralism, but they cannot normally have both' (Huntington 1968: 137). He suggested, as did the colonial advocates of indirect rule, that focusing purely on organic solutions to development, waiting for economic growth to develop a middle-class basis for liberal democracy, would result in 'political decay' and weak states falling to communist revolution. This innately political understanding of the problem of development meant that Huntington had little time for the 'apolitical' or technocratic approaches which focused on the state in isolation from society (Huntington 1968: 404).

The institutional focus for Huntington, as for Lord Lugard, was not a bureaucratic one, but a political one. This much more 'political' approach to development reflected the Cold War framework of US foreign policy which sought to support 'friendly' authoritarian regimes in order to maintain international stability and order, rather than concern itself with questions of narrow economic policy or with representative democracy. It was not until the late 1970s and 1980s that the international financial institutions and the former colonial powers concerned themselves with the domestic politics of African states, once the threat of Soviet competition and the resistance movements which they sponsored came to be lifted. In this period, the discourse of development and local ownership went into abeyance, to return in the late 1990s.

Climate change

From the 1990s onwards, development and local ownership have returned to the top of the international agenda and local agency has been key to the reinterpretaton of the development problematic. In many ways, the discourse draws upon the past: on the late-colonial discursive emphasis on the poor as the central subjects of development but also on the post-colonial discursive problematization of development, highlighting its destabilizing effects. However, within the framework of post-liberal governance, the relationship between development and autonomy is differently conceived. For the previous colonial and post-colonial discourses, development was held to be the precondition for liberal frameworks of autonomy and the lack of development used to justify restrictions on autonomy, in the form of colonial rule or external support for authoritarian regimes. For post-liberal frameworks, autonomy is taken as a given and, in fact, as the explanation for the lack of development or for its unevenness. Rather than development being used to justify the lack of autonomy, the lack of liberal rights-based conceptions of government, autonomy is used to justify or explain the lack of development. The autonomy of the post-colonial subject is here at the forefront of the policy discourse. Development in terms of economic material factors is displaced by autonomy in terms of the decision-making capabilities of the post-colonial subject. Within this framework, the emphasis is much more upon the resilience of post-colonial societies and individuals and their autonomous capacity to adapt to their circumstances than upon the need for economic or social transformation.

Here, there is neither the faith that the African state can manage or lead the development of society's productive forces nor that external intervention can direct African development, either through international financial institutions or by NGO management of service provision. Rather than development being understood as an attempt to transform the economic and social environment of the post-colonial individual, development is seen as developing the autonomy of the individual. Development as autonomy – 'development as freedom' – focuses on the individual's adaptation to their environment rather than to the collective shaping or transformation of it. The subject of development is increasingly seen to be the autonomous individual, in need of institutional frameworks which develop their capabilities and capacities for resilience, particularly in relation to climate change and environmental sustainability.

Sub-Saharan Africa is particularly vulnerable to climate fluctuations because of a lack of material economic development. The lack of development means that 70 per cent of the working population (90 per cent of Africa's poor) rely on agriculture for a living, the vast majority of them by subsistence farming (NEF 2006: 12). It is no coincidence that the continent with the lowest per capita greenhouse gas emissions is also the most vulnerable to climate change. Rather than the problems of Africa being seen as a lack of material development resulting in dependency upon climate uncertainties, the problem of development has increasingly been reinterpreted in terms of the problem of individual lifestyle choices and the survival strategies of the poor.

The framework of post-liberal governance views African development in terms of external assistance to an 'adaptation agenda', essential to prevent the impact of climate change from undermining African development (see, for example, UNFCCC 1994). According to the UK Government white paper on development, *Making Governance Work for the Poor*, 'climate change poses the most serious long term threat to development and the Millennium Development Goals' (DFID 2006). The poverty agenda and the climate change agenda have come together in their shared focus on Africa. In the wake of international support for poverty reduction and debt relief, many international NGOs, international institutions and western states, have called for climate change to be seen as the central challenge facing African development. African poverty and poor governance are held to combine to increase Africa's vulnerability, while the solution is held to lie with international programmes of assistance, funded and led by western states, held to be chiefly responsible for global warming.

This agenda appears to be more pro-African than the interventionist agendas of the 1990s in which good governance and democracy promotion seemed to put western states in the position of lecturing and hectoring African states. Building on the poverty reduction and debt-relief approaches of the early part of that decade, assistance to cope with climate change is billed as empowering and learning from Africa in an attempt to develop 'shared approaches to shared problems'. The 'adaptation agenda' highlights the increasingly interventionist demand for 'grand strategies' and new, more comprehensive, western agendas to manage Africa. In the midst of the Make Poverty History campaign, which won the support of millions of people for debt-relief and poverty reduction strategies linked to the Development Millennium Goals, a group of major international NGOs already questioned the lack of strategic linking of the UK government's chief themes – Africa and climate change. The NGO Working Group on Climate Change and Development (which comprises over twenty leading international NGOs, including ActionAid International, CAFOD, Christian Aid, Friends of the Earth, Greenpeace, Oxfam, RSPB, Tearfund, World Vision and WWF) called for a new test for every international policy and aid project, 'in which the key question will be, "Are you increasing or decreasing people's vulnerability to the climate?"'. The threat of climate change in Africa was held to necessitate 'a new flexibility and not a one-size-fits-all, neoliberal-driven approach to development' (Simms 2005: 2).

The 'adaptation agenda' brings together the concerns of poverty reduction and responses to climate change by understanding poverty not in terms of income, or in relation to social and economic development, but in terms of 'vulnerability to climate change'. This position has been widely articulated by the international NGOs most actively concerned with the climate change agenda. Tony Jupiter, executive director of Friends of the Earth, argues that: 'Policies to end poverty in Africa are conceived as if the threat of climatic disruption did not exist' (McCarthy and Brown 2005). Nicola Saltman, from the World Wide Fund for Nature, similarly feels that 'All the aid we pour into Africa will be inconsequential if we don't tackle climate change' (McCarthy and Brown 2005). This position is shared by the UK Department for International Development, whose chief scientific adviser, Professor Sir Gordon Conway, states that African poverty reduction strategies have not factored in the burdens of climate change on African capacities. He argues that: 'there are three principles for adaptation: 1. Adopt a gradual process of adaptation. 2. Build on disaster preparedness. 3. Develop resilience' (Conway 2006).The focus of the adaptation agenda puts the emphasis on the lives and survival strategies of Africa's poor. Professor Conway argues that, with this emphasis:

> Africa is well prepared to deal with many of the impacts of climate change. Many poor Africans experience severe disasters on an annual or even more frequent basis. This has been true for decades. The challenge is whether we can build on this experience.
>
> (Conway 2006)

The focus on the survival strategies of Africa's poor is central to notions of strengthening African 'resilience' to climate change. This approach has been posed contrary to development approaches which focus on questions of socio-economic development, dependent on the application of higher levels of science and technology and the modernization of agriculture. As the Working Group report states:

> Recently the role of developing new technology has been strongly emphasized . . . There is a consensus among development groups, however, that a greater and more urgent challenge is strengthening communities from the bottom-up, and building on their own coping strategies to live with global warming.
>
> (Simms 2005: 2)

Despite the claims that 'good adaptation also makes good development', it would appear that the adaptation to climate change agenda is more like sustained disaster-relief management than a strategy for African development (Simms 2005: 4). The focus on 'bottom-up' approaches which can increase communities' resilience to climate change transforms the previous discourses of development and autonomy through focusing on the autonomy and choices of the individual in post-colonial society. This shift in development focus, away from societal perspectives and towards individual choices, follows the work of Amartya Sen.

Sen has been central to the development of post-liberal individual rational choice framings of the problematic of development and autonomy, redefining development away from material indicators, such as income or GDP and instead focusing on the 'individual capabilities' of the most marginal members of society (see also, Sen 1992, 1999). Andrew Simms, policy director of the New Economics Foundation and lead author of the *Africa – Up in Smoke?* report, challenges the 'top-down' focus on poverty reduction of the G8 aid and debt-relief provisions, arguing that resilience (vulnerability to externalities) should be seen as the key problem:

> What hasn't been thought through at all is whether the development package attached to the proposed debt relief and increased aid-flows makes people more or less vulnerable to climate change. Minor enhancements of debt relief pale into insignificance compared to the negative impacts of global warming. Many places in Africa are overwhelmingly dependent on rain-fed agriculture and so they are vulnerable to even the early phases of climate change: any slight exaggeration of peaks and troughs of climate extremes hits them instantly.
>
> (McCarthy and Brown 2005)

The adaptation agenda focuses on individuals' vulnerability to climate change rather than looking at the possible responses from 'top-down'. This is discursively framed as empowering and 'community-focused': the 'bottom-up' approach, focusing on community resilience, suggests that large-scale development projects which seek to industrialize agricultural production are unnecessary. According to Simms:

> [T]here has been a lot of emphasis on the commercialization of agriculture. But people have not thought about whether the development of luxury horticulture from the west coast is going to enhance the resilience of people in the face of massive shifts in climate, when what you may really need is a massive amount of support to small-scale agriculture.
>
> (McCarthy and Brown 2005)

In re-describing development problems as 'vulnerability to climate change', there is a rejection of aspirations to modernize agriculture; instead there is an emphasis on reinforcing traditional modes of subsistence economy. Rather than development being safeguarded by the modernization and transformation of African society, underdevelopment is subsidized through the provision of social support for subsistence farming and nomadic pastoralism. Once poverty is redefined as 'vulnerability' then the emphasis is on the survival strategies of the poorest and most marginalized, rather than the broader social and economic relations which force them into a marginalized existence. According to the NGO Working Group:

> [T]he majority of the continent's poorest and most undernourished people live in rural areas – especially smallholders, nomadic pastoralists, and women. The joint effort to eradicate poverty promised by African governments and donor governments must therefore deliver rural policies that involve and prioritise these vulnerable groups. Even small improvements in what they produce and earn, in access to health, education and clean water, will have major impacts in reducing hunger, as well as driving equitable growth. The need to give much more support to small-scale farming comes up again and again from the field experience of development groups.
>
> (NEF 2006: 3)

The Working Group's follow-up report, *Africa – Up in Smoke 2*, argues that the problem is not one of underdevelopment in Africa, instead, 'it is primarily politics' which explains, for example, the poverty of nomadic pastoralists. To this end, Oxfam and others have put pressure on the Kenyan government to do more to support nomadic groups, arguing that with the right government policies 'pastoralism could still, despite climate change, be not only a viable way of life, but a profitable one too' (NEF 2006: 10).

Aid agencies, like Oxfam and Practical Action are encouraging the provision of a safety net of external subsidy to pastoral groups, by buying animals (usually goats which would die in drought conditions) at a fair price, slaughtering them and returning the meat and hide to the sellers, which they can then sell on to buy provisions (NEF 2006: 10). Other social safety-nets include the provision of cash for work, direct cash relief, free veterinary services, seed distribution, etc. Policies which make sense in a temporary emergency situation, where famine can be prevented through the provision of government relief, are now promoted as the way forward to increase the 'resilience' of the poor to climate change. Famines, in this framing are caused by individual responses to a variety of fluctuations in economic conditions (amenable to institutional intervention) rather than a lack of food or the economic and social context of dependencies (see Sen's work in this area, for example, 1981; and Drèze and Sen 1990). Pastoralism is therefore seen as unproblematic in itself. The fact that pastoralists live a life of dependency on the weather and are consigned to poverty is seen as a problem of 'climate vulnerability' to be ameliorated by correct government intervention and sponsorship.

The NGO Working Group on Climate Change argues that community and individual empowerment has to be at the centre of the adaptation agenda:

> [I]t has to be about strengthening communities from the bottom up, building on their own coping strategies to live with climate change and empowering them to participate in the development of climate change policies. Identifying what communities are already doing to adapt is an important step towards discovering what people's priorities are and sharing their experiences, obstacles and positive initiatives with other communities and development policy-makers. Giving a voice to people in this way can help to grow confidence, as can valuing their knowledge and placing it alongside science-based knowledge.
>
> (NEF 2006: 3)

African 'voices' are central to climate change advocacy as the science of climate change leaves many questions unanswered, particularly with regard to the impact of climate change in Africa (the problems of climate monitoring capabilities, particularly in Africa, are highlighted in UNFCC 2006: 4–5). Information, to support the urgency of action in this area, is often obtained from those in Africa, seen as having a 'deeper' understanding than that which can be provided by 'western' science. For example, the views of Sesophio, a Masai pastoralist from Tanzania, are given prominence in the *Africa – Up in Smoke 2* report:

> It is this development, like cars, that is bringing stress to the land, and plastics are being burnt and are filling in the air. We think there is a lot of connection between that and what is happening now with the droughts. If you bring oil and petrol and throw it onto the grass it doesn't grow, so what are all these cars and new innovations doing to a bigger area? Every day diseases are increasing, diseases we haven't seen before.
>
> (NEF 2006: 10)

Climate change advocates patronisingly argue that they are empowering people like Sesophio by 'valuing' his knowledge and giving him a 'voice', rather than exploiting Sesophio's lack of knowledge about climate change and the fears and concerns generated by his marginal existence.

Western advocates are more than happy to find their own views mirrored by African villagers. For example, John Donnelly at the *Boston Globe*, found that in the remotest villages of Somalia, village elders – like 70-year-old Habiba Hassan, who he interviewed, trudging from a failed field of sorghum toward her village of Beniday, 6 miles away – knew the reasons for the crop failure: 'She said everyone in her village knew the reason for the drought. "It's global warming", she said, adding that villagers had learned much about the potential effects from climate change from radio programs aired on BBC's daily Somali service' (Donnelly 2006). Views gleaned from the BBC, from hand-cranked radios, are then recycled as 'African voices' and prominently profiled in NGO reports and the Western media (see NEF 2006: 9; Lean 2006). The focus, on the 'real lives' of the poorest and most marginalized African communities has gone along with the problematization of autonomy and the individual choices made by the African poor. The NGO Working Group suggests that the problems of African development lie with the survival strategies of the most marginalized in African society:

> To survive the droughts, people have had to resort to practices that damage their dignity and security, their long-term livelihoods, and their environment, including large-scale charcoal production that intensifies deforestation, fighting over water and pastures, selling livestock and dropping out of school.
>
> (NEF 2006: 10)

The dominant view is that poor institutional frameworks have led individuals to make the wrong choices with regards to climate change and that this lack of capacity for adaptation or resilience, rather than underdevelopment per se, is responsible for poverty. This perspective results in an outlook that tends to blame local survival strategies, such as cutting down trees to make some money from selling charcoal. When these views are reflected back to western advocates, African poor reflect western views that they are part of the problem:

> In nearby Goobato, a village with no cars, no motorcycles, no bicycles, no generators, no televisions, no mobile phones, and dozens of $5 radios, Nour, the village elder, said increased temperatures bake the soil . . . Nour also said villagers share the blame: 'We cut trees just to survive, but we are part of the problem.'
>
> (Donnelly 2006)

The strategy of adaptation and promoting resilience, tends to problematize African survival strategies because, by talking-up isolated positive examples of adaptation under international aid, it inevitably problematizes the real life choices and decisions which African poor have to make. The 'adaptation agenda' allows western governments, international institutions and international NGOs to claim they are doing something positive to address the impact of global warming but the result is that the African poor are problematized as responsible for their own problems. 'Learning from the poor', 'empowering the poor' and strategies to increase their 'resilience', end up patronizing Africa's poor and supporting an anti-development agenda which would consign Africa to a future of poverty and climate dependency.

Conclusion

The discursive framing of development and autonomy, within the international statebuilding paradigm, is that of understanding social and economic problems, most sharply posed by the problems of subsistence agriculture in sub-Saharan Africa, as those of individual lifestyle choices. The framework of engagement is not to see the lack of development as a problem but the institutional frameworks in which these lifestyle choices are made. 'Development as freedom' understands the problems of a lack of development, most clearly highlighted in the dependence on climate stability in sub-Saharan Africa, in terms of the freedom of the individual to make the right choices in response to the external environment. Rather than push for material development, the statebuilding paradigm of 'development as freedom' suggests that the solution lies with the empowerment of individuals and communities and that therefore it is their lack of agency or inability to make the right autonomous choices that is the problem which external statebuilding intervention needs to address. In this respect, the current framing of development solutions seems little different from that of the pre-development, colonial period – discussed at the start of this chapter – where Britain's mission was not 'to alleviate Irish distress but to civilize her people' (Sen 1999: 174).

Development is a good example of the way socio-political questions are recast in the form of individual choices and decisions in the post-liberal paradigm. In this framing, the problem is not that of socio-economic relations at a global or national level but that of providing agency for the most vulnerable or marginalized individuals, through empowering them or unblocking their capacities. The problems of poverty and marginalization then top the development agenda; but not as an indictment of the economic and social system which produces them. In fact, it is the opposite: the fact that western states are held to have overcome problems of development is held to reflect their capacity for institutional learning and the internationalization of underdevelopment is then seen to reflect the care and concern felt around these issues. Once autonomy is seen to be the cause of underdevelopment, development becomes no longer an issue of western defensiveness but expresses a new moral agenda of promoting African 'agency' and 'responsibility'.

8 Race, culture and civil society

Statebuilding and the privileging of difference

Introduction

This chapter seeks to draw out an understanding of the role of narratives and discourses of race, culture and civil society, within the paradigm of international statebuilding, through the location of the discourse of culture as a transitional stage between interventionist and regulatory discourses of race and civil society. It particularly seeks to highlight that the discourse of culture is key to understanding the post-liberal paradigm of international statebuilding intervention and policy regulation as it has become cohered over the last decade. This is all the more important as the discourse of culture has in many respects been displaced by the discourse of civil society. In drawing out the links between the framings of race, culture and civil society, this chapter seeks to explain how the discourse of civil society intervention has been reinvented on the basis of the moral divide established and cohered through the discourse of culture and how the discourse of civil society contains a strong apologetic content, capable of legitimizing and explaining the persistence of social and economic problems or political fragmentation while simultaneously offering statebuilding policy programmes on the basis of highly ambitious goals of social transformation.

In the policy framings of international statebuilding, the concept of civil society is used very differently to how the concept was deployed in traditional political discourses of liberal modernity. This chapter will clarify some of these differences and highlight that, whereas for traditional liberal conceptions of civil society, autonomy was seen as a positive factor, in the international statebuilding discourse, autonomy is seen as a problematic factor and one which necessitates regulatory intervention. Civil society discourse highlights the problematic nature of autonomy, understood as irreducible differences which risk conflict if not regulated via the correct institutional mechanisms. In the distinctive use of difference in this context of external engagement, the concept of civil society is used in ways which reflect and draw upon pre-modern concepts of difference, especially the pre-existing colonial and post-colonial discourses of race and culture. The way in which civil society relates to earlier framings of race and especially of cultural distinctions will be a central part of the following analysis.

Civil society will be understood less as a really existing set of institutions and practices or as a sphere of policy intervention, than as a discursive framework capable of producing meaning, i.e. as a policy paradigm through which the problems (and solutions) of statebuilding intervention are interpreted. In this respect, civil society is the third of a series of interconnected and overlapping policy paradigms through which western engagement and intervention in the colonial and post-colonial state has been negotiated and reflected. The first paradigmatic framing was that of race, in which the hierarchical division of the world was given a natural basis. As this framework of division was questioned and problematized, race was gradually displaced by the paradigm of culture as a prism through which the divide between the west and the post-colonial world could be understood in moral and psychological terms, initially reflecting the desire to perpetuate colonial power through the emphasis upon the incapacity of the non-western other and gradually shifting to explain the limits to post-colonial aspirations to equality on this basis. After 1989, this cultural paradigm served to give a moral framing for the problems and inequalities of post-communist transition and to justify exceptions to the norms of sovereign equality and non-intervention.

The cultural paradigm established a moral divide between formally equal polities in the west and in the post-colonial world, suggesting that the political subject of non-western orders was less capable of exercising autonomy in a rational and stable manner. This problematization of the post-colonial subject and moral framing of difference was reproduced in the paradigm of civil society, which reproduced the apologia of essentialized differences at the same time as understanding irrational or sub-optimal social, economic or political outcomes on the basis of rational choices made by autonomous subjects. The civil society framework views post-colonial societies from the standpoint of self-governing individuals (as in the liberal-democratic model) rather than as submerged and subjugated by collectivities of race, nation or religion (as in the framings of race and culture) and, to this extent, may appear to be more progressive. However, this would be misleading as the shift from a collective or communitarian model of culture to the paradigm of civil society individualism reshapes the problematic of external intervention and statebuilding in ways which extend the ethical duties of international statebuilders on the basis of the moral and civilizational divide between the west and the post-colonial or post-conflict other.

In the civil society approach of the post-liberal statebuilding paradigm, the hierarchical views of race and cultural difference are reproduced but through the focus on the autonomy and rationality of the post-colonial subject rather than through the focus on their alleged lack of rationality or lack of autonomy. This emphasis on the autonomy of the subject of statebuilding intervention presents external intervention as an act of empowerment or of capacity-building, consciously disavowing colonial discourses of fixed distinctions of superiority. We will now proceed to deconstruct the civil society paradigm to demonstrate, first, the reproduction of the moral and civilizational divides of the paradigms of race and culture and, second, the reproduction of the apologetic intent of these previous discourses of understanding, shifting the focus from racial or cultural framings of incapacity to the institutional frameworks alleged to hold back developmental possibilities.

The ideology of race

Colonial discourses of external intervention and regulation of non-western societies were premised on the idea of racial difference. With the development and modernization of western societies, distinctions with the rest of the world were increasingly posed in racial terms. The discourse of race reflected the power inequalities at play in external intervention, which was legitimized on the basis of what were understood to be inherent differences. The initial legitimacy for empire or colonialism was that the subject peoples, denied political equality, were racially distinct. The distinctions of race were held to legitimize the denial of equality and the direct domination of peoples on the basis of their incapacities. In the words of Kipling's 'White Man's Burden', the subject races were held to be 'half man, half child' and therefore incapable of self-government.

The ideology of race was used to justify differences in political rights of self-government and to legitimize external rule. Racial discourse developed and was used to posit the inequality of humanity as a natural fact. While some races were capable of self-government or of political autonomy, other races were not and therefore were destined to subordination. Initially, the ideology of race developed independently of the question of colour or ethnicity and was dependent upon the linking of economic and social inequality with gradations of political and social capacity, naturalizing inequality. In the response to the Enlightenment demands of universality and the French Revolution, which attempted to transform these demands into a framework of government, the conservative reaction was articulated in terms of race, as a defense of the hereditary claims of the aristocracy (Malik 1996). As Kenan Malik notes, the radical Enlightenment claim to universal equality was the precondition for the defensive and apologetic discourse of natural (racial) difference (Malik 1996: 42).

The question of race was intimately tied to the right to rule from its emergence. As long as the right to rule was a restrictive one, race played a central role in justifying political inequality as natural and inevitable. Over the course of the twentieth century, the denial of political equality on the naturalized terms of race was increasingly discredited, especially in the wake of the genocidal racial experiment of the Nazi regime and the weakening of the major European colonial powers through the two world wars (Furedi 1998). The post-Second World War order was one in which race could no longer play the role of apology for difference and inequality, nor could it provide legitimacy for colonial rule or the revival of interventionist policy-making in the post-1989 period.

The differentiation of culture

While race was discredited in the experiences of the mid-twentieth century, the inequalities of the international sphere were not overcome. In many ways, the arguments of racial distinction were taken over through the replacement of the concept of race by the concept of culture. The discourses of race had little to do with the physical characteristics of skin colour or appearance but with apologia for political and social inequality (Malik 1996). This discourse of apology in the essentialization or reification of difference took the form of discourses of cultural difference. Cultural differences were given the same determining weight as earlier distinctions of race on the basis that cultures were separate, homogeneous and with their own paths of development. Path dependencies were key to understanding culture in reified terms of dependency upon the past rather than as reflective of the social relations of the present. The hold of the past over the present thereby enabled a moral rather than a racial critique of the capacity of the colonial (and post-colonial) other.

Views of cultural difference were developed less in reaction to the colonies than as a projection of Anglo-American social sciences, which viewed the rise of mass participation as a threat to 'civilized' values and a danger to liberal democracy. This perspective was highlighted in elite theorizing, such as Gustave Le Bon's work on crowd psychology and Walter Lippman's 1922 study *Public Opinion* which warned that a large proportion of the electorate were 'mentally children or barbarians' and would be easily manipulated (Furedi 1994a: 112–13). The key point was that the masses of the United States and Europe were not ready for democracy as they were not cultured or rational enough to understand their own or the public interest and could easily fall prey to the irrational demands of demagogues.

This elitist view of the incapacity of the masses and a moral and cultural framing for understanding their 'irrational' demands and responses was easily transferred to the colonies and used as a framework for understanding and delegitimizing anti-colonial protest. As Edward Said noted in *Orientalism*, social and political movements of non-Western societies were interpreted in cultural rather than political terms by colonial theorists (1985). These interpretations always highlighted the psychological and non-rational underpinnings of demands and protests, which were seen to express the hold of tradition or the need to express identity, often in reaction to the civilizing impact of the colonial project (Said 1985: 236).

This moral critique of the non-western subject was based upon a culturalized framing of the subject as less rational than the liberal rights-subject of western democracy. Culture played an important role as apologia for colonial power and the limits to which colonial authorities were able to marginalize resistance to their rule. In this context, opposition was understood to be the product of a clash of cultures rather than a product of colonial frameworks of domination. This understanding of a clash of cultures took its sharpest form in the theorization of the problems of 'transition' or of 'hybridity' as an inevitable consequence of western influence.

Hybridity was seen to be a problematic consequence of colonial influence undermining traditional forms of social relations without establishing the basis for the widespread acceptance of western norms and values. Instead, the clash of cultures was seen to result in a 'spiritual', 'moral' or 'cultural' vacuum (Furedi 1994a: 123). Colonial intervention had resulted in the dilemma or contradiction of creating a maladjusted society, lacking the stability of either traditional society or of modern society. It was in the discourses of imperial apologia in the late 1940s that much of the post-liberal statebuilding framing of transition (in the 1990s) and hybridity (in the 2000s) have their intellectual roots.

One of the key concepts denoting the problematic nature of this clash of cultures was that of 'marginal man': the product of both colonial intervention and traditional culture, but a hybrid product, inhabiting neither culture but exhibiting the problems of this cultural clash. The theory of marginal man was first explored by Robert Ezra Park, one of the leading American sociologists in the interwar years and a former President of the American Sociological Society (Furedi 1994b: 52–53). Park explicitly raised questions about the moral integrity of the marginal man, developing the notion that an individual suspended between two cultural realities is marginal, resulting in difficulties in establishing a stable identity. Park's work was based on urban sociological study of the integration of immigrants while at the University of Chicago. His work on the problems of hybridity was more fully developed, in the colonial context, by his student Everett Stonequist, who explained different reactions to colonial domination as the product of maladjustment (Stonequist 1961).

The crisis of colonial rule was apologetically reinterpreted in terms of the psychological problems of the colonial subject and challenges and opposition to this rule were framed in terms of the maladjusted individual pursuing petty egotistic goals rather than political convictions or ideals. It seemed that colonial societies were doomed to be permanently stuck in transition due to the dilemmas of the cultural clash of the colonial experience and the hybrid consequences, which meant that societies lacked the moral and civilization ties necessary for a transition to autonomy and self-government. Marginal societies were held to lack the necessary civic culture and public values and those who sought to replace the colonial rulers were held to lack legitimate political and public aspirations, being driven instead by petty objectives of power and personal grandeur; their social and political weight being explained through their ability to have a demagogic influence over the gullible masses.

Where the discourse of race expressed the confidence of imperial rule and the essentializing of difference, the discourse of culture expressed the decline of the imperial project and a defence against the shifting international norms which expressed more sympathy for the claims of the colonial subject. The elitist assumptions of western superiority were no longer reproduced in the discourse of race, but those of the psychological problems of (post-)colonial transition and of cultural hybridity: these moral, psychological and cultural frameworks reflected the shift from naturalizing and legitimizing external rule to ways of negotiating imperial withdrawal, suggesting that the limited progress made to democracy and self-government and in terms of economic and social progress could be explained through the path-dependencies of culture and the irrational outcomes of the cultural clash between the liberal west and the traditional values and beliefs of the colonial other. This discourse of culture as apologia can be drawn out in relation to the three key themes of what we have described in this book as the post-liberal statebuilding paradigm: development, conflict and democracy.

Culture and development

In the post-1945 world, the international agenda was dominated by decolonization and while the concept of culture played a similar role to that of race, the questions of controversy were less those of rule and the justifications for political inequality, than those of economic and wealth division between the former colonial powers and the post-colonial world. By the 1970s and the end of the post-war economic boom of European reconstruction, the economic and social divisions between the 'developed' and the 'developing' world had become greater and were the subject of a number of critiques which understood the problem to be that of the world market system which reproduced the inequalities of power and opportunity despite the formal equalities of the international state system (for example, Wallerstein 1976; Gunder Frank 1967).

As discussed in earlier chapters, the framework of institutionalism entered international relations through political economy, as a direct apologetic defence of the status quo, asserting that, rather than capitalism, culture was the key to understanding developmental inequalities. Douglass North tackled the critics of underdevelopment directly through the assertion that there was no such thing as the logic of capitalism but rather many capitalisms, dependent on their institutional and cultural context (North 1990; see also, Foucault 2008: 164–65). The important point to highlight is that culture came to the fore as an explanatory concept with increasing disillusionment with the extent of economic and social progress in the post-colonial world. The shift from economic and social explanations to the realm of the cultural reflected the lowering of policy horizons, as culture operated as a limiting factor for international intervention. For North, there was little that international intervention could do as even institutional reform at the level of state policy would only have a limited impact unless the informal values and norms of post-colonial societies were in line with these policy goals. There was therefore little that could be done to externally assist post-colonial development as 'informal constraints that are culturally derived will not change immediately in reaction to changes in formal rules' and it was this 'tension between altered formal rules and the persisting informal constraints' which was held to produce counterproductive outcomes (North 1990: 45).

Culture, conflict and democracy

During the Cold War, the problems of the post-colonial world were framed defensively in an attempt to exculpate the colonial powers and explain the reproduction and institutionalization of inequalities independently of the impact of the workings of the world market. This culturalized framing of difference and inequality was given greater weight in the first decade after the end of the Cold War, as the end of super-power rivalry opened up the post-colonial world to more extensive international intervention.

Culture was a vital framing justifying new approaches to intervention in the 1990s. However, culture operated as a way of legitimizing intervention, in an international context where traditional views of sovereignty and non-intervention were formally dominant, rather than as a comprehensive framework for international engagement in the paradigm of international statebuilding. In this respect, culture already appeared to be a limiting framing in the 1990s. Perhaps the best examples of 1990s discussions of the role of cultural difference can be seen in Mary Kaldor's conception of 'new wars' and Francis Fukuyama's views of the role of culture in relation to civil society in democratic transitions. Here we see culture play the role of legitimizing external international engagement but also limiting it.

New wars

Kaldor developed the concept of new wars to describe conflicts in the post-colonial world in ways which constructed a moral divide between the understanding of war and conflict in the west and in the post-colonial world. The binary of old and new war has little to do with the spatial framing of conflict as intra-state rather than inter-state, for example, the US or Spanish civil wars would be construed as old wars rather than new wars (Kaldor 1999: 13–30). Following Kalevi Holsti's analysis of 'wars of the third kind' (Holsti 1996: 19–40), Kaldor drew a moral distinction where old wars were rational, constitutive of a collective or public interest, and politically legitimate, whereas new wars were understood to be irrational, driven by private interest and politically illegitimate. This moral divide then enabled Kaldor to argue that illegitimate political representatives had no right to hide behind the rights of sovereignty and that external humanitarian intervention was morally necessary and legitimate, casting international interveners as interest-free enforcers of emerging international legal norms rather than as undermining international law.

This understanding of a cultural and moral divide discursively facilitated and reflected the shifting practices of external intervention, recasting the rights of sovereignty as conditional upon external judgement. However, while the cultural, moral divide of the new wars thesis legitimized intervention it provided little in the way of a policy framework. The fact that the cultural divide depended on assertions of incapacity and irrationality was a limiting factor as it either invited intervention with little possibility of exit or it invited a non-interventionist policy on the basis that little could be done to prevent such atavistic and irrational behaviour. In fact, the statebuilding paradigm of extended and holistic intervention and prevention emerged in response to the either/or of the liberal framing of interventionist debates in the 1990s (see also, Chapter 6).

Culture and transition

As with Kaldor's analysis of new wars so Francis Fukuyama's view of the centrality of culture for democratic transition is also a perspective which relates to the specific policy practices of the 1990s. Like Kaldor, Fukuyama uses a culture paradigm to explain the limits to democratic transition and the restrictive nature of international recognition and institutional integration, suggesting that those former Soviet states which were not being engaged with (such as Belarus, Ukraine and Russia) lacked the cultural preconditions for transition. In calling for a lowering of expectations about the speed and extent of post-communist reform, he advocated an apologia based on the problem of underestimating the cultural gap:

. . . social engineering on the level of institutions has hit a massive brick wall: experiences of the past century have taught most democracies that ambitious rearrangements of institutions often cause more unanticipated problems than they solve. By contrast, the real difficulties affecting the quality of life in modern democracies have to do with the social and cultural pathologies that seem safely beyond the reach of institutional solutions, and hence of public policy. The chief issue is quickly becoming one of culture.

(Fukuyama 1995: 9)

For Fukuyama, civil society was lacking in many post-totalitarian societies, making assumptions of stable political transition problematic. Here civil society discourse was one of moral division, legitimizing exclusion from western structures, rather than one of extensive and preventive intervention. In this context, the lack of capacity for civil society was emphasized. Fukuyama stressed that while civil society may be a precondition for democratic transition, 'civil society in turn has precursors and preconditions at the level of culture' (1995: 7). For Fukuyama, the understandings needed to explain the slowness of cultural change required the expertise of sociologists and anthropologists rather than political theorists, who worked on the assumptions of classical liberalism (1995: 7).

The reinvention of civil society

Culture played a similar role to race in essentializing difference during the Cold War and early 1990s, in that it acted mainly as apologia and as a framework for policy-making intervention only by demarcating exceptions. Central to the continuity of discourses of race and culture and those of the more extensive interventionist frameworks of international statebuilding is the privileging of difference over universality. The coherent nature of the post-liberal paradigm of international statebuilding is dependent upon the dismissal of universal social, economic or political frameworks of understanding (central to the liberal tradition). The precondition for the reinvention of civil society as both explanatory factor and as a sphere of policy-making has been the understanding of the problems of post-colonial or post-conflict society as products of difference, located within the historic path-dependencies of social structures and institutions: there is no universalizing logic within which we can understand the actions and political expressions of these societies within the same framework as those of the western liberal-democratic subject, held to be capable of rational political and economic choices.

The key to understanding the role of the concept of civil society in the framework of international statebuilding is in how post-colonial or post-conflict societies come to be understood as open to manipulation or change through policy-intervention. In fact, the institution-building at the heart of international statebuilding is focused on a reframing of traditional liberal democratic conceptions of civil society rather than any shift in the formal understanding of the operation of state-level institutions. For this reason it is important to spend a little time on what is described here as the post-liberal framing of civil society and the governance framing of policy objectives which accompanies it (see also, Chapter 4).

The first point to establish is that the shift from cultural framings of the problems of colonial and post-colonial societies to a civil society framing operates on two levels: that of ideas or understanding, the comprehension of the nature of the problems themselves; and the practical or policy level, the kinds of external policy responses which might be appropriate to address these problems. On both these levels, it would be wrong to understand the civil society framing of problems or policy interventions as being narrowly focused upon something which we might seek to describe as civil society as a real sphere or set of relations. Foucault's work on biopolitics usefully draws our attention to the transformation of civil society framings as both ideational (operating as a 'network' or 'grid' of 'intelligibility', i.e. as a way of understanding the problematic of post-colonial or post-conflict society) and as facilitating a set of practices, making possible a series of policy interventions, which follow from civil society becoming a sphere of statebuilding intervention (becoming 'governmentalizable') (Foucault 2008: 252).

The second point, which Foucault also draws our attention to, is that this framing of civil society depends upon inverting or transforming the classical liberal doctrine of civil society as a sphere in which the autonomous subject interacts with positive outcomes. For Enlightenment theorists, civil society was conceived in political and juridical terms, as Foucault notes, 'civil society is absolutely indistinguishable from political society', for example, in classic liberal framings, such as John Locke's *Second Treatise of Government* (Foucault 2008: 297). This view of the rights-bearing autonomous subject of civil society is also clear in the classical treatment in Adam Ferguson's *Essay on the History of Civil Society* which conceives civil society as the political reflection of Adam Smith's economic analysis, in which the autonomous interaction of rational interest-bearing individuals results in the collective development of the social good.

The foundational basis of the classical rights-based liberal framing of civil society is the autonomous interaction of subjects free from governing intervention. The rights- and interest-bearing subject of liberal theorizing exists prior to the institutions of government and civil society is understood to be grounded in human nature as an indispensable and constant factor of human existence (Foucault 2008: 298–99). The difference between civil society and political society is not in the subjects comprising it but the lack of a formal contract establishing or constituting sovereignty, the reciprocal relations are the basis of market relations and liberal-democratic forms of political-legal relations but exist independently and prior to these.

The subject of civil society – the autonomous rational individual – is the foundational subject of both halves of the liberal equation of government: the subject of both rights and interests. With regard to both, the individual subject's pursuit of self-interest coincides with the collective good as interests converge either through the market mechanism or through the reasoned debate of the political sphere. The liberal subject is not open to government intervention, but rather, establishes the rationality of laissez-faire (Foucault 2008: 270). This subject is very different from the statebuilding conception of the post-colonial or post-conflict subject who is assumed to be unable to pursue their interests or rights in a civic way, which contributes to the collective good of society. In this framing, the problems of post-conflict or post-colonial societies are understood as problems with the frameworks or institutional contexts of these societies, as reflected in the choices made by individuals. This enables these choices to become understood as being amenable to policy intervention.

The third crucial point to highlight is that the policy interventions which can impact on these choices do not necessarily have to be restricted to the narrow sphere of what might be described as civil society in 'reality'. In the civil society paradigm of international statebuilding, international policy practices assume that the rational choices made by post-colonial and post-conflict subjects are irrational due to the institutional context and that this institutional context can be reformed in specific ways to facilitate the making of different choices. In this way, the divisive context of policy-making hierarchies can be legitimized (as in racial and cultural understandings) but the problem of the autonomy of the post-colonial subject is brought to the fore. In the civil society approach there is no assumption that external interveners can make policies on behalf of the post-conflict subject.

The task of international statebuilding intervention, in this paradigm of understanding, is that of the indirect influencing of outcomes through institutional means. The framework of civil society enables management at a distance, where intervention is understood as necessary but never as sufficient, as the post-colonial subject is the means and end of intervention. Civil society will only have been achieved when this subject makes the 'right' or 'civil' choices revealing a rationality and maturity with regard to collective interests. The task of international intervention is to help facilitate this through policy intervention at the level of institutional frameworks, facilitating the compatibility of individual choices with collective outcomes.

Civil society becomes central to the international statebuilding paradigm of understanding only when the classical liberal framing is transformed: when civil society becomes a sphere of external or international policy-intervention rather than an unproblematic sphere of autonomy, as under rationalist framings of the liberal polity. Civil society becomes a way of understanding social problems and policy interventions on the basis of reconceiving cultural discourses which understood problems as deeply rooted and not amenable to policy intervention. In fact, policy intervention only becomes possible with the expansion of civil society as a framework for understanding and managing social problems. By removing civil society from the political-juridical framing of rights-based liberalism it opens up 'a new object, a new domain or field' for policy intervention (Foucault 2008: 295) on the basis of which post-colonial and post-conflict society can become the object of policy.

Foucault points towards how civil society is transformed. Whereas cultural understandings (as racial framings before them) understood social problems as being the product of collective identification and belonging, the civil society framework privileges the individual and understands social outcomes as the products of individual choices. These choices are understood to be rational in so far as they can be understood as non-arbitrary responses to institutional contexts in which the individual finds themselves. Civil society becomes the mediating link in which individuals respond to 'environmental variables' (Foucault 2008: 269). Methodologically, the shift from the collective of race, ethnicity or culture, to the privileging of the individual (see also, Chapter 7), enables civil society to be formulated as a sphere of intervention.

The statebuilding policy framework depends on the relationship between the state and society being inversed. Rather than society being natural and the state as the product of societal relations, the state is prior and society and social relations are seen to be the product of state-shaped institutions at both formal and informal levels. In this way, society (of interest-pursuing individuals) is held to be highly malleable. This malleability is based upon viewing social and political outcomes from the viewpoint of individual choices. As Foucault notes, in the shift from culture to civil society 'we move over to the side of the individual subject' but not as the subject of rights but as an object open to policy interventions (2008: 252).

Civil society and conflict

The transformation of cultural framings of conflict in post-colonial or post-conflict societies into civil society framings can be highlighted through a comparison of Kaldor's 1990s new wars thesis with the 'greed and grievance' framework developed by Paul Collier and Anke Hoeffler in the mid-2000s (Collier and Hoeffler 2004; Collier *et al.* 2006). It could be argued that the intention of the Collier thesis is little different from Kaldor's: that of morally delegitimizing political actors in contexts of post-colonial conflict, however, Collier's reconstruction of conflict, in the rational choice framework of institutionalist approaches, facilitates a much broader or holistic range of policy interventions than does Kaldor's.

Rather than morally distinguishing the post-colonial context from that of the west, making it seem merely 'irrational' or 'backward', the rational choice framing of Collier seeks to develop an understanding of post-colonial societies in the universalist terms of economic frameworks of individual choices. In their critique of theorists who sought to understand conflict in the rational terms of political rights (struggles over grievances), Collier and his Oxford University-based team sought to understand conflict in terms of individual economic interests. In this framing, grievance no longer becomes an explanatory or a legitimating factor; it is the opportunity for rebellion that has explanatory value. Essentially, if finance is easily available (for example, due to easy access to primary commodity exports) and there is little opportunity cost (i.e. few other avenues to earn income, if access to secondary education is low and the economy is stagnant) then conflict 'entrepreneurs' will arise who do not necessarily have any stake in furthering the interests or needs of their alleged constituents (Collier and Hoeffler 2004).

Conflict is entirely removed from the political-juridical framing of modern liberal understandings. For Collier's project: 'where rebellion is feasible, it will occur without any special inducements in terms of motivation' (Collier *et al.* 2006: 19); 'motivation is indeterminate, being supplied by whatever agenda happens to be adopted by the first social entrepreneur to occupy the viable niche' (2006: 20). Once conflict is understood as the product of the choices of individuals, within an economic (rather than a political) framework of understanding, the possibility of reshaping the institutional context, and therefore the outcome of decision-making, arises. This approach of indirectly influencing the conduct of individuals on the basis of this shift from a rights-based to an economic or rational-choice framework of understanding is the civil society approach which has displaced cultural framings within the policy-practices of international statebuilding.

To reiterate, the civil society framework can best be understood as an ideational paradigm or discourse, facilitating a certain 'governmental rationality'. This perspective is rather different than those which have a narrower focus on civil society as a reality. Intervention in the narrower field of civil society is just one set of policy interventions within this framework and often is not the most important. For example, in the work of Collier and his team, who have been highly influential in the policy developments of the World Bank, this civil society framing leads to a range of policy interventions, of which work in and upon civil society itself is not necessarily the key concern. Bearing in mind the framework of opportunities, rather than political or ideological concerns, policy is organized around modifying institutional frameworks in ways which seek to minimize the opportunities and raise the costs of rebellion. Such policies might include: the development of international regulatory institutions concerning the trade in primary goods, preventing rebel groups having easy access to world markets; the sharing of sovereignty or international institutional control of income sources to prevent state capture being the source of aggrandizement; policies which prevent barriers to job creation or educational opportunities, thus raising the opportunity costs of engagement in rebel activities; external support to enhance the capacity of the state military to more easily deter rebel movements, etc.

Civil society and the problem of autonomy

This framing of civil society intervention can be understood within the post-liberal paradigm of international intervention and good governance as the precondition for a broad range of policy intervention through the perpetuation of a cultural and moral distinction between the post-colonial subject and the liberal-democratic subject of the west. This distinction presupposes that the rationalist assumptions made with regard to the liberal-democratic subject do not hold in the post-colonial context of statebuilding interventions. The assumption is that the autonomous operation of civil society is problematic rather than positive. Whereas the liberal-democratic tradition argues that social conflicts can be resolved through rational deliberation and societal engagement, the post-liberal paradigm does not assume that conflicts within civil society can be resolved through democratic processes and therefore opens up the sphere of civil society to policy intervention in order to structure institutional frameworks which can contain conflicts.

This active, interventionist approach to civil society argues that external intervention by government or external actors is necessary to challenge or disrupt irrational or counterproductive forms of political identification through institutional modification to multiply frames of political identification. In this respect, interventionist civil society policy has become central to international statebuilding as a framework in which political and social collectivities are understood and engaged with as products of irrational mindsets shaped by institutional legacies of the past but nevertheless as potentially open to transformation. In this framing, civil society intervention is often presented as a way of challenging criminal, ethnic, regional, or nationalist conceptions of political identity and providing a policy framework through which these identifications can be substituted with a variety of alternative identifications, such as those of women, youth, unemployed, small businesses and so forth; the precondition being that these alternative identities transgress and cross-cut those which are considered to be irrational and problematic. This multiplication of political identities is then held to pluralize the political process, with barriers to progress in statebuilding goals overcome through the means of civil society intervention.

As Audra Mitchell and Stephanie Kappler highlight, this post-liberal framing of civil society as a sphere of policy intervention, draws upon internal western discourses critiquing liberal rationalist approaches (much as earlier colonial discourses drew upon internal western elite concerns) (Mitchell and Kappler 2009). Concerns with difference and the inability of the liberal-democratic process to overcome particularist and conflicting identities have been expressed clearly by critics of the rationalist assumptions of modern framings of the political. Perhaps, most influential in this respect have been agonistic frameworks which suggest that conflict is inevitable and that differences are irreconcilable through liberal democratic frameworks (Honig 1993) but that conflict can be accommodated and transformed through civil society intervention with the goal of multiplying political identifications. This has been expressed by, for example, William Connolly, in terms of the development of 'agonistic respect' (Connolly 2002), or by Chantal Mouffe, through reviving the left/right distinction (Mouffe 2005). The key point about the agonistic critique of rationalist approaches to democracy is that civil society becomes problematized as a sphere of irreconcilable difference at the same time as it becomes transformed into a sphere of policy intervention. Transferred to the sphere of international intervention, in the statebuilding policy framework, a whole set of policy practices open up, based upon the thesis that – through engaging with and transforming uncivil post-colonial or post-conflict societies – irrational antagonistic conflict can be transformed into rational agonistic contestation. Through institutionalist practices, external intervention is held to be able to build or constitute civil societies as a basis upon which the problems of societal development, inclusion and security can be resolved.

As noted earlier, with regard to the moral or cultural understanding of the problem of post-colonial society, the starting assumption is that civil society lacks the rational or civic qualities of civil society in the west. The focus of policy analysts is on group, ethnic, religious or regional identifications which are understood to be products of the past or path-dependencies of conflict, or colonial or Soviet rule. Civil society is understood to be hybrid, in the sense of reflecting the divisions or traditions of society but as open to intervention and transformation through informal institutional change (change of the norms and values of society). The statebuilding discourse of civil society intervention is therefore quite distinct from liberal framings of the 1980s and early 1990s, where writers and commentators tended to juxtapose civil society as a sphere of pristine values and civic norms vis-à-vis the sphere of formal politics and state power which was seen to be self-seeking and exclusionary. Civil society as a sphere of external statebuilding intervention is necessarily hybrid and the field of both strategic calculation and tactical engagement; as a leading policy authority states:

> Strategically, the promotion of civil society cannot occur in a platitudinous fashion that sees all civil society as an inherent good for peace and democratization. Quite the contrary, there needs to be a sharp strategy of differentiation in civil society promotion by which international donors are quite discriminating in identifying three types of non-state actors to support: those that cross-cut identity lines or fissures of conflict . . ., those that are moderate but reflecting primarily one perspective or protagonist social group, and those that are more extreme but which, through coaxing and inclusion, can become moderate . . .
>
> (Sisk 2008: 255)

In the statebuilding literature, the goal of external intervention is to transform civil society forms of voluntary association from existing and divisive forms (of bonding social capital) to pluralist and inclusivist forms (of bridging social capital) (Putnam 2000). The clash of cultures, in the self-understanding of international statebuilders, is played out in the policy interventions which attempt to transform traditional (non)civil society into a civic polity in which social and political divisions are submerged, mitigated or disappear. For this reason, civil society cannot be left to its own devices,

> effective international action requires identifying and working diligently against those civil society groups that are deemed not constructive to peacebuilding aims, either because of their irredeemably extreme nature and positions or because they have other interests or activities . . . that work against progress toward peace or democracy.
>
> (Sisk 2008: 255–56).

Civil society is seen as the sphere capable of generating the solutions to problems of conflict, the barriers to development or to democracy. The focus on civil society rather than social or economic transformation builds on the moral and cultural discourses of the colonial period, with their emphasis upon 'maladjustment' and their psychological framings of social and political questions. The problems are perceived to be in the hold of the past over the minds of post-colonial subjects rather than the social relations of the present. The precondition of civil society intervention is the assumption of the irrationality of the informal institutional frameworks – of the mindsets – of post-colonial subjects.

These irrational mindsets are held to be capable of transformation through policy intervention; it is held that irrational values and identities can be challenged by education and social interaction which encourages the pluralization of political identities. It is for this reason that (in this narrower framing) civil society intervention takes two main forms. First, there is support for 'democracy groups'; NGOs and international bodies, such as the OSCE, engage in policy advocacy or civic education which directly seeks to promote the politics of inclusion and civic principles. Roberto Belloni argues that these groups contribute by:

> . . . stressing the importance of developing multiple civic identities, pluralism, equal opportunity, tolerance, and the government's accountability. They attempt to defend and enlarge spaces for negotiation and compromise – islands of civility and dialogue in a context polarized by mutual fear and mistrust. They strive for inclusion, participation and equal access and place emphasis on the need to negotiate and cooperate in view of building consensus rather than repeating adversarial, zero-sum positions.
>
> (Belloni 2008: 189)

The second group, consisting mainly of internationally-funded NGOs, comprises those actors which, while not directly advocating democracy and civic values, attempt to pluralize political identification on the basis of ascribed identities held to be capable of breaking down primary collective affiliations, such as those of women, youth or small and medium business enterprises. In post-conflict situations, often any framework for engaging people across ethnic or ideological divides is considered productive for changing people's mindsets and breaking them from the hold of dominant and problematic political identities (Chandler 1999: 40).

Apart from being a framework that makes a broad range of policy interventions both possible and legitimate, the discourse of civil society is flexible enough to also offer an understanding of the limits to policy success or to societal transformation (as with the previous discourses of race and culture). As Carothers and Ottaway note, civil society intervention, as a key framing of policy-making, evolved with the extension of statebuilding mandates and goals in response to the perceived failures of democratic transition in the mid-1990s (2000: 7). During the Cold War, there was no discussion of civil society intervention as part of democracy-promotion; intervention was limited to indirect support for economic development or support for moderate political parties against political extremes. There was little support for societal movements which were often seen to be too much under the influence of leftist programmes. The exception was in Eastern Europe where social protest opposed communist rule. The end of the Cold War enabled greater societal intervention as well as associating civil society movements with democratic transition.

Carothers and Ottaway highlight that civil society intervention is intervention on the cheap. Rather than undertaking major projects of economic and social transformation or undertaking major institutional reform at the level of government, which would be seen as hugely expensive and ambitious, civil society intervention claims to address problems of development, conflict and democracy but without an ambitious programme of societal transformation. The actual programmes of civil society support, while ubiquitous as part of every international statebuilding project of international intervention, involve fairly small sums of money (2000: 8). This money is generally allocated to NGOs with tenuous roots with their own societies rather than to social movements. Donors focus on a very narrow set of organizations, usually highly professionalized and relating to the state through advocacy work or engaging in society through civic educational campaigns. The disjunction between the asserted aims of civil society intervention and the limited resources and limited success of this intervention (Ottaway and Carothers 2000) can only be understood by grasping civil society intervention within the statebuilding policy problematic.

Civil society becomes a focal point of international intervention and the statebuilding project because it posits a framework in which international engagement can be legitimized on the basis of the autonomy of the post-colonial subject. Cultural frameworks posit autonomy as problematic and act as apologia for the limited success of external intervention but cannot provide a framework of legitimacy for intervention or for a set of policy prescriptions. In civil society interventions, the autonomy of the post-colonial subject is both apologia and the mechanism and goal of intervention. Intervention in civil society is seen to be the precondition for the autonomy of the subject to be exercised unproblematically, with civil society – harmonious or conflict-free interaction – as the ongoing aim of intervention.

Conclusion

International statebuilding is increasingly operating in a holistic paradigm of preventive intervention and indirect regulation, external intervention not on the basis of overtly controlling states or societies but enabling them to safely manage their autonomy. The discourse of race, which legitimized and reflected the overt inequalities of colonial rule and direct domination, is no longer one that reflects the relationship management of international statebuilding, which presupposes the relationship of formal equality and of autonomy. The discourse of culture which replaced that of race as an essentializing explanation for inequality fits uneasily with the interventionist framework of international statebuilding. The emphasis on differential cultures provided an apologia for economic and social inequalities but little purchase for regulatory intervention. It is only once cultural differences were understood as social constructs that could be shaped and reshaped through institutional intervention that civil society could become a central concept within the international statebuilding policy framework.

The focus upon civil society maintains the role of race or culture in rationalizing difference and inequality, on the basis of distinctive 'path dependencies' created in specific contexts of interaction between states and societies, but also – through positing these differences as the rational choices of the individuals within those societies – opens up society as a sphere of external policy intervention. Civil society enables difference and inequality to be articulated and explained but locates these distinctions as products of the choices of these societies themselves. In taking over a classic liberal concept that depended upon a positive framing of individual autonomy, positing individual decision-making capacity, the statebuilding discourse tends to be much more judgemental and moralistic about drawbacks to policy interventions as the fault of individual and collective 'choices', at the same time as expanding the interventionist policy remit of international statebuilding beyond that made explicable or rational through the framework of cultural or racial division.

9 Conclusion

Introduction

The previous chapters have elucidated the ways in which international state-building can be understood as a paradigm through which the world can be comprehended and policy framed in a certain way. This paradigm, described here as one of post-liberal governance, is drawn out well by Douglass North, in his explanation of how behaviouralist rational choice approaches can become a template for the social sciences:

> Building a theory of institutions on the foundation of individual choices is a step toward reconciling differences between economics and the other social sciences . . . The strength of microeconomic theory is that it is constructed on the basis of assumptions about human behavior . . . Institutions are a creation of human beings. They evolve and are altered by human beings; hence our theory must begin with the individual. At the same time, the constraints that institutions impose on individual choices are pervasive. Integrating individual choices with the constraints institutions impose on choice sets is a major step toward unifying social science research.
>
> (1990: 5)

At first sight, this paradigm may appear to be little different to the classical liberal paradigm which is established on the basis of individual autonomy (decision-making individuals are at the centre). However, the fact that individuals are autonomous decision-makers is, in this paradigm, the central problem and explanatory nexus for differences in outcomes, in terms of security, development and democracy.

Rather than individual autonomy producing the collective good – as in rationalist framings of liberal polities and market societies – and therefore being an unproblematic starting assumption; in the post-liberal framing, stable polities and markets are seen to be merely an ideal which must be constantly striven towards, through removing the institutional blockages which are held to prevent individual autonomy from producing these rational, secure and progressive outcomes. The existence of institutional blockages at both formal and informal institutional levels – is held to explain why reality always diverges from the 'naturalistic', liberal ideal. 'Only when we understand these modifications in the behavior of actors can we make sense out of the existence and structure of institutions and explain the direction of institutional change' (North 1990: 17). The paradigm of post-liberal government seeks to explain and rectify the disjunction between liberal ideal behavioural outcomes and the world that exists, through a study of how institutional frameworks modify and shape human behaviour. International statebuilding only makes sense on the assumption that problems can be addressed through external actors modifying the behaviour of other states and societies through indirect forms of intervention at the level of institutional structures.

In this brief concluding chapter we will summarize the three key aspects that mark out the international statebuilding paradigm as one which can heuristically be described as shaped and cohered by the framework of post-liberal governance. All three of these aspects are interlinked and depend on the transformed view of the human subject at the heart of the post-liberal paradigm. These three aspects have formed the core of the previous chapters and together mark out a coherent, largely accepted, paradigmatic understanding of the world we live in, the way in which we should construct its problems, and the policy frameworks in which these problems might potentially be mitigated: the privileging of difference over universality; the privileging of preventive intervention over autonomy; and the privileging of governance over government.

The privileging of difference over universality

As North states, in his development of the institutionalist approach, which we have described as central to the post-liberal paradigm, the assumptions about the operation of human behaviour – individual autonomy – are very different from those of the classic liberal paradigm. Rather than liberal assumptions of the universal individual – homo œconomicus – the rational pursuer of self-interest, there is instead the privileging of difference:

> [The] traditional behavioral assumptions [that] actors possess cognitive systems that provide *true* models of the worlds about which they make choices or, at the very least, that the actors receive information that leads to convergence of divergent initial models [are] patently wrong . . . Individuals make choices based on subjectively derived models that

diverge among individuals and the information the actors receive is so incomplete that in most cases these divergent subjective models show no tendency to converge.

(North 1990: 17, emphasis in original)

Difference is the starting presumption for post-liberalism, rather than universality. Human behaviour cannot be understood on the basis of a pre-social conception of individuals as rational, autonomous, interest-bearing actors; except as an abstract ideal which differs from concrete reality. The differences between individuals and societies are understood to be the products of their own choices and the institutional frameworks constructed through these choices, which have resulted in irrational or suboptimal outcomes. Difference is privileged above universality as at every level, from the state down to the family and the individual's own mind-set, institutions have modified the liberal assumptions of universal capacities for autonomous, rational, instrumental, goal-directed behaviour. Assumptions about the positive and beneficial nature of autonomy – that the free play of market choices or of choices at the ballot box will lead to collective outcomes which are beneficial to society – thereby cannot be assumed to apply (see also, Chapter 4).

For the institutionalist approach of post-liberal governance, the free play of autonomy has resulted in, and can only result in, the segmentation of difference. Rather than differences being progressively overcome – through the development of the material forces of society, greater participation in the political process, or the equalization of the market – the post-liberal framework argues that liberal universalist or teleological views of progress take as natural that which needs to be constructed and shaped through institutional modification. In this framing, the meta-narratives of liberalism need to be deconstructed to understand the centrality of difference: not the natural or essentialized difference of colonial ideas of race (see Chapter 8), but the contingent and open-ended production and reproduction of difference through human activity and human choices, which shape the institutional frameworks through which we see the world, and necessarily blind us to the possibility of any one 'truth'. The privileging of difference over universality is seen to alert international statebuilders to the dangers of any 'one size fits all' understanding of state–society relations and to caution against any assumption that institutional solutions can just be imported from outside. The most that can be done is the constraining of decision-making autonomy through the rule of law and the gradual experimentation with institutional modification through the framings of good governance.

The 'lessons learned', which can be gleamed from the raft of studies on the practices of intervention and statebuilding, all converge on the need to reject liberal universalist assumptions (see Chapter 2) and to appreciate that international statebuilding can only operate on the basis that differences are understood and adapted to. The methodological starting point of the individual, isolated from a socio-political context, necessarily leads to an understanding of difference which serves as apologia for the status quo. This individual or 'agent-centred' view locates the problems of international society with those who have the least access to global wealth and resources and are held to have blocked themselves from achieving this access, through the conscious choices and decisions of the people and/or their political elites. It is the societies and states being statebuilt that are thereby seen to be the main barriers to the resolution of their problems (see also, Chapter 7). Any resistance to the capacity-building and empowering preventive interventions of the international community, in this framing, can only be conceived as evidence of their lack of capacity and the urgency of interventionist measures (see Chapter 6).

The privileging of preventive intervention over autonomy

The international statebuilding paradigm views autonomy as necessitating intervention, rather than as a barrier to intervention (see also, Chapter 5). This transformed understanding of autonomy – from a sphere of freedom and non-intervention, in the classical liberal paradigm, to a sphere necessitating intervention, in the post-liberal paradigm – has been at the heart of this book. Autonomy, in this framing, is the presupposition of interventionist practices, rather than a policy goal or end product. It is only once we clarify this transformation in the role and understanding of autonomy that the transformed nature of the post-liberal paradigm becomes apparent. As a study of a key issue of international relations, this book has emphasized the impact that this reframing of the problematic of autonomy has had with relation to the conception of sovereignty (for example, in Chapters 3, 5 and 6).

In the traditional rights-based framing of international relations, sovereign status was synonymous with autonomy – self government. A state which lacked formal policy-making autonomy could not be considered to be a sovereign equal. From within the paradigm of international statebuilding, this view of sovereignty has been superseded in policy practice, if not in terms of formal international legal frameworks. The recognition of sovereign equality and rights to equal treatment is increasingly held to be dependent on the voluntary limitation of policy-making autonomy. In the unbundling of sovereignty (considered in Chapter 3) the formal quality of sovereignty as autonomy is held to be the presupposition for external statebuilding intervention to ensure the development of sovereignty as the capacity to accept limits and constraints on autonomy, through binding commitments to international institutions and the acceptance of the prerogatives of good governance.

This framing can be described as post-liberal as the starting assumption is that the autonomy of post-colonial states is potentially problematic for both their citizens and international society as a whole. As considered in Chapter 6, the policy discourse of international security has shifted from discussions of intervention – as a 'reaction' to the problems of failing or weak states, especially in relation to conflict, war crimes and human rights abuses – to a perspective which argues that preventive intervention needs to take place as soon as possible in order to prevent states and societies from making the wrong autonomous choices which are understood to lead to conflict and disintegration. In this framework, unconstrained autonomy – decision-making in institutional frameworks which are not internationalized – risks the possibility of violence and human rights abuse and thereby necessitates external intervention. The starting assumption is that external intervention is necessary as a precondition for social harmony, rather than that intervention is an exception or reaction to the breakdown of social peace.

The privileging of governance over government

In Chapters 4 and 5, we focused on the post-liberal framings of the rule of law and good governance as frameworks in which autonomy was seen to be constrained; governmental or sovereign agency was reconstructed as facilitating or capacity-building subjects, rather than as capable of directing society or bearing more than indirect responsibility for policy outcomes. It is important to understand that this framing of the incapacity of government to know, to control, or direct – central to the discourse of good governance – is as much a framing shaping the self-understanding of western statebuilding policy practice (of leading governments and international institutions) as it is a prescription for how post-colonial states should safely govern themselves.

It is important to see the post-liberal paradigm as a retreat from the aspirations of social and economic transformation which were central to earlier framings legitimizing international intervention (see Chapter 7). This is highlighted in the shift in expectations, as the statebuilding paradigm cohered around post-liberal understandings, in the 2000s. In the 1990s, the post-Second World War examples of the international occupation of Germany and Japan were regularly called upon to justify the interventionist practices of international statebuilding and suggest that long-term engagement and international administrative control could result in rapid transformations towards democracy and economic growth. In the 2000s, the examples of Germany and Japan have been rarely called upon to justify or legitimize the statebuilding project; in fact, they increasingly stand as an embarrassment beside the limited capacities and limited goals claimed by the advocates of international statebuilding today.

The post-liberal paradigm tends, in fact, to reject policy goals and is concerned more with processes of engagement, held to empower the other, enabling them to pursue their goals safely and within a framework of international constraints. In this understanding, external policy-making is concerned with technical and administrative frameworks, in order to facilitate the building of capacity, functionality, resilience and adaptation. These are understood as qualities of governance rather than as specific policy goals or targets. In fact, the essence of the post-liberal paradigm is the understanding that policy goals are not the right process of governing, as their implicit instrumentality will throw up unintended results. There is also the rejection of the idea that development, democracy or security can be goals in themselves rather than the outcomes of good management. This is why previously distinct policy areas, such as rights promotion, development or security, increasingly become merged into one: international statebuilding.

The post-liberal paradigm of international statebuilding is therefore one which is highly flexible. This flexibility also stems from the rejection of the clear lines of authority and accountability explicit in the liberal 'rights-based' paradigm of sovereign state relations, which emphasized the formal nature of political and legal processes. Just as post-colonial states are understood to be incapable of autonomy – of safely attempting to direct or control their own societies – and therefore to stand in need of international statebuilding; so the international statebuilders increasingly understand their own role, not in terms of taking responsibility or of controlling or shaping these societies or of achieving discrete policy-goals, but rather as allowing these states to 'own' their own problems and make their own decisions more safely and securely. This facilitates frameworks of intervention in which political subjects, accountable agents of policy, become increasingly indistinct (as discussed in Chapter 5).

Whereas, in the liberal paradigm, self-interests and collective (or national) interests were the stuff of goal-directed politics, in the post-liberal paradigm, political interests, or the clash of political interests, can only be understood as the product of a poor institutional framework (whether at the level of states or internationally). It is for this reason that the post-liberal framing understands traditional conceptions of ('zero-sum') politics as problematic and therefore in need of constraint. Good governance is privileged over the dangers of government: it is understood that government should not have interests (either sectional interests or those of a collective and distinct polity) which can only get in the way of the administratively conceived tasks of institutional modification. In this framework, the tasks of international statebuilding are understood as those of the export of good governance rather than the tasks of direction or control, which come with direct government in the form of empire. In this way, liberal conceptions of government – of sovereignty and also of the formal denial of sovereignty – are removed from our understandings of the international statebuilding process, which can no longer be understood in the traditional rights-based legal and political terminology of intervention and non-intervention.

Conclusion

The post-liberal paradigm of international statebuilding cannot be understood outside of its own terms of the problematizing of autonomy. It is hard to understand the evolution of this paradigm as a result of the emergence of new 'facts' or as a direct response to greater policy knowledge. There is little evidence that the policy-practices associated with this paradigm are any better at addressing the problems of post-colonial or post-conflict states than those alleged to have failed because of their 'liberal' assumptions of autonomy and self-government. There is little evidence that fragile states do not need economic development and high technological impacts to transform agricultural production and manufacturing, there is similarly little evidence that these states do not need political and policy autonomy to overcome conflict and to establish forward-looking collective projects capable of legitimizing the state and galvanizing society around a collective project.

The emergence of the post-liberal paradigm can only be grasped as a political shift, as reflecting a different subjective conception of the world. This political shift could be understood as being based on the defeat of the post-colonial world's aspirations for autonomy; as being dependent on the defeat of the post-colonial subject. However, the defeat of the post-colonial subject is only part of the explanation for the shifting paradigm of western policy-intervention and the development of the discourse of international statebuilding. The most striking aspect of this discourse is the collapse of confidence of western policy-actors in their own ability to intervene and to shape the world around them. The apologetic content of the discourse highlights the low horizons and low expectations of those who claim the mantle of intervention and their lack of desire to take responsibility for policy-making.

The post-liberal paradigm perhaps can be understood as parasitical on the defeat of the liberal political subject per se, and a phenomenon rooted in the western world rather than the post-colonial one; perhaps even as the last refuge of western elites who appear to lack their own programmes capable of taking society forward. This is a discourse which is self-legitimizing because it is based on the status quo. The lack of progress can be explained as due to the hold of history, expressed in terms of institutional path-dependencies, whereas the future is held to be a closed book which humanity lacks the capacity to shape. This is the paradigm of a world without a subject, where humanity is seen to have lost the capacity to shape and construct its future and the 'lessons' learned are always to be more humble.

References

Abrahamsen, R. (2000) *Disciplining Democracy: Development Discourse and Good Governance in Africa* (London: Zed Books).

Althusser, L. (2005) 'On the Young Marx', in L. Althusser, *For Marx* (London: Verso), pp. 49–86.

Ashdown, P. (2003) 'What Baghdad Can Learn from Bosnia', *Guardian*, 22 April.

—— (2007) 'The European Union and Statebuilding in the Western Balkans', *Journal of Intervention and Statebuilding*, 1:1, pp. 113–15.

Balkanologie (1999) Special issue, 'South-Eastern Europe: History, Concepts, Boundaries', *Balkanologie*, 3:2, pp. 47–127.

Barbara, J. (2008) 'Rethinking Neo-liberal State Building: Building Post-Conflict Development States', *Development in Practice*, 18:3, pp. 307–18.

Barnett, M. (2006) 'Building a Republican Peace: Stabilizing States after War', *International Security*, 30:4, pp. 87–112.

Barnett, M. and Zürcher, C. (2009) 'The Peacebuilder's Contract: How External Statebuilding Reinforces Weak Statehood', in R. Paris and T. Sisk (eds) *The Dilemmas of Statebuilding: Confronting the Contradictions of Postwar Peace Operations* (London: Routledge), pp. 23–52.

Beck, U. (1994) *Risk Society: Towards a New Modernity* (London: Sage).

—— (1997) *The Reinvention of Politics: Rethinking Modernity in the Global Social Order* (Cambridge: Polity).

—— (2005) *Power in the Global Age* (Cambridge: Polity).

Begby, E. and Burgess, P. (2009) 'Human Security and Liberal Peace', *Public Reason*, 1:1, pp. 91–104.

Bellamy, A. (2009) *Responsibility to Protect: The Global Effort to End Mass Atrocities* (London: Polity).

Bellamy, A. and Williams, P. (2008) 'Introduction: Thinking Anew about Peace Operations', in A. Bellamy and P. Williams (eds) *Peace Operations and Global Order* (London: Routledge), pp. 1–15.

Belloni, R. (2008) 'Civil Society in War-to-Democracy Transitions', in A. K. Jarstad and T. D. Sisk (eds) *From War to Democracy: Dilemmas of Peacebuilding* (Cambridge: Cambridge University Press), pp. 182–210.

BH EDI (n.d.) European Partnership for Bosnia and Herzegovina, *Medium Term Priorities Realisation Programme* (Sarajevo: European Directorate for Integration).

Bickerton, C. J. (2005) 'Rebuilding States, Deconstructing Statebuilding'. Paper presented at the SAID workshop, University of Oxford, 28 April.

—— (2007) 'State-building: Exporting State Failure', in C. J. Bickerton, P. Cunliffe and A. Gourevitch (eds) *Politics without Sovereignty* (London: University College Press), pp. 93–111.

—— (2009) 'Europe's Neo-Madisonians: Rethinking the Legitimacy of Limited Power in a Multi-Level Polity'. Unpublished paper.

Brown, G. (2006) 'Our Final Goal Must Be to Offer a Global New Deal', *Guardian*, 11 January.

Buchanan, A. (2007) *Justice, Legitimacy, and Self-Determination: Moral Foundations for International Law* (Oxford: Oxford University Press).

Butterfield, H. (1951) *History and Human Relations* (London: Collins).

Cammack, P. (2002) 'The Mother of All Governments: The World Bank's Matrix for Global Governance', in R. Wilkinson and S. Hughes (eds) *Global Governance: Critical Perspectives* (London: Routledge), pp. 36–53.

—— (2004) 'What the World Bank Means by Poverty Reduction and Why It Matters', *New Political Economy*, 9:2, pp. 189–211.

—— (2006) 'Global Governance, State Agency and Competitiveness: the Political Economy of the Commission for Africa', *British Journal of Politics and International Relations*, 8:3, pp. 331–50.

Carothers, T. and Ottaway, M. (2000) 'Introduction: The Burgeoning World of Civil Society Aid', in M. Ottaway and Carothers, T. (eds) *Funding Virtue: Civil Society and Democracy Promotion* (Washington, DC: Carnegie Endowment for International Peace), pp. 3–17.

Cerkez-Robinson, A. (2009) 'Bosnia's ethnic divisions are evident in schools', *Associated Press*, 24 August.

CfA (2005) Commission for Africa, *Our Common Interest*, 11 March.

Chandler, D. (1999) *Bosnia: Faking Democracy after Dayton* (London: Pluto).

—— (2005) 'From Dayton to Europe', *International Peacekeeping*, 12:3, pp. 336–49.

—— (2006a) *Empire in Denial: The Politics of International State-building* (London: Pluto Press).

—— (ed.) (2006b) *Peace without Politics? Ten Years of International Statebuilding in Bosnia* (London: Routledge).

—— (2006c) 'Back to the Future? The Limits of Neo-Wilsonian Ideals of Exporting Democracy', *Review of International Studies*, 32:3, pp. 475–94.

—— (2009a) *Hollow Hegemony: Rethinking Global Politics, Power and Resistance* (London: Pluto Press).

—— (2009b) 'Critiquing Liberal Cosmopolitanism? The Limits of the Biopolitical Approach', *International Political Sociology*, 3:1, pp. 53–70.

—— (2010a) 'Forget Foucault, Forget Foucault, Forget Foucault . . .', *International Political Sociology*, forthcoming.

—— (2010b) 'Globalizing Foucault: Turning Critique into Apologia – A Response to Kiersey and Rosenow', *Global Society*, forthcoming.

Chesterman, S., Ignatieff, M. and Thakur, R. (eds) (2005) *Making States Work: State Failure and the Crisis of Governance* (Tokyo: United Nations University).

Chopra, J. (2003) 'Building State Failure in East Timor', in J. Milliken (ed.) *State Failure, Collapse and Reconstruction* (Oxford: Blackwell), pp. 223–43.

Collier, P. (2007) *The Bottom Billion: Why the Poorest Countries are Failing and What can be Done about It* (Oxford: Oxford University Press).

Collier, P. and Hoeffler, A. (2004) 'Greed and Grievance in Civil War', *Oxford Economic Papers*, 56, pp. 563–95.

Collier, P., Hoeffler, A. and Rohner, D. (2006) 'Beyond Greed and Grievance: Feasibility and Civil War', (The Centre for the Study of African Economies/ Working Paper Series) *CSAE WPS/2006–10*, 7 August.

Commons, J. R. (1936) 'Institutional Economics', *American Economic Review*, 26, Supplement, pp. 237–49.

Connolly, W. (2002) *Identity/Difference: Democratic Negotiations of Political Paradox* (Minneapolis: University of Minnesota Press).

Conway, G. (2006) 'Climate Change and Development for Africa: The need to work together', speech by Professor Sir Gordon Conway KCMG FRS, Chief Scientific Adviser, Department for International Development, Addis Ababa, Ethiopia, April. Available at: http://www.dfid.gov.uk/news/files/speeches/climate-change-development.asp (accessed 29 March 2010).

Cooper, R. (2003) *The Breaking of Nations: Order and Chaos in the Twenty-first Century* (London: Atlantic Books).

Cordell, K. (ed.) (1998) *Ethnicity and Democratisation in the New Europe* (London: Routledge).

Cox, R. W. (1981) 'Social Forces, States and World Orders', *Millennium: Journal of International Studies*, 10:2, pp. 126–55.

Craig, D. and Porter, D. (2002) 'Poverty Reduction Strategy Papers: A New Convergence', draft, later published in *World Development*, 31:1, (2003), pp. 53–69.

Cramer, C. (2006) *Why Civil War is Not a Stupid Thing: Accounting for Violence in Developing Countries* (London: Hurst & Co.).

Crawford, G. (2006) 'The World Bank and Good Governance: Rethinking the State or Consolidating Neo-Liberalism?', in A. Paloni and M. Zanardi (eds) *The IMF, the World Bank and Policy Reform* (London: Routledge), pp. 115–41.

Cunliffe, P. (2007) 'Poor Man's Ethics: Peacekeeping and the Contradictions of Ethical Ideology', in D. Chandler and V. Heins (eds) *Rethinking Ethical Foreign Policy: Pitfalls, Possibilities and Paradoxes* (London: Routledge) pp. 70–89.

Dahrendorf, R. (1990) *Reflections on the Revolution in Europe: In a Letter Intended to Have Been Sent to a Gentleman in Warsaw, 1990* (London: Chatto & Windus).

Davidson, B. (1992) *The Black Man's Burden: Africa and the Curse of the Nation-State* (New York: Three Rivers Press).

De Angelis, M. (2003) 'Neoliberal Governance, Reproduction and Accumulation', *The Commoner*, 7, Spring/Summer, pp. 1–28. Available at: http://www.commoner.org.uk/07deangelis.pdf (accessed: 29 March 2010).

Deng, F. M., Kimaro, S., Lyons, T., Rothchild, D. and Zartman, I. W. (1996) *Sovereignty as Responsibility: Conflict Management in Africa* (Washington, DC: Brookings Institution).

Derrida, J. (1989) *Edmund Husserl's Origin of Geometry: An Introduction* (Lincoln: University of Nebraska Press).

Deutsch, K. W. (1966) 'Foreword: The Study of Nation-Building, 1962–66', in K. W. Deutsch and W. J. Foltz (eds) *Nation-Building* (New York: Atherton Press), pp. v–xi.

Devji, F. (2008) *The Terrorist in Search of Humanity: Militant Islam and Global Politics* (London: Hurst).

DFID (2005) UK Department for International Development, *Partnerships for Poverty Reduction: Rethinking Conditionality: A UK Policy Paper* (London: The Stationery Office).

—— (2006) UK Department for International Development, *Eliminating World Poverty: Making Governance work for the Poor* (London: The Stationery Office).

Dillon, M. and Reid, J. (2009) *The Liberal Way of War: Killing to Make Life Live* (London: Routledge).

Dobbins, J., Jones, S. G., Crane, K. and DeGrasse, B. C. (2007) *The Beginners' Guide to Nation-Building* (Santa Monica, CA: RAND Corporation).

Donnelly, J. (2006) 'Drought imperils Horn of Africa', *Boston Globe*, 20 February. Available at: http://www.boston.com/news/world/africa/articles/2006/02/20/drought_imperils_horn_of_africa/ (accessed 29 March 2010).

Drèze, J. and Sen, A. (eds) (1990) *The Political Economy of Hunger* (Oxford: Clarendon Press).

Duffield, M. (2001) *Global Governance and the New Wars: The Merging of Development and Security* (London: Zed Books).

—— (2007) *Development, Security and Unending War: Governing the World of Peoples* (Cambridge: Polity).

Easterly, W. (2006) *The White Man's Burden: Why the West's Efforts to Aid the Rest Have Done so Much Ill and so Little Good* (Oxford: Oxford University Press).

Emerson, R. (1960) *From Empire to Nation: The Rise to Self-Assertion of Asian and African Peoples* (Cambridge, Mass: Harvard University Press).

—— (1966) 'Nation-Building in Africa', in K. W. Deutsch and W. J. Foltz (eds) *Nation-Building* (New York: Atherton Press), pp. 95–116.

ESI (2007) European Stability Initiative, *The Worst in Class: How the International Protectorate Hurts the European Future of Bosnia and Herzegovina* (Berlin: ESI). Available at: http://www.esiweb.org/pdf/esi_document_id_98.pdf (accessed 29 March 2010).

EU (2001a) European Commission, 'Regional Strategy Paper 2002–6: CARDS Assistance Programme to the western Balkans', Brussels. Available at: http://www.mathra.gr/files/regional_strategy_paper_en.pdf (accessed 29 March 2010).

—— (2001b) European Commission, *European Governance: A White Paper*. Brussels, 25 July. Available at: http://eur-lex.europa.eu/LexUriServ/site/en/com/2001/com2001_0428en01.pdf (accessed 29 March 2010).

—— (2001c) European Commission, 'The Stabilisation and Association Process and CARDS Assistance 2000 to 2006', European Commission paper for the Second Regional Conference for South East Europe, Brussels.

—— (2001d) European Union General Affairs Council Report, 'Review of the Stabilisation and Association Process', European Commission, Brussels.

—— (2002) European Commission, 'The Stabilisation & Association process: First Annual Report', European Commission, Brussels, 4 April.

—— (2005) European Commission, *Kosovo (under USCR 1244) 2005 Progress Report*, SEC(2005)1423, Brussels, 9 November.

—— (2008) European Commission, *Instrument for Pre-accession Assistance (IPA)*. Available at: http://ec.europa.eu/enlargement/how-does-it-work/financial-assistance/instrument-pre-accession_en.htm (accessed 29 March 2010).

Evans, G. (2008) *The Responsibility to Protect: Ending Mass Atrocity Crimes Once and For All* (Washington, DC: Brookings Institution).

EWI (2001) EastWest Institute and European Stability Initiative, *Democracy, Security and the Future of the Stability Pact for South Eastern Europe: A Framework for Debate*. Available at: http://www.esiweb.org/pdf/esi_document_id_15.pdf (accessed 29 March 2010).

Farrell, D. (2008) *Democracy Promotion, Domestic Responsibility and the Impact of International Intervention on the Political Life of Republika Srpska*. Unpublished PhD thesis, National University of Ireland, Maynooth.

Fearon, J. D. and Laitin, D. D. (2004) 'Neotrusteeship and the Problem of Weak States', *International Security*, 28:4, pp. 5–43.

Feldman, N. (2004) *What We Owe Iraq: War and the Ethics of Nation Building* (Princeton, NJ: Princeton University Press).

FES (2005) Friedrich Ebert Stiftung, *Arithmetic of Irresponsibility – Political Analysis of Bosnian Domestic and Foreign Affairs* (Sarajevo: FES).

Finkelstein, L. S. (1995) 'What is Global Governance?', *Global Governance*, 1:3, pp. 367–72.

Foltz, W. J. (1966) 'Building the Newest Nations: Short-Run Strategies and Long-Run Problems', in K. W. Deutsch and W. J. Foltz (eds) *Nation-Building* (New York: Atherton Press), pp. 117–31.

Forest, J. and Mehier, C. (2001) 'John R. Commons and Herbert A. Simon on the Concept of Rationality', *Journal of Economic Issues*, 35:3, pp. 591–605.

Foucault, M. (2008) *The Birth of Biopolitics: Lectures at the Collège de France 1978–1979* (Basingstoke: Palgrave).

Frankfurt Institute (1973) *Aspects of Sociology* (London: Heinemann Educational Books).

Fraser, A. (2005) 'Poverty Reduction Strategy Papers: Now Who Calls the Shots?', *Review of African Political Economy*, No.104/5, pp. 317–40.

Fukuyama, F. (1995) 'The Primacy of Culture', *Journal of Democracy*, 6:1, pp. 7–14.

—— (2004) *State Building: Governance and World Order in the Twenty-First Century* (London: Profile Books).

Furedi, F. (1994a) *Colonial Wars and the Politics of Third World Nationalism* (London: I. B. Tauris).

—— (1994b) *The New Ideology of Imperialism: Renewing the Moral Imperative* (London: Pluto Press).

—— (1998) *The Silent War: Imperialism and the Changing Perception of Race* (London: Pluto Press).

Ghani, A. and Lockhart, C. (2008) *Fixing Failed States: A Framework for Rebuilding a Fractured World* (Oxford: Oxford University Press).

Ghani, A., Lockhart, C. and Carnahan, M. (2005) 'Closing the Sovereignty Gap: an Approach to State-Building', *Overseas Development Institute Working Paper*, No.253, ODI, September. Available at: http://www.odi.org.uk/publications/ working_papers/wp253.pdf (accessed 29 March 2010).

Giddens, A. (1994) *Beyond Left and Right: The Future of Radical Politics* (Cambridge: Polity Press).

—— (1998) *The Third Way: Renewal of Social Democracy* (Cambridge: Polity Press).

Gould, J. and Ojanen, J. (2003) *'Merging in the Circle': The Politics of Tanzania's Poverty Reduction Strategy*, Institute of Development Studies, University of Helsinki Policy Papers. Available at: http://www.valt.helsinki.fi/kmi/english/ pub_merging.htm (accessed 29 March 2010).

Grabbe, H. (2003) 'Europeanization Goes East: Power and Uncertainty in the EU Accession Process', in K. Featherstone and C. M. Radaelli (eds) *The Politics of Europeanism* (Oxford: Oxford University Press), pp. 303–30.

—— (2006) *The EU's Transformative Power: Europeanization through Conditionality in Central and Eastern Europe* (Basingstoke: Palgrave).

Gunder Frank, A. (1967) *Capitalism and Underdevelopment in Latin America* (New York: Monthly Review Press).

Gunther, R.,Diamandouros, N. P. and Puhle, H.-J. (1996) 'Debate: Democratic Consolidation: O'Donnell's "Illusions": a Rejoinder', *Journal of Democracy*, 7: 4, pp. 151–59.

Hamilton, A., Madison, J. and Jay, J. (1948) *The Federalist: Or, The New Constitution* (Oxford: Basil Blackwell).

Harrison, G. (2001) 'Post-Conditionality Politics and Administrative Reform: Reflections on the Cases of Uganda and Tanzania', *Development and Change*, 32:4, pp. 634–65.

—— (2004) *The World Bank and Africa: The Construction of Governance States* (London: Routledge).

Hatzopoulos, P. (2005) 'Non-Nationalist Ideologies in the Balkans: The Interwar Years'. Unpublished PhD thesis, London School of Economics.

Heartfield, J. (2007) 'European Union: A Process without a Subject', in C. J. Bickerton, P. Cunliffe and A. Gourevitch (eds) *Politics without Sovereignty: A Critique of Contemporary International Relations* (London: UCL Press), pp. 131–49.

—— (2010) The Dynamic of European Integration. Unpublished PhD thesis, University of Westminster.

Hehir, A. (2008) *Humanitarian Intervention after Kosovo: Iraq, Darfur and the Record of Global Civil Society* (Basingstoke: Macmillan).

Held, D. (1983) *Introduction to Critical Theory: Horkheimer to Habermas* (London: Hutchinson).

Helman, G. B. and Ratner, S. R. (1993) 'Saving Failed States', *Foreign Policy*, 89, pp. 3–21.

Herbst, J. (2004) 'Let Them Fail: State Failure in Theory and Practice: Implications for Policy', in R. I. Rotberg (ed.) *When States Fail: Causes and Consequences* (Princeton, NJ: Princeton University Press), pp. 302–18.

Herz, J. H. (1951) *Political Realism and Political Idealism* (Chicago, IL: Chicago University Press).

Hobbes, T. (1978) *Leviathan: Or the Matter, Forme and Power of a Commonwealth Ecclesiastical and Civil* (London: Collier Macmillan) (originally published in 1651).

Holsti, K. (1996) *The State, War, and the State of War* (Cambridge: Cambridge University Press).

Honig, B. (1993) *Political Theory and the Displacement of Politics* (New York: Cornell University Press).

Huntington, S. (1968) *Political Order in Changing Societies* (New Haven: Yale University Press).

Husserl, E. (1970) *The Crisis of European Societies and Transcendental Phenomenology* (trans D. Carr) (Evanston, IL: Northwestern University Press).

ICB (2005) International Commission on the Balkans, *The Balkans in Europe's Future*. Available at: http://www.becei.org/DOKUMENTI/Report.pdf (accessed 29 March 2010).

ICISS (2001) *Report of the International Commission on Intervention and State Sovereignty: The Responsibility to Protect* (Ottawa: International Development Research Centre).

Ignatieff, M. (2003) *Empire Lite: Nation-Building in Bosnia, Kosovo and Afghanistan* (London: Vintage).

—— (2005) 'Human Rights, Power and the State', in S. Chesterman, M. Ignatieff and R. Thakur (eds) *Making States Work: State Failure and the Crisis of Governance* (New York: United Nations University Press), pp. 59–75.

Jabri, V. (2007) *War and the Transformation of Global Politics* (Basingstoke: Macmillan).

Jackson, R. H. (1990) *Quasi-states: Sovereignty, International Relations and the Third World* (Cambridge: Cambridge University Press).

Jacoby, T. (2007) 'Hegemony, Modernisation and Post-War Reconstruction', *Global Society*, 21:4, pp. 521–37.

Jahn, B. (2007a) 'The Tragedy of Liberal Diplomacy: Part I', *Journal of Intervention and Statebuilding*, 1:1, pp. 87–106.

—— (2007b) 'The Tragedy of Liberal Diplomacy: Part II', *Journal of Intervention and Statebuilding*, 1:2, pp. 211–29.

Kahler, M. (2009) 'Statebuilding after Afghanistan and Iraq', in R. Paris and T. Sisk (eds) *The Dilemmas of Statebuilding: Confronting the Contradictions of Postwar Peace Operations* (London: Routledge), pp. 287–303.

Kaldor, M. (1999) *Old and New Wars: Organized Violence in a Global Age* (Cambridge: Polity Press).

Keck, M. E. and Sikkink, K. (1998) *Activists beyond Borders: Advocacy Networks in International Politics* (Ithaca: Cornell University Press).

Keohane, R. O. (1984) *After Hegemony: Cooperation and Discord in the World Political Economy* (Princeton: Princeton University Press).

—— (1988) 'International Institutions: Two Approaches', *International Studies Quarterly*, 32:4, pp. 379–96.

—— (2002) 'Ironies of Sovereignty: The European Union and the United States', *Journal of Common Market Studies*, 40:4, pp. 743–65.

—— (2003) Political Authority after Intervention: Gradations in Sovereignty', in J. L. Holzgrefe and R. O. Keohane (eds) *Humanitarian Intervention: Ethical, Legal and Political Dilemmas* (Cambridge: Cambridge University Press), pp. 275–98.

Keohane, R. O., Macedo, S. and Moravcsik, A. (2007) 'Democracy Enhancing Multilateralism', *Institute for International Law and Justice (IILJ) Working Paper*, 2007/4, Global Administrative Law Series, New York University School of Law.

King, A. and Schneider, B. (1991) *The First Global Revolution: A Report of the Council of Rome* (New York: Pantheon Books).

Klein, N. (2005) 'Baghdad Year Zero', in N. Klein *et al.*, *No War: America's Real Business in Iraq* (London, Gibson Square Books).

Krasner, S. (1983) *International Regimes* (Ithaca, NY: Cornell University).

—— (1999) *Sovereignty: Organized Hypocrisy* (Princeton, NJ: Princeton University Press).

—— (2004) 'Sharing Sovereignty: New Institutions for Collapsing and Failing States', *International Security*, 29:2, pp. 85–120.

—— (2005) 'The Case for Shared Sovereignty', *Journal of Democracy*, 16:1, pp. 69–83.

Kratochwil, F. and Ruggie, J. G. (1986) 'International Organization: A State of the Art on the Art of the State', *International Organization*, 40:4, pp. 753–76.

Kuhn, T. (1996) *The Structure of Scientific Revolutions* (Chicago, IL: Chicago University Press) (Third edition; originally published in 1962).

Laitin, D. D. (1985) 'Hegemony and Religious Conflict: British Imperial Control and Political Cleavages in Yorubaland', in P. B. Evans, D. Rueschemeyer and T. Skocpol (eds) *Bringing the State Back In* (Cambridge: Cambridge University Press), pp. 285–316.

Lean, G. (2006) 'African Apocalypse: The continent burning into a desert', *Independent*, 29 October. Available at: http://news.independent.co.uk/world/africa/article1938393.ece (accessed 29 March 2010).

Léautier, F. A. and Madavo, C. (2004) 'Foreword', in B. Levy and S. Kpundeh (eds) *Building State Capacity in Africa: New Approaches, Emerging Lessons* (Washington, DC: IBRD/World Bank).

Leonard, M. (2005) *Why Europe Will Run the 21st Century* (London: Fourth Estate).

Leys, C. (1996) *The Rise and Fall of Development Theory* (Oxford: Indiana University Press).

Lugard, Lord (1923) *The Dual Mandate in British Tropical Africa* (Abingdon: Frank Cass).

Lyotard, J.-F. (1989) *The Postmodern Condition: A Report on Knowledge* (Manchester: Manchester University Press).

McCarthy, M. and Brown, C. (2005), 'Global warming in Africa: The hottest issue of all', *Independent*, 20 June. Available at: http://news.independent.co.uk/world/africa/article226561.ece (accessed 29 March 2010).

Maclean, S. M., Black, D. R. and Shaw, T. M. (eds) (2006) *A Decade of Human Security: Global Governance and New Multilateralisms* (Aldershot: Ashgate).

Malik, K. (1996) *The Meaning of Race: Race, History and Culture in Western Society* (Basingstoke: Macmillan).

Manners, I. (2002) 'Normative Power Europe: A Contradiction in Terms?', *Journal of Common Market Studies*, 40:2, pp. 235–58.

March, J. G. and Olsen, J. P. (1984) 'The New Institutionalism: Organizational Factors in Political Life', *American Political Science Review*, 78:3, pp. 734–49.

Meszaros, I. (1989) *The Power of Ideology* (London: Harvester Wheatsheaf).

Meurs, W. van and Weiss, S. (2005) 'Qualifying (For) Sovereignty: Kosovo's Post-Status Status and the Status of EU Conditionality', Discussion Paper, 6 December. (Guetersloh: Bertelsmann Stiftung).

Mitchell, A. and Kappler, S. (2009) 'Transformative Civil Society and the EU Approach to Peacebuilding', paper presented at the *Millennium: Journal of International Studies* conference 'After Liberalism', London School of Economics, London, 17–18 October.

Mitrany, D. (1975) *The Functional Theory of Politics* (London: Martin Robertson and Co.).

Morgenthau, H. J. (1970) *Truth and Power: Essays of a Decade, 1960–1970* (New York: Praeger).

Morris, N. (2009) 'Bosnia is back on the brink of ethnic conflict, warns Hague: Shadow Foreign Secretary Fears "Europe's Black Hole" is Slowly Falling Apart Again', *Independent*, 12 August. Available at: http://www.independent.co.uk/news/world/europe/bosnia-is-back-on-the-brink-of-ethnic-conflict-warns-hague-1770638.html (accessed 29 March 2010).

Mouffe, C. (2005) *On the Political* (London: Routledge).

Muehlmann, T. (2008) 'Police Restructuring in Bosnia-Herzegovina: Problems of Internationally-led Security Sector Reform', *Journal of Intervention and Statebuilding*, 2:1, pp. 1–22.

NEF (2006) New Economics Foundation, *Africa – Up in Smoke 2: The second report on Africa and global warming from the Working Group on Climate Change and Development* (London: NEF), October. Available at: http://www.neweconomics.org/sites/neweconomics.org/files/Africa_Up_in_Smoke_2.pdf (accessed 29 March 2010).

Newman, E., Paris, R. and Richmond, O. P. (eds) (2009) *New Perspectives on Liberal Peacebuilding* (New York: United Nations University Press).

North, D. C. (1981) *Structure and Change in Economic History* (New York: Norton).

—— (1990) *Institutions, Institutional Change and Economic Performance* (Cambridge: Cambridge University Press).

North, D. C. and Thomas, R. P. (1973) *The Rise of the Western World: A New Economic History* (Cambridge: Cambridge University Press).

NSS (2002) *The National Security Strategy of the United States of America*. Available at: http://www.globalsecurity.org/military/library/policy/national/nss-020920.pdf (accessed 29 March 2010).

O'Donnell, G. (1996) 'Illusions about Consolidation', *Journal of Democracy*, 7:2, pp. 34–51.

Ohmae, K. (1990) *The Borderless World: Power and Strategy in the Interlinked Economy* (London: HarperCollins).

—— (1995) *The End of the Nation State: The Rise of Regional Economies* (London: HarperCollins).

ORI (2007) Oxford Research International report for the United Nations Development Programme, *The Silent Majority Speaks: Snapshots of Today and Visions of the Future of Bosnia and Herzegovina*. Available at: http://europeandcis.undp.org/ cpr/show/161BE7CD-F203-1EE9-BD4C1FDAE001EFBC (accessed 29 March 2010).

Ottaway, M. and Carothers, T. (2000) 'Conclusion: Toward Civil Society Realism', in M. Ottaway and T. Carothers (eds) *Funding Virtue: Civil Society and Democracy Promotion* (Washington, DC: Carnegie Endowment for International Peace), pp. 293–310.

Paris, R. (2002) 'International Peacebuilding and the "Mission Civilisatrice"', *Review of International Studies*, 28:4, pp. 637–56.

—— (2004) *At War's End: Building Peace after Civil Conflict* (Cambridge: Cambridge University Press).

Paris, R. and Sisk, T. (eds) (2009a) *The Dilemmas of Statebuilding: Confronting the Contradictions of Postwar Peace Operations* (London: Routledge).

Paris, R. and Sisk, T. (2009b) 'Introduction: Understanding the Contradiction of Postwar Statebuilding', in R. Paris and T. Sisk (eds) *The Dilemmas of Statebuilding: Confronting the Contradictions of Postwar Peace Operations* (London: Routledge), pp. 1–20.

—— (2009c) 'Conclusion: Confronting the Contradiction', in R. Paris and T. Sisk (eds) *The Dilemmas of Statebuilding: Confronting the Contradictions of Postwar Peace Operations* (London: Routledge), pp. 304–15.

Pender, J. (2001) 'From "Structural Adjustment" to "Comprehensive Development Framework": Conditionality Transformed?', *Third World Quarterly*, 22:3, pp. 397–411.

Poels, J. (1998) 'Bosnia and Herzegovina: A New "Neutral" Flag', *Flagmaster*, 98, pp. 9–12.

Pugh, M. (2005) 'The Political Economy of Peacebuilding: A Critical Theory Perspective', *International Journal of Peace Studies*, 10:2, pp. 23–42.

Pugh, M., Cooper, N. and Turner, M. (eds) (2008) *Whose Peace? Critical Perspectives on the Political Economy of Peacebuilding* (Basingstoke: Macmillan).

Pupavac, V. (2007) 'Witnessing the Demise of the Developing State: Problems for Humanitarian Advocacy', in A. Hehir and N. Robinson (eds) *State-Building: Theory and Practice* (London: Routledge), pp. 89–106.

Putnam, R. D. (2000) *Bowling Alone: The Collapse and Revival of American Community* (New York: Simon & Schuster).

Pye, L. W. (1962) *Politics, Personality, and Nation Building: Burma's Search for Identity* (New Haven: Yale University Press).

Richmond, O. P. (2005) *The Transformation of Peace* (Basingstoke: Macmillan).

—— (2008a) *Peace in International Relations* (London: Routledge).

—— (2008b) 'Reclaiming Peace in International Relations', *Millennium: Journal of International Studies*, 36:3, pp. 439–70.

Richmond, O. P. and Mac Ginty, R. (2007) Special Issue 'The Liberal Peace and Post-War Reconstruction', *Global Society*, 21:4.

Risse, T., Ropp S. C. and Sikkink, K. (eds) (1999) *The Power of Human Rights: International Norms and Domestic Change* (Cambridge: Cambridge University Press).

Roberts, D. (2008) 'Hybrid Polities and Indigenous Pluralities: Advanced Lessons in Statebuilding from Cambodia', *Journal of Intervention and Statebuilding*, 2:1, pp. 63–86.

—— (2009) 'The Superficiality of Statebuilding in Cambodia; Patronage and Clientelism as Enduring Forms of Politics', in R. Paris and T. Sisk (eds) *The Dilemmas of Statebuilding: Confronting the Contradictions of Postwar Peace Operations* (London: Routledge), pp. 149–69.

Rosenau, J. N. (1995) 'Governance in the Twenty-first Century', *Global Governance*, 1:1, pp. 13–43.

Rotberg, R. I. (2004) 'The Failure and Collapse of Nation-States: Breakdown, Prevention and Repair', in R. I. Rotberg (ed.) *When States Fail: Causes and Consequences* (Princeton: Princeton University Press), pp. 1–49.

Rowden, R. and Irama, J. O. (2004) *Rethinking Participation: Questions for Civil Society about the Limits of Participation in PRSPs*, Action Aid USA/Action Aid Uganda Discussion Paper, Washington, DC, April. Available at: http://siteresources.worldbank.org/CSO/Resources/AA_Rethinking_Participation_by_Action_Aid.pdf (accessed 29 March 2010).

Ruggie, J. G. (ed.) (1983) *The Antinomies of Interdependence* (New York: Columbia University Press).

Ruggie, J. G. (1993) 'Territoriality and Beyond: Problematizing Modernity in International Relations', *International Organization*, 47:1, pp. 139–74.

Sachs, J. (2005) *The End of Poverty: How We Can Make It Happen In Our Lifetime* (London: Penguin).

Said, E. (1985) *Orientalism* (London: Penguin).

Schmitt, C. (2003) *The Nomos of the Earth: In the International Law of the Jus Publicum Europaeum* (New York: Telos).

Schmitter, P. C. and Karl, T. L. (1991) 'What Democracy is . . . and is Not', *Journal of Democracy*, 2:3, pp. 4–17.

Sen, A. (1981) *Poverty and Famines: An Essay on Entitlement and Deprivation* (Oxford: Clarendon Press).

—— (1992) *Inequality Reexamined* (Oxford: Oxford University Press).

—— (1999) *Development as Freedom* (Oxford: Oxford University Press).

Sen, A. and Drèze, J. (1989) *Hunger and Public Action* (Oxford: Clarendon Press).

Simms, A. (2005) *Africa – Up in Smoke? The second report from the Working Group on Climate Change and Development* (London: New Economics Foundation), June. Available at: http://www.oxfam.org.uk/resources/policy/climate_change/downloads/africa_up_in_smoke.pdf (accessed 29 March 2010).

Sisk, T. D. (2008) 'Peacebuilding as Democratization: Findings and Recommendations', in A. K. Jarstad and T. D. Sisk (eds) *From War to Democracy: Dilemmas of Peacebuilding* (Cambridge: Cambridge University Press), pp. 239–59.

Sjursen, H. (ed.) (2006) 'Special Issue: What Kind of Power? European Foreign Policy in Perspective', *Journal of European Public Policy*, 13:6.

Snyder, J. (2000) *From Voting to Violence: Democratization and Nationalist Conflict* (New York: W. W. Norton).

Stonequist, E. V. (1961) *The Marginal Man: A Study in Personality and Culture Conflict* (New York: Russell and Russell).

Storey, H. (1995) 'Human Rights and the New Europe: Experience and Experiment', *Political Studies*, 43, pp. 131–51.

Tadjbakhsh, S. and Chenoy, A. M. (2007) *Human Security: Concepts and Implications* (London: Routledge).

Thakur, R. and Schnabel, A. (2000) 'Unbridled humanitarianism: Between justice, power and authority', in A. Schnabel and R. Thakur (eds) *Kosovo and the Challenge of Humanitarian Intervention* (Tokyo: UN Press), pp. 496–504.

Trauner, F. (2009) 'From Membership Conditionality to Policy Conditionality: EU External Governance in South Eastern Europe', *Journal of European Public Policy*, 16:5, pp. 774–90.

UN (1960) United Nations, *Declaration on the Granting of Independence to Colonial Countries and Peoples*. Available at: http://untreaty.un.org/cod/avl/ha/dicc/dicc.html (accessed 29 March 2010).

—— (1970) United Nations, *Declaration on Principles of International Law Concerning Friendly Relations and Co-Operation among States in Accordance with the Charter of the United Nations*. Available at: http://www.hku.edu/law/conlawhk/conlaw/outline/Outline4/2625.htm (accessed 29 March 2010).

—— (2004) United Nations, *Report of the High Level Panel on Threats, Challenges and Change: A More Secure World: Our Shared Responsibility* (New York: United Nations).

—— (2005a) United Nations, Report of the Secretary-General, *In Larger Freedom: Towards Development, Security and Human Rights for All* (New York: United Nations).

—— (2005b) United Nations, *General Assembly 2005 World Summit Outcome Document*, A/60/L.1, 15 September.

—— (2009) United Nations, *Implementing the Responsibility to Protect: Report of the Secretary-General*, A/63/677, 12 January.

UNFCCC (1994) Secretariat of the United Nations Framework Convention on Climate Change, *United Nations Framework Convention on Climate Change*, 21 March. Available at: http://unfccc.int/resource/docs/convkp/conveng.pdf (accessed 29 March 2010).

UNFCC (2006) Secretariat of the United Nations Framework Convention on Climate Change, *Report of the African Regional Workshop on Adaptation*, September. Available at: http://www.iisd.ca/ymb/adaptationaccra/images/pdficonsm0.gif (accessed 29 March 2010).

UNMP (2005) UN Millennium Project, *Investing in Development: A Practical Plan to Achieve the Millennium Development Goals*. Available at: http://www. unmillenniumproject.org/reports/index.htm (accessed 29 March 2010).

Venneri, G. (2008) 'The EU's "Hands-Off" Statebuilding: From Bosnia-Herzegovina to Kosovo'. Paper presented at the International Studies Association's 49th Annual Convention, San Francisco, USA, 26 March.

Walker, R. B. J. (1992) *Inside/Outside: International Relations as Political Theory* (Cambridge: Cambridge University Press).

Wallerstein, I. (1961) *Africa: The Politics of Independence* (New York: Vintage).

Wallerstein, I. (1976) *The Modern World System* (New York: Academic Press).

WB (1989) World Bank, *Sub-Saharan Africa: From Crisis to Sustainable Growth: A Long-Term Perspective Study* (Washington, DC: World Bank).

—— (1992) World Bank, *Governance and Development* (Washington, DC: World Bank).

—— (1997) World Bank, *World Development Report 1997: The State in a Changing World* (Washington, DC: IBRD/World Bank).

—— (1998) *Assessing Aid: What Works, What Doesn't, and Why. A World Bank Policy Research Report* (New York: Oxford University Press).

—— (2000) World Bank, *Reforming Public Institutions and Strengthening Governance: A World Bank Strategy* (Washington, DC: IBRD/World Bank). Available at: http:// www1.worldbank.org/publicsector/Reforming.pdf (accessed 29 March 2010).

Weiner, J. (2001) 'Globalization and Disciplinary Neoliberal Governance', *Constellations*, 8:4, pp. 461–79.

Wendt, A. (1987) 'The Agent-Structure Problem in International Relations Theory', *International Organization,* 41:3, pp. 335–70.

—— (1992) 'Anarchy is What States Make of It: The Social Construction of Power Politics', *International Organization*, 46:2, pp. 391–425.

—— (1999) *Social Theory of International Politics* (Cambridge: Cambridge University Press).

Wheeler, N. and Booth, K. (1992) 'The Security Dilemma' in J. Bayliss and N. J. Rengger (eds) *Dilemmas of World Politics: International Issues in a Changing World* (Oxford: Clarendon Press), pp. 29–60.

Whitlock, C. (2009) 'Old Troubles Threaten Again in Bosnia: 14 Years After War, Leaders Suggest U.S. Should Step In to Rewrite Treaty', *Washington Post*, 23 August. Available at: http://www.washingtonpost.com/wp-dyn/content/ article/2009/08/22/AR2009082202234.html (accessed 29 March 2010).

Wight, M. (1966) 'Why Is there No International Relations Theory?', in H. Butterfield and M. Wight (eds) *Diplomatic Investigations* (London: George Allen & Unwin), pp. 17–34.

—— (1979) *Power Politics*, eds H. Bull and C. Holbraad (Harmondsworth: Penguin).

Yannis, A. (2002) 'The Concept of Suspended Sovereignty in International Law and its Implications in International Politics', *European Journal of International Law*, 13:5, pp. 1037–52.

Young, O. R. (1986) 'International Regimes: Toward a New Theory of Institutions', *World Politics*, 39:1, pp. 104–22.

Zakaria, F. (2003) *The Future of Freedom; Illiberal Democracy at Home and Abroad* (New York: W. W. Norton).

Zaum, D. (2007) *The Sovereignty Paradox: The Norms and Politics of International Statebuilding* (Oxford: Oxford University Press).

Index

Lightning Source UK Ltd.
Milton Keynes UK
UKOW06f2339161115

262867UK00009B/172/P